Doctors within Borders

Colonialisms

Jennifer Robertson, General Editor

Doctors within Borders

Profession, Ethnicity, and Modernity in
Colonial Taiwan

MING-CHENG M. LO

University of California Press

BERKELEY   LOS ANGELES   LONDON

University of California Press
Berkeley and Los Angeles, California

University of California Press, Ltd.
London, England

Library of Congress Cataloging-in-Publication Data

Lo, Ming-cheng Miriam.
    Doctors within borders : profession, ethnicity, and modernity in
colonial Taiwan / by Ming-cheng M. Lo.
        p.   cm.—(Colonialisms ; 1)
    Includes bibliographical references and index.
    ISBN 0-520-22946-0 (cloth : alk. paper)—ISBN 0-520-23485-5 (pbk. :
alk. paper)
        1. Physicians—Taiwan—History—20th century.   2. Medicine—
Taiwan—History—20th century.   3. Sino-Japanese Conflict, 1937–
1945—Medical care—Taiwan.   I. Title.   II. Series.

    R644.T28 L6 2002
    610'.95124'9—dc21   2002001622

11   10   09   08   07   06   05   04   03   02
10   9   8   7   6   5   4   3   2   1

To my parents

Contents

Illustrations and Tables

Foreword

Jennifer Robertson, General Editor, Colonialisms

In 1921, Dr. Jiang Weishui publicly diagnosed the condition of Taiwan as a male suffering from symptoms of immorality, an impoverished spiritual life, superstition, and poor hygiene caused by "intellectual malnutrition." He prescribed "maximum doses" of basic education and libraries to correct the condition. As Ming-cheng Lo explains in this creatively and subtly argued book, Jiang's diagnosis cleverly articulated the analogy between physical illness and social disease, medicine and social action, in venturing a "modernist critique" of Japanese colonial administrators who had occupied Taiwan since 1895. Physicians like Dr. Jiang were at the forefront of anti-colonial resistance against Japan, even though, as Japanese-trained doctors and agents of modernity, they embodied hybrid and ambivalent ethnic, cultural, and professional identities. Ironically, the culture of "modernity" accompanying the professionalization of medicine in Taiwan under the aegis of Japan in turn enabled both a critique of Taiwanese traditional practices and a critique of Japanese colonialism, which was premised on the harshly enforced institutionalization of social and ethnic inequality.

Lo's book exemplifies the intellectual mission of the Colonialisms series, which is to explore and analyze the historical realities, present-day significance, and future ramifications of imperialist and colonialist practices outside of "the West." In addition to demonstrating the theoretical and methodological strengths of interdisciplinary scholarship, Lo's book puts into practice the criteria that books in the series must be empirically grounded and written in accessible prose. Moreover, the series seeks to emphasize the "cultural," or the practical, experiential, affective, and aesthetic, strategies and dimensions of imperialist agendas and colonialist projects. Here, "cultural" includes the differential experiences of females and males, as well as the experiences of other categories of people defined by race and ethnicity, religion, sexuality, class and caste, age, and health in colonial situations. Lo's book on the life and work experiences of Taiwanese physicians subjected to Japanese colonial rule will stimulate the development of new theories about the cultural dimensions of colonial and imperial systems.

Acknowledgments

I have incurred a large number of debts to an endless list of individuals during the years that were spent on this project. Although my limited space here does not allow me to identify all of them, I hope that they will know how much I appreciate their generosity.

Some individuals must be acknowledged more specifically. I thank Michael Kennedy for introducing me to critical theory and the sociology of professions and helping me formulate the conceptual categories in this project when it was still a dissertation. Jennifer Robertson gave timely and inspirational support at every stage of this project. Julia Adams's thoughtful and judicious comments have challenged me and moved my work in fruitful directions. I am also grateful to my other dissertation committee members, Mayer Zald and Marty Whyte, for their encouragement, comments, and criticisms. Peggy Somers's graduate seminar on historical sociology at the University of Michigan profoundly influenced my intellectual growth. Christopher Bettinger, Margaret Weigers, Sandra Ma, Jenny Sell, Naomi Galtz, Pauline Gianoplus, and many other friends from graduate school patiently listened to me wrestling with my arguments and challenged me with their insights and questions in our countless late-night conversations. I am grateful to have been blessed with such great friendships. With his characteristic kindness, Christopher Bettinger also tolerated my frequent deviations from our collaborative project and allowed me to impose many conversations about this book on him.

Vicki Smith, Diane Wolf, Fred Block, Susan Mann, and John Hall generously made themselves available to read drafts of the manuscript or portions of it; without them the insights in this book would have been far poorer. Craig Calhoun, Renee Anspach, Takie Lebra, Michelle Yeh, Thomas Gold, Fred Wakeman, Wen-hsin Yeh, Elizabeth Berry, Ron Aminzade, and Norma

Field provided very useful comments on parts of the argument in this book as it was presented in different forums. Kyu Hyun Kim, Sophie Volpp, Ryken Grattet, Laura Grindstaff, Sean O'Riain, and David Kyle dropped many useful hints over coffee and in the hallway and sustained my confidence with their support throughout the process. Ken Pomeranz, Steven Harrell, and two other anonymous reviewers helped me to make significant improvements in the manuscript with their careful and critical readings. Special gratitude is due to Julia Adams, Vicki Smith, Fred Block, Diane Wolf, and John Hall for their invaluable professional guidance.

I am deeply indebted to many individuals in Japan and Taiwan for sharing with me their advice and contacts. Professor Shozawa Jun generously offered his published and unpublished work and his knowledge of the educational system in colonial Taiwan, and he kindly introduced me to my first informant. Dr. Zhang not only gave me access to his life stories and his personal holdings of some precious historical materials, but also introduced me to many other informants. I also benefited from the insights of Professors Wu Wenxing, You Jianming, Wakabayashi Masahiro, Xu Xueji, Mr. Mita, and Mr. Chen Junkai, as well as the encouragement and support from Fan Yun, Hong Yuru, He Yiling, and Liu Xiaru. Most of my informants will have to remain anonymous, and I regret that I cannot acknowledge each of them here to express my deepest gratitude for their kindness in offering me their stories, memories, and opinions. I also thank the staffs at the Tokyo University Library, the National Diet Library, the Taiwan Association, the Diplomatic Record Office of the Ministry of Foreign Affairs in Japan, the Taiwan Division at the National Central Library, and the Research Library at the National Taiwan University.

Financial assistance for this book was provided by the following sources: the International Institute of the University of Michigan, the University of Michigan's Center for Chinese Studies, the Horace H. Rackham School of Graduate Studies at the University of Michigan, the Chiang Ching-Kuo Foundation for International Scholarly Exchange, the University of California–Davis Washington Center, the UC Davis Faculty Research Grants, and the UC Davis Publication Assistance Funds. I also thank Shizuko Oyama and Clare Stacey for their research assistance, and Jaime Becker for her editorial assistance. Colleagues and friends at the University of Michigan and UC Davis have provided a constantly stimulating intellectual milieu in which this project was conceptualized and completed. The editor for the Colonialisms series, Jennifer Robertson, and my editor at the University of California Press, Sheila Levine, were two vital figures that enabled the production of this book and deserve my deepest gratitude.

Finally, I must acknowledge one man whose memory inspired this book in the first place. Growing up with hearing whispers about my grandfather, I never knew what caused his death to be so early and so silent. Not until I entered graduate school in the United States did I begin to learn the details about the Taiwanese popular uprising in 1947, in which my grandfather, an engineer trained at Waseda University in Japan, was killed on his way to work by the Chinese Nationalists. But even after I learned more about his death, I still knew little about his life. During the endless hours in the archives, I read through old diaries, school records, and newspaper articles written by or about the educated elite in colonial Taiwan, who, like my grandfather, bravely confronted the complicated web of relationships among the Taiwanese, Japanese, and Chinese. As this book approached completion, I was also beginning to be rewarded with a deeper understanding of this man whom I never met but have loved from childhood.

A Note on Romanization

This book uses the pinyin and the Hepburn styles of romanization in rendering Chinese and Japanese terms, respectively. For place names and personal names that are familiar in the English-speaking world, however, the familiar spellings are given instead (e.g., Taipei instead of Taibei, and Tokyo instead of Tōkyō). The romanization of some personal names follows the form used by the individuals themselves in their published works (e.g., Ching-chih Chen instead of Chen Qingqi).

1 Taiwanese Doctors under Japanese Rule

Confronting Contradictions and Negotiating Identities

A creative yet peculiar campaign poster greeted the Taiwanese public during the 1995 legislative election. The candidate, wearing an iconic white lab coat, presented himself as "the new-generation physician for the independence of Taiwan." The implied connection between medicine and politics was elaborated in the text of the poster: "Perform an operation on congress. Cure the diseases which ail Taiwan. This generation's physician for the independence of Taiwan is Chen Qimai. From curing human diseases to medicating societal problems, to care for the community is the noblest fate of students of medicine."

The candidate explicitly grounded his claim to healing in the unique history of Taiwanese doctors. On the top half of the poster he placed pictures of older Taiwanese physicians who were active in past cultural and social reforms; on the bottom he put a picture of himself, creating a visual chronology (see figure 1). After outlining the lives of the older physicians, the poster concluded: "Through his participation in the legislative election, Chen Qimai, the physician for the independence of Taiwan, now chooses to enter congress in order to do direct battle with the forces of evil. From Dr. Jiang Weishui [an activist in the colonial period] onward, they [the doctors] have bequeathed a precious tradition: The conscientiousness of the medical arena should serve to glorify the conscientiousness of Taiwan."

This campaign poster is not an isolated creation authored by a particularly innovative campaign staff; rather, it signals an important legacy in the cultural and political repertoire of past and present Taiwan: the blending of nationalism and professionalism in the physician. This legacy is also illustrated by the Medical Professionals Alliance in Taiwan (MPAT). The MPAT

Figure 1. Dr. Chen Qimai's 1995 Campaign Poster

was founded in 1992 by Dr. Li Chen-yuan—the figure on the lower right in Dr. Chen's campaign poster. On its English homepage on the internet, the MPAT describes itself as an organization that seeks to "[unite] medical and health professionals dedicated to enhancing the *health and dignity* of Taiwanese society and its citizens" (http://www.worldhealth.org.tw/english/profile_e.htm; my emphasis). Functioning as an important link between health professionals working in private and government institutes, the MPAT has allegedly "become an important discussion forum, reaching out to potentially around 150,000 Taiwanese" (ibid.). Like medical associations elsewhere, the MPAT engages in various health-related activities that aim to improve medical education, practice, ethics, policy, and social welfare. What is unique about this organization, however, is that the MPAT's official agenda includes the promotion of Taiwan's democratization and global participation, and it is actively involved in the development of Taiwanese nongovernmental organizations (NGOs).[1] These dual concerns were vividly visualized by a 1997 "Taiwan for WHO" picture, in which the MPAT juxtaposed its two major appeals: "health for all" and the recognition of Taiwan as a member of the international community (see figure 2).[2] This picture gestured at an attempt to integrate the political and medical dimensions of "healing." The MPAT's dual roles, then, parallel Dr. Chen Qimai's prescription that the Taiwanese medical profession take the lead in healing the nation, both medically and politically. The health of the nation, in this sense, can only be secured by both further developing the medical profession in Taiwan and actively confronting the island's current political problems.

As the stories of Dr. Chen Qimai and the MPAT suggest, Taiwanese physicians are noted for both their professional specialization and national-

1. "MPAT has developed partnerships with organizations such as the Geneva-based International Service for Human Rights and the Sydney-based Diplomacy Training Program for the People of Asia to improve human rights education and training of Taiwanese NGOs" (http://www.worldhealth.org.tw/english/v4.htm).

2. In narrative form, the MPAT explains how it conceptualizes the relationship between these two issues: "We firmly believe that it is crucial for the Asia-Pacific region that Taiwan be allowed to directly contribute to the international health community. This is necessity if the goal of 'Health for All' is to be reached by the year 2000. Taiwan has been a responsible and sovereign member of the international community. Its people have contributed to many international health projects and have often played a pioneer role in primary health care and eradication of communicable infectious diseases in the region. MPAT, therefore, considers it as one of our main objectives to help Taiwan gain its membership at the WHO and the UN. It is a fundamental right of the Taiwanese people and also a right for all other peoples who benefit from Taiwan's international presence and contributions" (http://www.worldhealth.org.tw/english/v5.htm).

Figure 2. 1997 Taiwan for WHO (Source: Medical Professionals Alliance in Taiwan)

ist mobilization. Indeed, since the colonial period, doctors have been recognized as the first modern and the most prestigious professional group in Taiwan. As early as the 1920s, Taiwanese doctors devoted themselves to numerous anticolonial struggles. After World War II, their political mobilization developed at several significant points: during the initial confrontation between Taiwan and China in the late 1940s, during the post-1987 period of democratization, and, as we just saw, during recent elections and campaigns. While this social legacy is readily recognized in contemporary Taiwan, neither its historical genesis nor its theoretical implications have been adequately addressed. This book takes up this task by providing an analysis of the Taiwanese medical profession under Japan's "scientific colonialism." This empirical case provides both a more adequate historicization and theorization of the tensions and ambiguities within Japanese colonialism and, through a historical sociology of the professions, a more complete appreciation of the diverse politics in the making of the "modern."

INTERSECTIONS OF COLONIZATION AND PROFESSIONALIZATION

The unique legacy of the Taiwanese medical profession offers both a historical lesson about Japan's colonial designs in Taiwan and a theoretical challenge to the historical sociology of the professions. Formed at the intersection of colonization and professionalization, the medical profession in Taiwan vividly illustrates the central tensions and ambiguities of Japan's "scientific colonialism" (described below). At the same time, this history poses a sociological question about the embeddedness of the "modern" profession in ethnic or national communities and, more broadly, about the politics of the localization of aspects of "modernity."

With the annexation of Taiwan in 1895, Japan successfully established itself as the first and only Asian colonial force, and the Japanese colonial officials were determined to build a showcase out of this first colony. As an Asian nation engaged in colonizing other Asians, the Japanese Empire imagined and sustained itself through a set of power relations which, in contrast to the stories of European colonialism, were often articulated through alleged cultural and racial affinities between the colonizers and the colonized. In this peculiar formulation of imperial categories of race and ethnicity, Japan constructed its role as the "anticolonial colonizer," that is, the leader of Asia in the battle against European and American imperialism. With this self-imposed mission in mind, and through diligent comparative studies of colonialism, Japanese colonial officials developed one of their central colonial theories, "scientific colonialism." According to these officials, Japanese colonialism was scientific in two senses: it featured a scientific and research-oriented approach, and it aimed to bring science and civilization to the colonies.

The achievements in colonial medicine provided one of the most pivotal examples of Japan's "scientific colonialism" in Taiwan. During the early years of the colonial age, upon the realization that the success of colonial medicine relied heavily on the existence of a body of well-trained, native agents, the Japanese state made a great effort to promote and institutionalize medical education in Taiwan. As a result, in less than two decades, doctors emerged as the first modern native professionals in Taiwan, and their professional practices endowed them with very favorable market positions and high social status.

The very success of colonial medicine under scientific colonialism, however, created an elite native class positioned to articulate and promote anticolonial politics. In the second half of the colonial period (1920–1945), the medical profession in Taiwan deviated from the expected colonial plan and underwent a series of transformations. In the 1920s, following the transition from military rule to civilian government in 1919, many Taiwanese doctors channeled their resources and power into anticolonial struggles, positioning themselves as major movement leaders in the nascent Taiwanese civil society. As many scholars have observed, the development of a civil society in

Taiwan initiated a turbulent decade of social movements and reformist efforts (Mukōyama 1987; Ng 1989; Wu 1992). In this context, many cosmopolitan physicians emerged as leading activists,[3] despite the fact that they were among the greatest beneficiaries of colonial rule (Chen 1992; Tsurumi 1977; Oda 1974).

Turning to their course of action in subsequent years (a history that is much less well understood than that of the 1920s) reveals important changes in the spirit and activities of the Taiwanese medical community. In the early to mid-1930s, as Japan progressed toward war, and political control at home and in the colony increased, the majority of anticolonial physicians, along with other activists, were demobilized and retreated into a relatively private civil society. But in the following period of imperial expansion, known as the *kōminka* period (1937–45), doctors became the professionals who carried forth Japanese colonial modernity at a time when the ethnic distinction between Taiwanese and Japanese in that imperial project was being blurred. If at one point doctors were more active than other social groups in anticolonial activities, they now appeared more ready than other social groups to embrace the modernity they perceived to be represented by the colonizers' civilization.

Through these historical phases (the anticolonial, the demobilized, and the assimilated), doctors drew upon their experiences to imagine and articulate collective narratives about their group identities. In their anticolonial

---

3. I follow Dunn (1976) and Leslie (1976) in using the term "cosmopolitan medicine" to refer to what is alternatively called "modern medicine," "scientific medicine," and "Western medicine." Dunn and Leslie caution us against the biases implied by these terms. Leslie explains that the terms "modern medicine" and "scientific medicine" carry the assumption that all medicine other than cosmopolitan medicine is antimodern or unscientific. The term "Western medicine" is even more problematic. According to Leslie, "The scientific aspects of Western medicine are transcultural. Ethnic interpretations of modern science are the aberrations of nationalistic and totalitarian ideologies or, in this case, a reflex of colonial or neo-colonial thought. . . . The social organization of cosmopolitan medicine . . . is as Japanese as it is Western" (1976, p. 8). For these reasons, Dunn proposes the term "cosmopolitan medicine," and Leslie favors it over alternative terms. Susan Long (1980) later employs the term "cosmopolitan medicine" in her study of the careers of Japanese physicians.

For all these reasons, I also use the term "cosmopolitan medicine" (or "cosmopolitan physician"). However, it would be wrong to paper over the fact that many Japanese health administrators and Taiwanese physicians precisely assumed that "good medicine" was distinctly "modern and scientific." Thus, in order to avoid confusing these people's self-description with my analysis of them, I preserve the terms "modern medicine" or "scientific medicine" in their narratives and use the term "cosmopolitan medicine" in my own.

activities, they developed a collective identity as "national physicians." This legacy was lost later in their collective demobilization. A new identity as "medical modernists" was subsequently constructed as they became assimilated. Because they were the native agents for the colonial medical project—the benchmark of the colonizers' design of rule—the transformations of these doctors' identities are indeed intriguing and remarkable. The logic of scientific colonialism dictated that modern sciences and professions be utilized in the service of colonialism. As the telling story of Taiwanese doctors shows, however, such political policies led to unintended and unpredictable interactions between the processes of professionalization and colonization.

Grounded in this intriguing history, the book analytically articulates the social positionality of ethnic professionals. I situate these social agents in their in-between position, where their ethnicity is allegedly ascribed and particularistic in nature, and their professional status and culture are considered attained and modern. With their ethnicity and profession figuring centrally in their lives, ethnic professionals are deeply embedded in two sets of cultural heritages, institutional practices, and group interests. Positioned at such a structural location, they interpret, deploy, and negotiate with these two categories of identities. More specifically, ethnic professionals draw from their multiple cultural heritages to claim membership in their ethnic community as well as the larger society.

Taking this mutual embeddedness of ethnicity and the profession as its central "problematique," this inquiry aims to push boundaries of scholarship on three fronts: studies of Japanese colonialism, the historical sociology of professions, and understandings of the making and unmaking of "modernity." First, adopting a perspective that focuses on the social experiences of a colonized group—Taiwanese doctors in this case—I trace the cultural and structural intersections of professionalism and colonialism at which the Taiwanese medical profession formed and transformed its collective identity. In so doing, this book addresses an important gap in studies of Japanese colonialism—in particular, the social experiences of those groups commonly referred to by the category of "the colonized." Despite differing emphases, most studies of Japanese colonialism are more concerned with the structural forces of colonialism than the individual and group experiences of this history (e.g., Gann 1996; Gold 1988; Cumings 1995). As a result, although Japanese colonialism has been well documented as a system of governing and management that embodied the tensions and ambiguities stemming from its self-proclaimed role as the "anticolonial colonizer," little is known about the experiences of the colonized population who *lived* such tensions and ambiguities. The "Japanese colonial landscape" was populated by living, active people whose identities encompass a much richer and more complex array of social experiences than those understood as a direct derivation of the structures of colonial rule.

By emphasizing the identity formation process of an important social group, this endeavor is part of recent scholarly efforts to rescue our understandings of Japanese colonial legacies from Western-centered social science categories (e.g., Barlow 1997). This inquiry asks how colonial subjects confronted the tensions and ambiguities of colonial relations within an empire whose legitimacy, as constructed in its official ideology, rested on the shared racial similarities and cultural past of the colonizers and the colonized. This approach, focused on the identity formation process of Japan's colonial subjects, contributes to the new conceptual terrain in which frameworks suggested by studies of European orientalism are subjected to critical reappraisal. As Barlow puts it, "[In Japanese colonialism,] the proper borders separating Self and Other are never sufficiently drawn, as Tomiyama implies they are in European orientalism. The [Japanese] national Self can neither maintain distinctions nor conceive of nonexploitative, nonincorporative relations outside its own discursive regimes. And this, Tomiyama suggests, may be the unique and distinguishing quality of Japanese colonial discourse" (1997, p. 13). That Japanese colonial discourses defined an "other" that appeared surprisingly similar to the "self" generated many unique ambiguities in Japanese colonial relations. Taking this theorization of the ambiguities in the Japanese colonial discourses as my point of departure, I seek to understand how Japan's colonial subjects experienced, interpreted, and potentially altered such colonial ambiguities. By focusing on the formation of an ethnic professional social group at the intersections of multiple social processes engendered by "scientific colonialism," this book traces how the colonized confronted such ambiguities in the diverse moments (the anticolonial, the demobilized, and the assimilated) in which their identity formation process took place.

Second, this reading of Japanese scientific colonialism brings to the fore a rigorous historical perspective on professions not yet fully established in American sociology. In recent decades, scholars have significantly advanced the sociology of professions with debates about how to properly situate professions in the developments of capitalist market and state, viewing professions alternatively as culprits of capitalist rationalization (Larson 1977) or as bearers of the third logic that counterbalances bureaucracy and the market (Freidson 2001), portraying institutionalized expertise alternatively as facilitators of state intrusion (Larson 1984; Johnson 1995) or as one palatable solution to the crisis of ungovernability in contemporary liberal democracy (Halliday 1987). Furthermore, with an increasing awareness of the field's Anglo-American bias, scholars have turned their attention toward continental Europe, shedding light on the unfamiliar paths of "professionalization from above," exposing the theoretical malaise of Anglo-American ethnocentrism (Jarausch 1990; McClelland 1991), and have "brought the private Anglo-American discussion of the professions to an end" (Burrage 1990, p. 13). The historical sensitivities and comparative visions in these studies are key to garnering our current rich understandings of the varying relationships of the professions, market, and state.

But to the extent that these are still private American-European discussions, we have not gone far enough. Broadening the efforts to understand how professionalization interacts with other macro-social processes, we must look beyond the West and interrogate how, in the rest of the world, the genesis of modern professions is often embedded in the forces of colonialism. Current theories of professions provide a useful framework for studying the intersection of professionalization and colonialism, while such analyses in turn challenge us to rethink major parameters in our theories. As one cannot escape the centrality of race and ethnicity in the social formation of professions under colonialism, these studies inevitably raise a general question about the relationships of racism and professionalization elsewhere. Much in the same ways that feminist scholarship has helped sociologists to see the need to "gender the agents" of professionalization (Witz 1992, p. 39), so analyses of colonial professions can help "racialize the agents" and situate professionalization in the histories and structures of racism and nation building.

Third, at a more macro level, this study views the intricate relationships between ethnicity and the profession as part of the history of a community's effort to claim modernity and, from this perspective, problematizes the "agents" of modernity in its localization process. Does it matter *by whom* science is being delivered to a local community, so long as it is delivered? This is a central question in any attempt to achieve a nuanced understanding of "East Asian colonial modernity" and, more broadly, other formations of modernity—an understanding that avoids both the Euro-American assumption of a singular, unified modernity and an open-ended monologue of cultural relativism.

One familiar critique of Japanese imperialism concerns the arrogance of the assumption that the Japanese alone were the sole legitimate agents for developing modernity in Asia. While careful historical studies reveal an element of idealism in some of Japan's efforts to deliver "modernity" to the Chinese continent, the lack of meaningful examination of their leadership position, however, ultimately turned Japan's best intentions into something indistinguishable from aggressive imperialism (e.g., see Young

1998; Reynolds 1989). This critical appraisal of Japan's monopoly of agency should be further expanded to accommodate understandings of colonial subjects' struggle to attain their own agency. While Taiwanese doctors' struggle to craft a coherent identity between ethnicity and their profession was marked by contradictions and silence, this very struggle suggests a trace of agency in their attempt to "claim modernity" and, in so doing, to indirectly challenge the colonizers' monopoly of modernity on the island. In this sense, the modernity project is as much about the development, consolidation, and legitimization of the imagination of particular groups as it is about the delivery of science, education, and so on. Modernity, as Barlow (1997) urges, should not be assumed to exist "prior to" imperialism; modernity as we know it has always been defined within particular (e.g., Japanese or Taiwanese) frameworks of values and ideologies and by particular groups of people. That the modernity project is "always already" localized constitutes one central lesson of the Japanese colonial legacy in Taiwan, and more broadly the category of East Asian colonial modernity.

As one of the "wild cards of modernity" (Tiryakian 1997), this lesson contributes to a timely update of our paradigms of modernity, many of which, "although . . . [with] a distinguished genealogy extending back to the Enlightenment, . . . need to be updated with a more amorphous and dynamic perspective" (p. 148). Foucault and many others have forcefully debunked the Enlightenment tradition by analyzing modernity as a disciplinary regime. Taking this one step further, Latour (1993) claims that we have never been modern in the way "modern" is traditionally conceptualized. For Latour, such conceptualizations of modernity rest primarily on a fundamental—and fundamentally ahistorical—division between the realms of knowledge about the human (social, political, and cultural) and nonhuman (natural) spheres. Latour argues for the denaturalization of such a division and the historicization of the human aspects of science. Standing on the giant's shoulders, I wish to accentuate the importance of the "agents" of modernity by attending to how different social groups negotiate between the powerful narrative of the universality of science and the concrete political and social relationships through which science is delivered and developed. I call for a perspective that recognizes "modernity" as always rooted in specific communities without losing sight of the power carried by the fiction of the universality of modernity. This book attempts to develop such a perspective by examining the complicated webs of relationships in which a particular group of "science-deliverers" were embedded, and the difficulties and creativity with which they made sense of the modern-local encounter.

FROM CATEGORICAL TO RELATIONAL THINKING

The experiences of social groups that occupy an in-between position often appear to be marginal, atypical, and perhaps less deserving of our scholarly attention when mapped onto the more conventional knowledge enterprises that are built with categories and variables. Most people, however, never live singularly in any given category or variable, nor do they derive meanings about their lives and identities from these conceptual constructs without their own intervention (Abbott 1992a, 1992b). In reality, a great portion of people's lived experience falls between the conceptual constructs we use to describe those experiences. A recent discussion of the need for sociology to study more systematically these large domains in between sociological categories resulted in the call: *"Entities of the World—Relate!"* (Emirbayer 1997, p. 312, n. 47; emphasis in original). Focusing on the in-between locations and identities of Taiwanese doctors, my case lends itself to furthering the call for "relational thinking" and to better operationalizing some abstract concepts in this trend of thought.

It is noteworthy that relational thinking has deep roots in the writings of classical sociologists. Marx, for example, argues that "society does not consist of individuals, but expresses the sum of interrelations, the relations within which these individuals stand" (Marx, quoted in Emirbayer 1997, p. 288). Simmel, with his dominant concern with forms of social interactions, also tends to situate individuals in relational contexts. Even Parsons, "especially after the development of his later 'interchange model' and theory of 'generalized media' . . . moves decisively in the direction of a relational, transactional point of view" (Emirbayer 1997, p. 291). What I wish to propose here, then, is not so much the invention of a new paradigm. Rather, I am taking as my point of departure sociology's fundamental concern with social relations and insist on studying just as seriously those social relations that are not fully captured by major categories in Western sociology.

To this end, I borrow insights from several recent sociological endeavors that have implicitly or explicitly built toward a "relational" vocabulary. For example, drawing from Bourdieu (1977), Giddens (1984), and others, Sewell (1992a) offers a general proposal for how to situate human actors in a web of *relationships* of structural forces, including culture.[4] He suggests

---

4. Following the tradition of Bourdieu (1977), Swidler (1995), Sewell (1992a), and many others, I emphasize the structural nature of culture. "There is now an abundance of work—that of Foucault and Bourdieu, but also many others (Wuthnow 1987; Sewell 1985, 1990, 1992)—arguing that culture constitutes social experience

that (1) multiple structures intersect with one another, (2) resources are subject to different interpretation and use, and (3) human agency can transform and be transformed by structural forces (pp. 16–20).[5] Similarly, Ortner's (1989) "theory of practice" sensitizes us to the ways in which people's lives are constrained by vast socio-structural forces. She also stresses that individuals and groups can derive imagination and power from the very tensions and intersections they encounter within this web of macro social forces. Like Bourdieu, Swidler also accentuates "the active role social agents play in reproducing [and inevitably redefining] social structures" (1996, p. 2). In short, this line of conceptualization makes salient the interconnectedness of social structures and the active role of human agency in making sense of their structural environments, implicitly pointing to a "relational" sociology.

The emphasis of Sewell and others on the intersections of structural forces is more explicitly articulated by scholars who wish to denaturalize "society," "nation-state," and other conventional units of analysis. For example, Michael Mann suggests that "society" should be conceived as "multiple overlapping and intersecting sociospatial networks of power" (1986, p.1). Similarly, Somers replaces the term "society" with "relational settings" or "relational configurations," which she defines as "a patterned matrix of institutional relationships among cultural, economic, social and political practices" (Somers as quoted in Emirbayer 1997, p. 295). What is significant here is that such a perspective "does not invalidate the historical-comparative study of national states or 'countries' . . . , but it does prescribe considerable caution in assuming their primacy as units of sociological analysis" (Emirbayer 1997, p. 295).

Furthermore, conceiving such relational settings as fluid, dynamic configurations that change over time, Somers and other relational thinkers are particularly sensitive to the temporal dimension in sociological analysis. For example, Somers develops the notion of "causal emplotment," highlighting how, as the "plot" of the relational configuration unfolds over time, its

---

and social structure, that *culture should be seen as socially organized practice rather than individual ideas or values,* that culture can be located in public symbols and rituals rather than in ephemeral subjectivities" (Swidler 1995, p. 31; my emphasis).

5. "What is needed [for a theory of change] is a conceptual vocabulary that makes it possible to show how the ordinary operations of structures can generate transformations. To this end, I propose five key axioms: the multiplicity of structures, the transposability of schemas, the unpredictability of resource accumulation, the polysemy of resources, and the intersection of structures" (Sewell 1992a, p. 16). Here I reformulate Sewell's ideas in order to make them easier to operationalize.

dynamics, shape, or patterns may also change.[6] Here Somers joins many others in comparative historical sociology to focus on "process" and "transformation" (see Abbott 1992a, 1992b).[7] Although the emphasis on historical processes could sometimes be misunderstood as a preoccupation with descriptions at the expense of analyses, this is not the case with relational thinking. With the concept of "causal emplotment," alternatively referred to as an "explanatory plot" (Abbott 1992a), scholars in this line of inquiry trace historical processes analytically in that they organize a particular social process as a story that consists of sequentially ordered, theoretically understandable bits. Here one is reminded of what Stinchcombe suggests for constructing social explanation: "For the purpose of advancing causal understanding, the unique sequence that brought Stalin to power has to be broken up into theoretically understandable bits. When those bits get back into the narrative, *having been theoretically interpreted,* the narrative will also be improved by being grounded in general ideas" (1978, p. 14; my emphasis). In short, these scholars emphasize *both* causality and temporality, situating social events in their time sequence as well as interpreting them via the analyst's chosen theoretical framework. The inclusion of the temporal dimension refines, rather than replaces, the analytical dimension.[8]

The emphasis of Sewell and other structuration theorists on human agency, which I discussed earlier, is also further developed by the more self-consciously relational thinkers. While in more conventional perspectives, agency is "commonly identified with the self-actional notion of 'human will,' . . . the relational point of view sees agency as inseparable from the

6. Relatedly, Somers develops the concept of "narrativity" to describe the unfolding of her "relational configurations." "Narratives are constellations of relationships (connected parts) embedded in time and place, constituted by what I call causal emplotment" (1992, p. 601). For Somers, "it is causal emplotment that gives significance to independent instances, not their chronological or categorical order. . . . As a mode of explanation, then, causal emplotment is an accounting (however fantastic or implicit) of why a narrative has the story line it does. . . . In fact, it is emplotment of narrative that allows us to construct a significant network or configuration of relationships" (Somers 1992, p. 601–2). See also Janet Hart, Mary Jo Maynes, Luisa Passerini, William H. Sewell Jr., Margaret R. Somers, George Steinmetz, and others, in the pages of *Social Science History* (1992) for discussions of various uses and implications of the term "narrative approach."

7. See also Quadagno and Knapp 1992; Sewell 1992b; and Steinmetz 1992 for discussions of related concepts (e.g., path dependence, historical contingency, sequentiality, etc.).

8. For a debate on this issue, see the exchange between Somers (1998, pp. 722–84) and Kiser and Hechter (1998, pp. 785–816) in the *American Journal of Sociology* 104, no. 3. Goldstone's, Calhoun's, and Boudon's articles in the same issue of the *AJS* also offer important comments.

unfolding dynamics of situations, especially from problematic features of those situations. . . . Agency is always 'agency *toward* something,' by means of which actors can enter into relationship with surrounding persons, places, meanings, and events" (Emirbayer 1997, p. 294; emphasis in original). Somers expresses a similar view in her discussion of "causal emplotment." For her, emplotment involves not only the temporal unfolding of events and the theoretical meaning of such unfolding (as explained earlier); it also centrally concerns the ways in which people write stories about themselves under certain constraints.

This perspective shifts the focus of the discussion about human agency from human will to identity formation. As actors embed themselves in a web of structural and cultural relationships, their understandings about how they situate themselves in these different sets of relationships are at the same time stories about their perceived self-identity in this context. Thus, the formation of social identities can be seen as a process that parallels the formation of relational configurations.[9] In these processes, groups of social actors generate "[collective] narratives attached to cultural and institutional formations larger than the single individual, . . . [which] range from the narratives of one's family, to those of the workplace (organizational myth), church, government, and nation" (Somers 1994, p. 619). These collective narratives are one concrete manifestation of a social group's collective identities.[10]

Swidler's (1995) proposal for a sociology of culture "from outside in" is helpful in clarifying this conception of group narratives. Acknowledging that individuals may possess different cultural values and ideas, Swidler nevertheless argues for the possibility—and indeed the need—to study culture at a collective level. From various empirical studies, Swidler suggests, we learn that a powerful social context that is collectively confronted by a social group helps crystallize the influences of a collective culture in that context. She invokes a famous example in the study of social movements to illustrate her points:

> Gamson's *Talking Politics* (1992), for example, looks carefully at discourse—at what ordinary people say about politics when they are stimulated to think about it in a group situation. . . . While respondents demonstrate intelligence and occasional indignation over social wrongs,

9. Janet Hart (1996) provides us with a detailed empirical example of narrative analysis in social science. She also concurs with Somers in identifying emplotment to be "the most important element in the construction and deconstruction of narratives" (1992, p. 48).

10. Steinmetz (1992) coined the term "collective narrative," and Somers (1992), in the same arena, used the term "public narratives."

their information is fragmentary, their conversation meandering, and their worldviews concatenations of numerous overlapping frames, many of which are nearly self-canceling. (Swidler 1995, p. 38)

How, then, can one possibly study group culture, let alone group identity? Swidler answers this question by pointing out that "[perhaps] this search for a popular culture that could support activism starts in the wrong place. How people organize the cultural resources at their disposal depends very much on the kinds of institutional challenges they face" (ibid.).

Thus, group culture, like group identity, is not something that is shared equally by every member of the group. Collective narratives should not be seen simply as narratives about the collective; rather, they are patterned ways of thinking that exist in the social space of the group instead of the subjective consciousness of individuals and often become crystallized only in contexts that confront the group collectively. Without denying individual differences, we should regard group identity as a (changing) group narrative that is communicated through their public statements in response to certain social situations, and through cultural symbols, communal rituals, group organizations, and so forth. Alternatively, scholars have located such group narratives/identities in the cultural products of social movement organizations, submerged networks, or the organizations that serve as the "reputation entrepreneurs" of a community. All of these group organizations/ networks are not participated in equally by each group member, but they speak from the social space of the collective, reflect upon the position and identity of the group, and their narratives become legacies in the cultural repertoire of the group.[11] In this sense, collective narratives provide concrete documents that allow us to trace the seemingly abstract story of collective identity.

11. For example, Melucci (1989) and Mueller (1994) discuss how the collective identity of a social movement is often developed in one or more movement-related "submerged networks," alternatively described as "cultural laboratories," which are the informal group networks that experiment with new ideas, circulate information, and collectively try on new group identities. While these submerged networks are not participated in equally by everyone in the movement, and even less so by the individuals of the group whose cause the movement advocates, their cultural products become part of the cultural properties of the larger group. Similarly, in his discussion of the formation of community identities, Fine (1998) points out that the task is "accomplished primarily by communal reputational entrepreneurs," namely, those who "choose to speak for the community" (p. 84). Although other members of the community may disagree with the reputational entrepreneurs, "the absence of dissension regarding these claims indicates that these claims are uncontroversial, if not commonly accepted" (p. 84).

The relational approach enables us to center on those social groups whose experiences fall on the margin or outside of dominant conceptual categories. This perspective, which turns its attention toward those social locations at structural and cultural intersections—unstable, changing "relational settings"—and toward social actors' struggles to meaningfully relate to their environment and thereby articulate their identities, offers a useful conceptual vocabulary to address the experiences of the in-between. These emphases guide my analysis of the history of Taiwanese doctors. I write my analytical story by tracing the temporal unfolding of the specific cultural and structural intersections where these doctors were located and by reconstructing their collective narratives at these locations.

CONCEPTUALIZING THE INTERSECTIONS

Coming from this conceptual angle, I designed my research to explicate the processes by which structural forces form the central relational configurations where my actors are embedded. Particularly informative for identifying the key dimensions that shape this relational configuration are the literatures on professions and (anti)colonialism. While these two bodies of literature both cover a huge and diverse field, they converge on the major parameters of the social experiences in each domain, namely, the organizational, the cultural, and the material.

First, the literature on professions has long identified the attainment of market position or group interests as one major defining feature and mobilizing incentive of professional groups (Larson 1977; Jarausch 1990; Freidson 1994). Second, this literature also views occupational autonomy as a defining feature of the system of professions, the key element which differentiates professions from the class system and which is garnered through the administrative, knowledge, and moral authority vested in professional organizations (Freidson 1994).[12] Third, several recent studies have explored the importance of unique professional cultures (Hoffman 1989; Kennedy 1990, 1991; Haber 1991; Halliday 1987; Rothblatt 1995). These studies suggest that

12. In *Professionalism Reborn,* Freidson explores the attainment of professional autonomy and describes how it is achieved through a separation of the "occupational principle" from the administrative one:

> When the central, strategic task of an organization is formulated, controlled, and evaluated primarily by the workers, as it is in the case of the established professions, management does perform logistic functions, but is essentially stripped of what Weber considered to be the prime characteristic of administrative authority—the legitimate right to exercise imperative coordination. . . . Professionalization includes the establishment of authority to coordinate a division of labor. (Freidson 1994, pp. 64–65)

upholding particular moral visions, worldviews, and cultural orientations is part of a process whereby professionals build identity and mobilize.

Scholars of colonialism and anticolonial activism vary about the explanatory power of economic inequality, but they almost uniformly accept it as a primary variable in the formulation of nationality (Gellner 1964; Hechter 1975; Nairn 1977; Hechter and Levi 1979; Balibar and Wallerstein 1991). Similarly, whether ethnic traditions are considered primordial (Smith 1986, 1991), are "invented" by the state (Giddens 1985; Hobsbawm and Ranger 1983), emerge from the intertwined histories of political institutions and cultural idioms (Breuilly 1982; Hroch 1985, 1993; Brubaker 1992), are "imagined" collectively via modern communication networks (Anderson 1991), or are seen as a misleading creation of global imperialism (Young 1985; Chatterjee 1993), the importance of culture in colonialism and nationalism is undeniable. In addition to the communicative networks that sustain the "imagined community" (Anderson 1991), formal movement organizations and informal community networks are also important sites where anticolonial activities, like other contentious actions, develop and mobilize.

The material, cultural, and organizational dimensions of professions and (anti)colonialism are rarely discussed independently of the state and civil society. Professional autonomy is often discussed in contrast to state control or, in a more critical vein, in the context of professionals' withdrawal from civil society (Marshall 1965; Habermas 1989). The role of the state is inevitably centralized in discussions of colonialism and anticolonialism, while civil society is variously regarded as a stage or the goal of resistance,[13] or more dubiously seen as a corrupted forum that tends to betray "the community" (Chatterjee 1993).

Drawing on these literatures, I analyze a central relational configuration:

---

13. A few examples that illustrate the roles of civic organizations (as a stage, an agent, or a goal) in anticolonial struggles follow:

1. The Council of the Indonesian People (headed by Madjalis Rakyat) in Dutch Indonesia, which eventually became linked with an underground anti-Dutch organization, combining the efforts of Indonesian elites with the Japanese and the organizational support of Radio Tokyo

2. The Independence Club of Korea (1876–1910), which marked the effort of Korean nationalist elites to convert public attention from devotion to the Yi monarch to the Korean nation in order to fend off China's and later Japan's imperialist claims

3. The emergence of an "Islamic sphere" in French West Africa, which marked the effort to consolidate an Islamic identity across borders and separate from colonial control

4. The plea for oriental universities in British India, which represented a local demand for respect for indigenous customs and traditions.

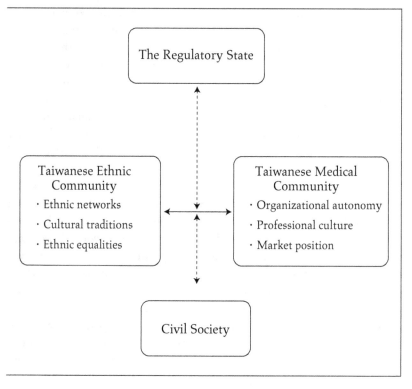

Chart 1. Conceptualizing the Structural Intersections

the intersections of ethnicity and the profession along the material, cultural, and organizational axes in colonial Taiwan. More specifically, these are, first, the profession's organizations, its knowledge and cultural system, and its group interests (often discussed in terms of its market position); and, second, ethnic networks within the Taiwanese community, Taiwanese cultural traditions, and the institutionalized and non-institutionalized inequality between Taiwanese and Japanese. Furthermore, this relational configuration is situated in the context of the colonial state and nascent Taiwanese civil society. The relational configuration unfolds in the context of changing policies and new developments in these two arenas. In sum, professions, ethnicity, the state, and civil society interact and intersect to create historically specific settings for the actors I am studying (see chart 1).[14]

14. However, not all the dimensions that constitute these four domains are equally important in shaping the structural conjunction at all times. As Abbott

As I examine the evolving relational configurations at the intersection of ethnicity and the profession, I foreground the ways in which these doctors situate themselves in, and construct their self-identity out of, the cultural and structural tensions and contradictions around them. In other words, I analyze the ways in which the doctors recognize, portray, or, to use Somers's term, "narrativize" their collective public identity as "Taiwanese physicians." They do so, as Somers, Swidler, and others would suggest, by relating themselves to the structural and cultural intersections surrounding them and thereby reflecting upon their own social roles. By attending to the doctors' understanding and interpretations of their own social positions, I trace the processes and patterns of their self-recognition, formed in partial interaction with recognition by others.[15]

Structural conjunctions and narrative identities together constitute the building blocks, or the "theoretically understandable bits" (to quote Stinchcombe once again), of my analytical narrative. Since I focus on the transformation of one historical case, I conduct an internal comparison over time. I identify specific patterns of relational configuration and narrative identity for each of the three time periods and then discuss the differences in these patterns across time. In my effort to establish these patterns, I highlight the impact of historical legacies, which challenge the perception of macrostructures as timeless. For example, regardless of how much or little political change these physicians achieved, their very participation in anticolonial struggles left a meaningful imprint of nationalism on the Taiwanese medical profession thereafter—as suggested by the two examples we encountered at the opening of this book.

---

explains, "the case/narrative approach to explanation thus differs from the population/analytic one in important ways. It ignores 'variables' . . . when they aren't narratively important, whereas population/analytic approaches must always treat all included variables as equally salient (although perhaps differing in coefficient). This means that case/narrative explanation follows the causal action. Rather than assuming universal or constant relevance, it explains only 'what needs to be explained' and lets the rest of things slide along in background. This selective attention goes along with an emphasis on contingency" (Abbott 1992a, p. 68).

15. Self-recognition and recognition by others, as Calhoun (1994) explains, is a key dimension in "identity politics." One problem with current literature is that the issue of self-recognition is often naturalized. According to Calhoun, discussions of identity politics deal more with the process and mechanism of the struggle for recognition by others and less, if at all, with how self-recognition of an identity is achieved in the first place. This problem is shared by Habermas's theory, with its famous inattention to difference, and by many forms of identity politics rooted in claims to difference which simply take "difference" as a "pre-given point of departure" (Judith Butler, quoted in Calhoun 1994, p. 23).

METHODOLOGY

My data consists of archival materials, in-depth interviews, published oral histories, interviews, memoirs, and secondary sources. The following institutes host a wealth of archival materials that this book draws upon: Guoli Zhongyang Tushuguan Taiwan Fenguan (the Taiwan Division at the National Central Library) and Guoli Taiwan Daxue Yenjiu Tushuguan (the Research Library at the National Taiwan University) in Taiwan, and Taiwan Kyōkai (Taiwan Association), the Gaimushō Gaikōshirōkan (the Diplomatic Record Office of the Ministry of Foreign Affairs), and Kokkai Toshokan (the Diet Library) in Japan. Like all other historical researchers, I encountered a few constraints in my data collection process. The varying conditions of historical materials limited my effort at uncovering the histories that produced them: I was unsuccessful in locating the names of doctors dispatched to the South during the war. The missing holdings make it difficult to conduct a more detailed analysis of wartime state regulation of medical practitioners. I was similarly limited in my capacity to document the development of the professional culture. While a fairly complete collection of the *Journal of the Medical Association of Formosa* can still be found today, the publications of smaller, local medical associations from the colonial period are largely unavailable. Thus, in order to assess the professional culture in the medical community during this time, I supplemented the *Journal of the Medical Association of Formosa* with other sources, such as newspapers, memoirs, and oral interviews.

I interviewed ten physicians: eight in Taiwan and two in Japan. Nine of my ten interviewees were male. All ten came from middle- to upper-middle-class families. Each interview lasted for an average of two to three hours. Two informants, who seemed particularly interested in my project, agreed to be reinterviewed two to three times after our initial conversation. These doctors were typically in their early to mid-seventies at the time of the interview, but one doctor, who was mainly offering information about his physician father, was in his early fifties.

In addition to archival materials and oral interviews, I collected published life stories, autobiographies, memoirs, and oral histories of physicians in prewar Taiwan. To document the general political and economic backgrounds and activities of the time, I drew upon the abundant, well-researched secondary materials written in English, Chinese, and Japanese. Unless indicated otherwise, quotations from Chinese and Japanese materials are my translations. A more detailed discussion of the strengths and weaknesses of my data and a reflection of the complexities of interviewing about colonial experiences in contemporary Taiwan are provided in the appendix.

Consistent with my engagement with the move from categorical to relational thinking, this book employs a case-study approach. Cases are not simply "found," as Ragin and Becker (1992) rightly note. Rather, the delineation of cases and their boundaries always represent an interactive process between theoretical deliberations and empirical investigations. The story of Taiwanese doctors in this book is composed both as a specific, empirical contribution to the study of Japanese colonialism and as a new theoretical exploration of general social trends in the twentieth century. With intense empirical effort, I define a previously unexplored case in a more inductive manner. At the same time, I engage general theoretical concepts to define what this is *a case of* and, in the medium of this previously unexplored history, am led to consider existing theories in unconventional ways. In this sense, the specific contour of the case coalesces only through the course of research.[16]

This book, then, brings theory and data to bear upon each other. The literatures on professions and (anti)colonialism are drawn upon to identify the

16. Ragin (1992) offers a useful conceptual map for understanding what a case is. He suggests that the nature of a case can be considered along two dimensions: cases as specific or general and cases as empirical units or theoretical constructs. This classification yields four possible understandings of cases:

1. Cases are found (specific-empirical). Researchers who conceptualize their cases in this way see them as "empirically real and bounded, but specific. They must be identified and established as cases in the course of the research process" (p. 9).

2. Cases are objects (general-empirical). In this line of thinking, researchers "also view cases as empirically real and bounded, but feel no need to verify their existence or establish their empirical boundaries in the course of the research process, because cases are general and conventionalized. These researchers usually base their case designations on existing definitions in research literatures" (pp. 9–10).

3. Cases are made (specific-theoretical). Researchers can also "see cases as specific theoretical constructs which coalesce in the course of the research. Neither empirical nor given, they are gradually imposed on empirical evidence as they take shape in the course of the research" (p. 10).

4. Cases are conventions (general-theoretical). Finally, researchers may "see cases as general theoretical constructs, but nevertheless view these constructions as the products of collective scholarly work and interaction, and therefore as external to any particular research effort" (p. 10).

Researchers, argues Ragin, often think along more than one of these four dimensions when selecting and/or constructing their cases. This conceptual map helps to clarify what kind of case my study concerns; one can say that my case study evolves a process of "casing" along the lines of (1) and (3).

major dimensions in the relational configurations enveloping these doctors, as explained above. This historical investigation in turn poses new challenges to and questions about these two literatures, as it centralizes and pursues the theoretical question of how "modern" (e.g., the professional) and "traditional" (e.g., ethnic) identity categories interact and are integrated. Specific aspects of the question concerning the blending of the "modern" and the "traditional" are taken up in the following chapters.

The next chapter begins with the specific historical settings of pre-Japanese Taiwan and discusses the traffic between various communities and colonial forces on the island. Although the island is small, Taiwan's location attracted visitors and immigrants from early on, including immigrants from the Malay-Indonesian-Philippine areas, Chinese and Japanese pirates, the Dutch and the Spanish imperialists, and a large number of Chinese settlers. Against this background, I examine how the Japanese, upon conquering Taiwan, confronted the difficult task of singularizing hegemony and in turn developed and implemented their theory of scientific colonialism.

Chapter 3 discusses the formation of the "national physician" identity crafted by doctors between 1920 and 1931, which located the central role of the profession in its service to the nation. During this time, doctors were situated in a relational configuration that confronted them with three sets of contradictions. First, they were closely regulated by the state, but they also enjoyed a certain degree of professional autonomy. Second, they encountered serious, institutionalized ethnic inequalities in the medical community, yet their professional culture challenged this very inequality. Third, Taiwanese doctors shared a sense of solidarity with their ethnic group, but their market position distanced them from other Taiwanese. I analyze how, within the context of a relatively liberal civil society at the time, doctors emphasized the liberal elements of their surrounding structural setting, actively devoted themselves to anticolonial activities, and developed a group identity as "national physicians." The chapter concludes with a theoretical discussion of the social formation of professions and a conceptualization of the possibilities for anticolonial resistance during Japanese colonialism.

Chapter 4 addresses the subsequent uncoupling of nationalism and professionalism and thus the silencing of the narrative of "national physicians." During the years between the Manchuria Incident in 1931 and the outbreak of the second Sino-Japanese War in 1937, rising state oppression and regulation diffused the activism, including that of the physicians, that characterized a once-agitated Taiwanese civil society. But uniquely, the medical profession was increasingly mobilized by the state in its imperial medical system. Professional autonomy gave way to state regulation in the formation of goals and directions. The expanding professional market, in part cultivated by intensified ties between state and profession, further integrated the Taiwanese medical community into the imperial medical system. The expanding professional market, together with other new economic trends in the colony, also sustained the continuation of class differences between doctors and the general Taiwanese population. The cultural connections between their professional and ethnic communities appeared muted during this time. Situated in this new in-between position, the profession failed to register a collective identity narrative, leaving merely silenced and fragmented discourses. These new developments represent a process by which the profession was at least partially uprooted from its ethnic community.

Chapter 5 analyzes the formation of the legacy of the "medical modernists" between 1937 and 1945. During this period, modernity, presented through the profession, was invoked as a source of identity in lieu of ethnicity, which became increasingly confused and tension-ridden. Taiwanese doctors were further domesticated by the surrounding relational configuration, which was characterized by the colonial state's domination over the organizational, material, and cultural dimensions of doctors' ethnic and professional communities. Meanwhile, the elevated market position of the profession and its weakened cultural connections to the ethnic community changed little. Situated in these structural conditions yet attempting to bracket them, Taiwanese doctors tended to ground their identity in professional experiences and culture and thereby developed an identity as "medical modernists." Through the cultural repertoire of their profession, doctors constructed an identity narrative that, for the most part, defined them as "modern" and read modernity as non-ethnic, registering profound confusion between Self and Other in an empire of the "anticolonial colonizers." If the story of the "national physicians" demonstrates the influence of the ethnic community on the professional one, the experiences of the "medical modernists" in turn illuminate the roles that the profession could play at moments of ethnic re-formation.

Chapter 6 provides the brief comparative case of Japan-funded hospitals and medical activities in China. This chapter discusses the process by which Japanese medical doctors and colonial officials, guided by the same principles of scientific colonialism, exported to China their self-conceived missionary religion of medicine. But behind this evangelistic gesture, Japanese medical personnel concentrated on the hegemonic competition with other imperial powers already present in China. The China case illuminates the diverse and complex roles of colonial medicine. This case also shows that when packaging the piece of modernity that it promises to deliver, the profession not only invokes the cause of common welfare but, by necessity, delivers comments about the tradition, culture, and other particularistic ties within both its originating nation and the foreign land. The nationality of the profession offers a powerful challenge to any universalistic implications of "modernity."

After the Japanese decamped at the end of World War II, Taiwanese doctors continued to confront changing structural and cultural forces and negotiate new identities. But this book has to impose a temporary closure on their story and, by way of concluding, reflect upon the theoretical implications of the changing positionality of these doctors, who lived with their compound identity as ethnic professionals, embedded in their Taiwanese community, and this thing called "modernity" that their profession was perceived to carry, at the heart of the tensions of Japanese colonialism.

2 Taiwan
A Nexus of Colonial Forces

What we have to do is to transform our empire and our people,
and make the empire like the countries of Europe and our people
like the people of Europe. To put it differently, we have to establish
a new, European-style empire on the edge of Asia.

Inoue Kaoru, Foreign Minister of Japan, in 1887

After the Meiji Restoration of 1868, the Japanese Empire completely
reversed its long-term policy of seclusion and eagerly sought to rank itself
among the "modern" nations of the world.[1] Modern nationhood, the Meiji
elites believed, "would put an end to Japan's humiliating, unequal treaties
with the Western nations; but their long-range goal was far greater than
this. Their aim was nothing less than a Japan capable of matching the industrial, military, and even colonial achievements of Europe and America"
(Tsurumi 1977, p. 1).

Modeling itself after Europe and America, Japan adopted the road of
imperial expansion as a "reasonable" way to strengthen itself. After the
Sino-Japanese War of 1894–95, Japan acquired its first colony: Taiwan.
Although there has been much debate as to whether Meiji imperialism was
planned or unplanned,[2] it is commonly agreed that Japan carefully designed its colonial policies in Taiwan with the hope that it would become a
"model colony." But what was this "model colony" like before the Japanese
intrusion?

---

1. "From the 1630s Japan was virtually cut off from outside contact, with the
exception of some trade with China and Holland through Dejima (Nagasaki). From
the 1790s increasing Western attempts were made to break Japan's isolation, but it
was not until the mid-nineteenth century that the increase in Pacific whaling and
trading made the United States determined to secure from Japan coaling stations and
supply and help facilities. . . . Eventually, under the 1854 Treaty of Kanagawa, Japan
agreed to open ports, provide supplies, help castaways, and later on exchange consuls.
This is followed by treaties with other powers and renewed pressures to extend
intercourse" (Hunter 1984, pp. 192–93). These foreign pressures caused major
domestic crises in Japan and eventually led to the Meiji Restoration of 1868.

2. For example, see Wray and Conroy 1983, chapter 5, "Meiji Imperialism:
Planned or Unplanned?" See also Jansen 1984.

EARLY HISTORY OF TAIWAN

The oval-shaped, mountainous island, Taiwan, measures about 240 miles from north to south, and 90 miles from east to west at its broadest point. Subtropical to tropical temperatures and excessive humidity characterize the climate. The island is divided into two parts by the Central Range which runs from north to south, with most of the arable lands concentrated on the western half. The U.S. Navy in 1944 registered a precise description of Taiwan's geography:

> Two-thirds of the area is mountainous. The center and eastern half of the island is a rugged mass which forms a central range running from the southern tip (Cape Garambi and Cape Byobito) to the Taihoku [Taipei] plain at 25° N. latitude. . . . On the north, east, and extreme south the mountains rise abruptly from the sea. . . . Between 24° 15' and 24° 35' N. the sea cliffs are among the highest and most precipitous in the world, rising perpendicularly for 300 feet or more and then sloping only a little less than perpendicularly to heights as great as seven thousand feet. (Office of the Chief of Naval Operations 1944, p. 4)

Although the island is small (13,807 square miles—slightly larger than the Netherlands), Taiwan's location attracted visitors from an early age on. Lying to the southeast of China, Taiwan is separated from the province of Fujian by the 150 miles of the Taiwan Strait. "To the South lie the Philippine Islands, . . . To the Northeast lies the Loochoo [Ryūkyū] group, stepping stones toward Japan" (Davidson 1988, p. 2). The earliest visitors to Taiwan were believed to come from these neighboring areas.

The first inhabitants on the island left traces of civilization from as early as 3000 B.C. Although generally referred to by the later settlers from China as "savages," these people actually belonged to different tribal divisions and had distinct dialects and customs. Scholars believe that "Taiwan served as a stepping-stone for the Austronesian (Malayo-Polynesian) people in their movement from south China into island Southeast Asia and the Pacific" (Shepherd 1993, pp. 27). The busy traffic in the pre- and protohistory of Taiwan cultivated a rich and diverse heritage among its aboriginal communities. For example, "linguists constructing the family tree of the Austronesian family of languages depict the Formosan languages as its earliest and most divergent branches" (Shepherd 1993, p. 28). For centuries, the aboriginal tribes settled on the island, where they hunted, fished, and farmed.

Historians believe that Chinese and Japanese pirates and sailors stopped off at Taiwan before any authorities laid claim to it. In the fifteenth century, Chinese and Japanese pirates set up headquarters on the south and the north of Taiwan respectively (Office of the Chief of Naval Operations 1944, p. 162). "The trade thus commenced by the pirates was regarded by the (Japanese) nation with hope and finally authorized by the government. . . . These merchants gave the island, or rather the belt of the island from Takao to Anping, the name of Takasago because the scenery so much resembled the scenery of Takasago in Harima, Japan" (Takekoshi, quoted in Office of the Chief of Naval Operations 1944, p. 162). But if the Japanese seem to have been more active and successful in trade, the Chinese were more numerous. The first known permanent Chinese settlement dates from the sixteenth century, during the decline of the Ming Dynasty (Mukōyama 1987).

In the following century, Taiwan was occupied first by the Dutch and then by the Spanish, in the course of these nations' imperialist expansions. The name Formosa, however, was actually given by the Portuguese, who sailed down the west coast of the island and "were struck by its beauty and gave it the name 'Ilha Formosa' (Beautiful Isle)." A Dutch navigator employed by the Portuguese recorded the name in his charts, and in Europe Taiwan eventually became known as Formosa (Davidson 1988, p. 10). Of the two European powers that did occupy Taiwan, the Dutch arrived earlier and stayed longer than the Spanish, gradually turning Taiwan into an "important entrepot in Holland's worldwide trading network" during the years 1624 to 1662 (Tsurumi 1977, p. 4). The Spanish established only partial control of the island during their brief presence in Taiwan between 1626 and 1642. After the Spanish left in 1642, the Dutch East India Company established island-wide jurisdiction and trade monopoly (Copper 1993).[3]

In 1662, the Dutch were expelled by Zheng Chengkong,[4] a Ming general who settled in Taiwan and attempted—unsuccessfully—to overthrow the mainland Qing regime, in the name of resurrecting the heritage of the Ming

---

3. For an excellent discussion of the history and legacies of the Dutch rule on Taiwan, see Shepherd 1993, chapter 3.

4. Zheng Chengkong is also known by a popular name "Guoxingye," or "Koxinga" in its Europeanized version, which literally means "lord of the imperial surname." Zheng gained this unusual appellation because, in his youth, the Ming court honored him by extending to him the surname of the imperial family. Zheng, born in 1624 in Japan, was the first son of his Chinese father and Japanese mother. He returned to China at a young age and made himself into a Confucian scholar and, later, a military general. Chinese novels and plays often portray Zheng Chengkong as a hero. In eighteenth-century Japan, Chikamatsu Monzaemon, who is referred to as the "Japanese Shakespeare," also wrote a play about Zheng entitled *The Battles of Koxinga*. The play was a great success and created a "Koxinga-mad public" all over Japan (Keene 1951).

dynasty. Under the Zheng family, Chinese-style schools were opened, and the Chinese legal system was adopted. Foreign trade with Japan, the Philippines, Indochina, Siam, and the East Indies was promoted (Copper 1993). During this period, "refugees from politics and famine in China proper flocked to the kingdom of Koxinga [Zheng Chengkong], in spite of the Ch'ing [Qing] defense policy of moving coastal dwellers inland and forbidding all contact with Taiwan" (Tsurumi 1977, p. 6). As a result, the Chinese population of the island continued to increase. In 1683, Zheng Chengkong's grandson surrendered Taiwan to the Qing regime.[5]

After Taiwan was formally incorporated into Chinese territory, it remained politically marginalized in the Chinese Empire. The turbulent history of the island included frequent uprisings and earned the inhabitants the reputation of being a "belligerent population"—as the Chinese later described to the Japanese. Even after the Chinese established official rule in Taiwan, the Emperor of China planned to abandon the island "now that the Ming loyalists were no longer a threat" (Tsurumi 1977, p. 256, n. 17). From 1729 to 1760, the Chinese government banned emigration to the island (Copper 1993; Tsurumi 1977). Not until 1887 was Taiwan made a formal province of China; eight years later it was ceded to Japan. Meanwhile, Taiwan also remained on the *cultural* periphery of the empire. A small scholar-gentry class did emerge by the nineteenth century, and members of this class began to sit for the imperial examinations, thereby encouraging the study of Chinese classical texts on the island. However, the scholar-gentry class remained small. As of 1810 "the total literati class comprised less than .5 percent of the population" (Tsurumi 1977, p. 8). Of course, in this immigrant society, imperial examinations were far from the only road to success. Many settlers accumulated lands and fortunes through agriculture and trade. Certain clans expanded their wealth by these means and, over the generations, came to constitute the landlord-merchant class of Taiwan (Tu [1991?]).[6] Shepherd offers a succinct summary of the Qing rule on Taiwan:

> Taiwanese society . . . remained turbulent and rebellious down through
> the nineteenth century. . . . The [Qing] state did nevertheless find its
> degree holders of service in the maintenance of control over the island,
> if only because of their assistance in recruiting loyalist militia to help
> put down the worst outbreaks. But frontier society did not provide an
> ideal environment for the practice of Confucian government by moral

5. See Shepherd 1993, chapter 4, for a discussion of the Zheng era on Taiwan.
6. See Meskill 1979 for a detailed analysis of the formation of one such clan, the Lins of Wufong.

influence, and the increasing number of degree holders (or of civil in proportion to military) did not by itself guarantee social order in Taiwan. Instead the central government ruled its strategic periphery on Taiwan through a greater than average density of civil and military officers; thus, Taiwan was not "neglected" by the Ch'ing [Qing] court. That is not to say, however, that the methods of control (and the means of financing that control) employed by the late imperial state were adequate to create a stable and nonviolent social order on the Taiwan frontier. (1993, pp. 213–14)

An account of the pre-Japanese history of Taiwan would not be complete if it did not provide a sense of the traffic between various communities and colonial forces throughout the island. Pre-Japanese Taiwan served as the stage for fierce and frequent struggles. For example, the Han settlers acquired lands from the tribal aborigines largely through forceful dispossession, and the aborigines often raided Han settlements in revenge. "Although some buying, trading, and cooperative work was achieved, the history of Chinese-aborigine relations has been that of a long and bloody struggle" (Office of the Chief of Naval Operations 1944, p. 141; see also Shepherd 1993, chaps. 4, 5, and 9). The Han settlers also experienced friction with the Dutch colonizers and organized their first rebellion against Dutch rule in 1630. This first act of rebellion was put down by the Dutch with the help of the Christian aborigines (Office of the Chief of Naval Operations 1944, p. 163), but Han-Dutch tensions persisted until the end of the Dutch rule.

In addition to contentious relationships with both the aboriginal tribes and the Dutch colonizers, the Han community experienced internal divisions. Settlers originating from the Fujian and the Guangdong provinces of China formed two major opposing factions. Later, subethnic feuds developed between the immigrants from Quanzhou and Zhangzhou prefectures in Fujian. The history of settlement was further complicated by the fact that more powerful immigrants offered support and protection to less powerful ones in exchange for service and gratitude, thereby creating deep lines of loyalty and divisiveness. Finally, after the 1860s, the Han subethnic strife subsided and gave way to a more stable, gentry-led society, although differences in lifestyle and dialect persisted.[7]

When the Japanese came in 1895, they were faced with the unfinished

---

7. See Shepherd 1993, chapter 10, for a detailed discussion of the history of ethnic and subethnic conflicts in Taiwan during this period. Shepherd also offers an excellent discussion of the Qing state's strategies to deal with these conflicts.

task of stabilizing the social order and singularizing hegemony, and they managed this task well over the following fifty years. In fact, in assessing Japanese rule in its final years, the U.S. Navy recognized the Japanese precisely for their "salutary" job of establishing a stable social order and single political authority on the island (Office of the Chief of Naval Operations 1944, p. 162). How was this task accomplished? While the U.S. Navy contended that it was achieved mainly through means of police control, the following sections paint a more complicated and complete picture of how control, co-optation, and the policies of what the Japanese called "scientific colonialism" all worked toward the establishment of a stable order and singular authority on Taiwan.

THE JAPANESE TAKEOVER: CONTROL AND CO-OPTATION

After the Sino-Japanese War, China and Japan began a series of negotiations which culminated in the Shimonoseki Treaty of 1895. Chinese representatives ceded Taiwan to Japan, but asked Japan to compromise on its other demands. The Chinese showed little sympathy or concern for the lives of the people on the island. When the two sides met to finalize the issue of Taiwan, the Chinese representative even refused to meet on the island, fearing that the "unruly" population of Taiwan would attack him (Ide 1988, p. 216; Ng 1989, p. 49).[8] He also advised the Japanese to keep in mind that, on the island of Taiwan, "the population was unusually belligerent."[9]

Although the Chinese government gave up Taiwan, it did not eradicate the sense of identification with the Chinese political and cultural order among the Taiwanese gentry. After they learned of China's resolution to give up Taiwan, the gentry in Taiwan formally declared independence on May 25, 1895, and named the then governor of Taiwan as president of the Taiwan Republic. They named their calendar Yongqing, meaning "forever Qing," in order to symbolize their continued loyalty to the Qing court in

8. The Chinese representative, Li Jingfang, said to the Japanese representative, "If I land on the island, I am afraid I will be assassinated [by the Taiwanese] immediately. Please allow me to stay away from the island [for our meeting]" (Ng 1989, p. 49).

9. At the Qing court in Beijing, many politicians contended that China should cede Taiwan, as Japan demanded, to bring peace back to their defeated empire as quickly as possible. Officials and intellectuals fought over the issue. But the former dominated the court and gradually formed the consensus on the relative insignificance of Taiwan. For a detailed explanation of the process and discussion of the ceding of Taiwan, see Huang 1992.

Beijing. However, the president of the Republic fled back to the mainland soon after the Japanese army landed on May 29, and the Republic itself lasted only till June 7 of the same year.

The Japanese continued to encounter local resistance after the collapse of the Taiwan Republic. As the legacy of a long history of conflict, both the immigrant and the aboriginal communities sought to foil Japanese rule, even though they probably did not share the gentry's loyalty to the Chinese court. Various Taiwanese groups organized themselves into anti-Japanese military forces, and Japanese troops faced stiff resistance in their five-month campaign to occupy the island. Officially, civil administration on the island began in April 1896, but insurrections continued long after that. Between 1895 and 1902, more than fifty local uprisings occurred, in which guerrillas attacked Japanese offices and police bureaus (Lin 1993).[10] Even the Imperial Parliament (*teikoku gikai*) in Tokyo began to worry about the issue of public order in Taiwan (Mukōyama 1987, p. 214).

Finally, the third governor-general, Kodama Gentarō, and his civil administrator, Gotō Shimpei, arrived in Taiwan in 1898 and effectively reformed the police system.[11] They forced the native armed forces to disband by 1902 and thereby laid the foundation for civil institutions (Tsurumi 1977; Wu 1992). After 1902 there was peace for about ten years, except for one major case of resistance in 1907, which was quickly suppressed. But then, between 1912 and 1915, perhaps inspired by the 1911 revolution on the Chinese mainland, Taiwanese dissidents organized nine major anti-Japanese uprisings, all of which were quickly put down by the Japanese police. After 1915, "peace more or less prevailed" (C. Chen 1984, p. 220; see also Lin 1993). Armed underground resistance gradually gave way to political and social movements aimed at reform and negotiation with the Japanese government.

Kodama and Gotō's reforms of the police system also laid the basis for the extensive reach of the state over the island. In some remote areas, the police served as the only representatives of the colonial government. In other areas, the police regularly assisted local governments in various administrative aspects.[12] The 1901 administrative reform divided Taiwan

10. See Mukōyama 1987, pp. 164–304 for a detailed discussion of these uprisings and Japan's various measures to suppress and control them.

11. Perhaps the most important police reform under Kodama was the incorporation of the Chinese self-policing system—the *baojia* (*hokō* in Japanese) system. Another important policing device was the establishment of the guard-line system that separated the Han Taiwanese from the mountain areas populated by the aborigines (See Chen 1967, 1984).

12. They "censored publications, supervised public rallies, controlled firearms and explosives, rendered summary judgment in minor criminal cases, curbed illegal

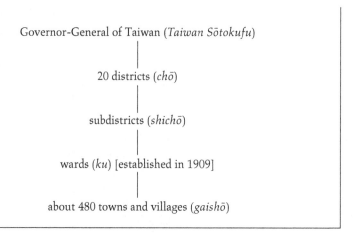

Chart 2. Structure of Colonial Administration in Taiwan, 1901–1920
(Source: Chen 1967, p. 150)

into twenty districts (*chō*), each headed by a civilian official (*chōchō*) who
supervised the police and other public services. Each district was further
divided into several subdistricts (*shichō*), which were then divided into
towns and villages (*gaishō*) (Chen 1967; Wu 1992). In 1909, the governor-
general redivided the island into twelve districts. Villages and towns were
grouped into wards (*ku*). But Kodama's 1901 system essentially remained
intact until 1920 (see chart 2).

The first civilian governor-general of Taiwan, Den Kenjirō, reformed the
1901 system in 1920. Den's reforms mainly aimed at the separation of police
and administration, as a response to both Taiwanese requests for self-
government and the government's need for better division of labor (Chen
1967; Wu 1992). The reforms divided the island into Western Taiwan and
Eastern Taiwan, which were further divided into prefectures (*shū*) in the
west and districts (*chō*) in the east. The prefectures of the west were composed of counties (*gun*) and cities (*shi*). County heads oversaw both administrative and police affairs, while city mayors exercised administrative power
only (Chen 1967). Eastern Taiwan inherited more of the old system. Its two
districts were divided into five subdistricts, and in each of these a police
inspector took charge of both administrative and police matters. Villages and

---

entry of laborers, kept domiciliary records, managed fire prevention, supervised
pawn shops, bath-houses, hotels, restaurants, slaughter houses, licensed prostitution,
administered sanitation matters, etc." (C. Chen 1984, p. 227).

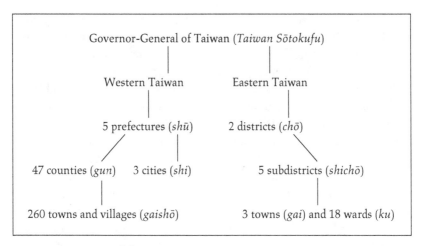

Chart 3. Structure of Colonial Administration in Taiwan, 1920–1945
(Source: Chen 1967, p. 151; Wu 1992, pp. 222-23)

towns remained the most elementary administrative unit in both east and
west (see chart 3). The heads of these administrative units were assigned by
the governor-general. The major change of 1920 that supposedly prepared
Taiwan for local self-government was the establishment of province, city,
town, and village councils. All the council members, however, were to be
elected by the government instead of the local residents, and they influenced
the formulation of local policies in very limited ways.[13] Although the governor-general took pride in these reforms, the educated Han-Taiwanese
often criticized it as a system of "distorted self-government" or "pseudo
self-government" (Wu 1992).

The governor-general relied on devices of co-optation as well as direct
control. In order to facilitate the "domestication" of the colonized population, "the Japanese government agreed to permit those who were unwilling
to remain under Japanese rule to dispose of their properties and emigrate to
China within two years after ratifications of the treaty were exchanged.
According to [the Treaty of Shimonoseki (Article 5)] they had to leave by
May 8, 1897, after which the Japanese government might regard those
remaining on the island as Japanese nationals" (E. Chen 1984, p. 245). Surprisingly few people chose to leave. Only about 5,460 persons of an esti-
mated total population of 2.8 million moved to China by the end of the two-
year period (E. Chen 1984, p. 245, n. 7). But the government was aware that

13. For a discussion of the role of the council members, see Wu 1992, pp. 222–23.

people might stay because of their attachment to their roots and properties in Taiwan, rather than to the new government. So from the start of the colonial rule, the governor-general took various measures to co-opt powerful Han-Taiwanese social groups, such as gentry and landlords.

The government attempted to recruit members of the gentry and landlord class, whose education and wealth gave them high social status and influence in their communities, to serve as advisors or low-ranking officials. The regime hoped to win the approval of these respected and influential people and thereby solidify its legitimacy among the natives. In these early years of colonial rule, some Han-Taiwanese elites refused government positions and withdrew from public life altogether. They tried to live the life of a Chinese-style elite under Japanese rule, organizing their own poetry clubs and Chinese schools.[14] But in general, the government's co-optive strategies succeeded. By 1901, as many as 49,174 Han-Taiwanese had accepted low-ranking or advisory positions in local government, were awarded the honorable title of gentry, or participated in government-sponsored meetings and activities (Wu 1992, p. 67). By the 1920s, positions in local government were highly desirable posts among Han-Taiwanese elites, who seemed more interested in competing among themselves for these positions than in articulating the voices of the general public that were critical of different forms of ethnic inequality in the colony.[15]

The administration of the aborigines differed greatly from that of the Han-Taiwanese; in the former case, the system was geared toward complete control and sustained primarily through violent means. The Japanese, incorporating the *aiyong* (*aiyū* in Japanese) system extant among the Han-Taiwanese,[16] established a guard-line to separate Han-Taiwanese communities from the mountainous areas populated by the aborigines (C. Chen 1984). They achieved this by cutting a path along the crest of the mountains and, at 120-yard intervals along the path, stationing guardhouses staffed by Japanese patrolmen, Han-Taiwanese *aiyong*, doctors, and others (ibid.). Violence was used liberally against rebellious tribes. According to U.S. Naval

14. For a more detailed discussion of these elites, see Wu 1992, pp. 24–42.

15. Several articles published in *Taiwan minpō*, the first non-state-affiliated newspaper (hereafter *MP*), criticized both the government and Taiwanese elites for ignoring the voices of the people. For example, see *MP* no. 123, p. 2; *MP* no. 138, p. 4; *MP* no. 139, p. 3; *MP* no. 196, p. 8.

16. "The Chinese immigrants to Taiwan had created their own organizations for dealing with hostile aboriginal tribes called the *aiyong* (*aiyū* in Japanese) system. Ad hoc as this system was, its general pattern was that of local elite employing a special force of able-bodied men to guard their estates and households" (C. Chen 1984, p. 218).

records, "[Japanese] naval units bombarded settlements from the coast, and army units (over 12,000 troops at a time) engaged in a series of campaigns which wiped out most recalcitrant groups. . . . It has been alleged from time to time that gas has been employed in scouting out elements of resistance" (Office of the Chief of Naval Operations 1944, p. 142). As late as 1930, tribal people attacked an official Japanese ceremony and, taking the Japanese by surprise, killed 190 Japanese. Known as the Musha Incident, the event spurred the Japanese to kill an entire generation of able-bodied men from one village (Mukōyama 1987).

Much like the Han-Taiwanese, the Japanese paid little attention to the existence of different cultures among the tribal divisions and labeled all aborigines as the "Takasago people" (Takasago-zoku). Since the Japanese had adopted the Chinese name Taiwan for the island, they reserved the old Japanese name Takasago for the aboriginal communities (Mukōyama 1987, p. 140). Within this general category, distinctions were made between "uncivilized savages" (*seibanjin*)—those who dwelled in the mountainous regions surrounded by the guard-line (called the Aboriginal Administrative Territory)—and "civilized savages" (*jukubanjin*)—those who lived on the plains and had been assimilated among the Han-Taiwanese. "Civilized savages" received the same treatment as the Han-Taiwanese, but "uncivilized savages" were overseen by the police and governed with a different set of laws and regulations (ibid.). In general, the Japanese policy toward tribal peoples was to suppress and isolate. Throughout the entire colonial period, the "uncivilized savages" were supervised closely and governed as a distinctly different community from the Han-Taiwanese.

Because of its distinct nature, the situation in the Aboriginal Administrative Territory lies beyond the scope of this book. Hereafter, unless otherwise specified, discussions of Taiwanese society will concern only the areas outside of the Aboriginal Administrative Territory.

"SCIENTIFIC COLONIALISM"

Strategies of control and co-optation allowed the Japanese to establish a measure of social order in Taiwan. But in order to truly transform the island into a "model colony," the colonial government needed more complex policies. The first few years of Japanese rule testified to the difficulty of the task. "Without a colonial tradition, literature, or policy, or a corps of trained administrators, it was difficult to translate self-satisfied pronouncements into effective colonial policy, as the first chaotic and haphazard attempts to govern Taiwan quite dismally revealed" (Peattie 1984, p. 83). With the appointment of Kodama Gentarō and Gotō Shimpei (1898), the Japanese at last began a policy of "scientific colonialism" geared toward building a model colony (Peattie 1984, p. 85).

Gotō, a German-trained physician, developed a theory of "scientific colonialism" based on his knowledge of German colonial policy.[17] He adopted a systematic and research-oriented approach to the development of Taiwan, conceiving of the island as a "laboratory." Research into the natural, social, and political environment of the colony would supposedly yield an understanding of its course of social change and evolution (Peattie 1984). To carry out his plan of scientific colonialism, Gotō enlisted outstanding Japanese scholars to carefully and extensively study the customs and laws of Taiwan. At his initiative, Tokyo University established a chair in Colonial Studies in 1908.[18] A deep, scholarly understanding of the colonies, Gotō believed, was essential to designing policies that would commence the "modernization" and "Japanization" of the territories with the utmost naturalness and ease. The idea of "scientific colonialism" left clear imprints on Japanese colonial attitudes and served to legitimize their domination of Taiwan and other Asian colonies as a form of paternalistic guidance. Those in the mainstream of Japanese colonial thought argued that "Japan's subject peoples should be introduced to the benefits of modern civilization—hospitals, railways, the telegraph, basic schooling—under the careful scrutiny of colonial authority" (Peattie 1984, p. 94).

After assuming control of Taiwan, the Japanese extensively and carefully planned the construction of modern infrastructure. Colonial officials invested heavily in railroads, harbors, roads, warehouses, and banking. Throughout the colonial period, "transportation and communication projects consistently absorbed the largest share of the colonial governments' investment" (Ho 1984, p. 352). The colonial government also initiated economic programs and, as a result, became financially independent of the central government's subsidies in 1905 (Ho 1984; Ng 1989). Most of the groundwork for "scientific colonialism" was laid during the Kodama-Gotō Era (1898–1906), except for the campaign to "contain" the aborigines, which was begun later, by Governor Sakuma Samata (1906–1915; see Ide 1988; Ng 1989).

In addition to the development of local infrastructure and economy, "sci-

---

17. See Peattie 1984, p. 85, n. 13 for a brief outline of the similarities between German colonialism and Japanese colonialism.

18. Gotō was the president of the South Manchuria Railroad Company at this time.

entific colonialism" aimed to gradually transform the native population. Through education, colonial officials carefully engineered the make-up of future generations of native elites. Japan's education policies in Taiwan were informed by observation of European and American colonies. The colonial officials in Taiwan, as Tsurumi points out, "were particularly keen students of comparative colonialism" (1977, p. 47) who observed in other colonies specific points to be avoided. Their comparative study of colonial situations convinced them that "to import systems, especially systems of education, from the mother country spelled disaster. To disseminate knowledge which encouraged an individualistic mentality was to poison the social order" (Tsurumi 1977, p. 48). The colonial government was as resolute to avoid these problems as it was committed to the training of native agents. Accordingly, the government strictly controlled both the curriculum and the student body of schools in Taiwan.

The colonial regime developed a well-calculated education policy. Having managed to control and co-opt most of the Han-Taiwanese gentry and land-lords, the governor-general consciously recruited students from gentry and landlord backgrounds to enter the "common schools," or *kōgakkō* (Tsurumi 1977). Only the few outstanding common school graduates were encour-aged to apply to the medical school or normal school (Wu 1992), whose graduates—doctors and teachers—constituted the two major elite groups throughout the colonial period. The rest of the common school graduates were encouraged to return to commerce or agriculture. Before 1918, "teach-ing and medicine were the [only] two main safety valves by means of which a small number of Taiwanese might legitimately seek upward mobility" (Tsurumi 1977, p. 77). Furthermore, the colonial government limited the expansion of higher education in Taiwan, despite increases in demand. Throughout the entire colonial period, only one medical school existed in Taiwan. A few vocational schools were founded after 1919, and a university was finally opened in 1928, mainly to accommodate Japanese youth on the island. In addition to ensuring the slow pace of the expansion of higher edu-cation, the colonial government controlled admission to most schools and preserved many spaces for Japanese students.

The state-engineered system of education produced major changes in the structure of Taiwanese elites. In the 1910s, the landlords and gentry (known as the "old elites") had begun to give way to the rising groups of professionals trained in colonial institutions. By the early 1930s, these new elites outnumbered old elites, and the growth of new elite groups continued until the end of the colonial era. Of existing literature on this topic, Wu Wenxing's study (1992) most tellingly captures the transition

Table 1. Taiwanese Elites in the 1910s, 1930s, and 1940s

	Old Elites	New Elites	Unknown Background
1910s	48.3%	43.4%	8.3%
1930s	23.9	64.0	12.1
1940s	4.1	83.9	12.0

SOURCE: Wu 1992, pp. 151–57

from old to new elites.[19] According to Wu's analysis of the 1916 *Who's Who in Taiwan (Taiwan jinshikan)*, gentry and landlords still maintained their social dominance, comprising 48.3 percent of all Taiwanese elites. Meanwhile, the emerging elites of the colonial school system, many of them from landlord and gentry families, still relied on family background, not education, for social prestige. Over 23 percent of all Taiwanese elites were doctors, and 6.6 percent were teachers. Other educated elites included common school and middle school graduates and Taiwanese graduates from colleges in Japan. Many of the educated elites were active in domains not related to their training, such as small business or low-level government administration.

Wu analyzed three additional volumes of *Who's Who in Taiwan*, one published in 1929 and two in 1934. His analysis indicates that by this time, the new, educated elites had grown to 64 percent of all elites, while the old elites had fallen to 23.9 percent. Doctors and teachers remained the most important educated elites, making up 17 percent and 18.9 percent of all Taiwanese elites respectively. Taiwanese graduates of colleges and vocational schools in Japan had increased to 16.7 percent. As opposed to the 1910s, social position was now achieved through a combination of education and family background. Wu's analysis of the 1943 *Who's Who in Taiwan* confirms the continuation

19. Wu's definition of "elites" draws more upon general descriptions than analytic categories. Wu stresses the importance of education as the means of achieving elite status, but he does not hold education as the criterion to define the category of elites. Instead, he uses the term "elites" to broadly include "people with greater power, reputation, or wealth in society" (Wu 1992, p. 5). According to Wu, during the Qing dynasty, the elites included "the scholar-gentry who had received official titles from the court, and the wealthy merchants, landlords, and scholars who had not received any official titles. Under the Japanese rule, elites mainly consisted of figures with important status in the political, economic, and cultural spheres" (ibid.).

of this trend. At this point, doctors constituted 17.9 percent of all Taiwanese elites, and teachers, 16.6 percent. Graduates of colleges and vocational schools in Japan now comprised 24.2 percent of total elites (see table 1).

Two professions largely accounted for the rise of the new educated elites: medicine and teaching. Their emergence, as the colonial government had hoped, caused little disruption for old elites, as the new professionals often came from families of gentry or landlords. The fact that the social genealogy of new elite groups roughly corresponded to old family genealogies contributed to social stability in these transitional years.

COLONIAL MEDICINE

The Japanese state was proud of its "scientific colonialism" and viewed it as a distinct characteristic of Japanese colonialism. Thirty some years after the acquisition of Taiwan, Gotō Shimpei proudly referred to this colony as an example of the superiority of Japanese colonialism. He argued that, based on its experiences in Taiwan, Japan had done better than various European colonial forces and had developed unique insights to offer to the discussion of colonialism.

> Our first colony, Taiwan, had developed so rapidly that it took every country by surprise. . . . In fact, these achievements were due to my suggestion of developing "biological colonial policies." In other words, we adhered to natural, instead of artificial, policies, which were developed and modified flexibly according to the abilities and characters of the colonized population. ("Asami kyōju cho Nihon ishokumin mondaijo," Kokkai Toshokan)

In both the theoretical discussions and the actual implementation of "scientific colonialism" in Taiwan, cosmopolitan medicine was often singled out as the foundation for this colonial enterprise. Japanese colonial officials thought that "medicine laid the basis for improvement of the health conditions and progress of society in Taiwan" (ibid.). At a more general level, it was argued that medicine was the key to political welfare and doctors the agents of modern civilization ("Gotō minsei chōkan enzetsu hikki," Kokkai Toshokan). Social hygiene, according to Gotō, should be understood broadly as "the protection of the people's lives, which was crucial to the foundation of politics" (ibid.). In his postwar writings, a former dean of the Medical College at Taipei Imperial University reported Gotō Shimpei's 1901 speech at a conference of public physicians in Taiwan:

If we take a look at colonial policies in other countries, we find that there is not a country which does not use religion to facilitate its rule. In other words, the aim is to increase the regime's popularity by resolving mental confusion for, and providing spiritual comfort to, the colonized. However, the native religion in our country [Japan] has not fully developed. But physical diseases, like mental confusion, are also a human weakness, which provides a space [in which the regime can alleviate people's pains in order to] enhance approval in the popular mind. That's why we adopted the system of public physicians. . . . Physicians will function in our colony the way missionaries did [in other colonies]. (Oda 1974, pp. 51–52)

Therefore, medicine was meant to be a tool both for civilizing the colonial subjects and for legitimizing the colonial regime, and, as subsequent chapters show, it was an effective instrument.

Before the Japanese systematically institutionalized cosmopolitan medicine in Taiwan, Western missionaries had already introduced cosmopolitan medicine to Taiwan thirty years prior to the arrival of the Japanese. In 1865, Dr. James L. Maxwell, dispatched by the British Presbyterian Church to introduce Christianity as well as to provide medical services in Taiwan, opened the era of "church medicine" on the island (Xie 1989). Dr. Maxwell founded a hospital in Tainan, and in the following years, Rev. George Leslie Mackay (see figure 3) of the Canadian Presbyterian Church and Dr. Calvin Russell of the British Presbyterian Church established hospitals at Danshui and Zhanghua. These hospitals, like the church itself, were greeted with mistrust and hostility at first, but the missionaries persisted. Gradually they attracted many Han-Taiwanese as well as aboriginal patients, and they converted some of these patients to Christianity. For example, in the 1880s, Dr. David Lan, successor to Dr. Russell, treated as many as 200–500 patients daily at his hospital (Li 1989, p. 118). These Christian hospitals also trained Taiwanese medical assistants, who could rightly be considered the first generation of Taiwanese practitioners of cosmopolitan medicine. Whether or not the Christians were merely "using" medicine to advance their religious missions, they did bring cosmopolitan medical services to many Taiwanese and are regarded as foundational figures in the medical history of the island (Li 1953; Oda 1974).

When Japan occupied Taiwan in 1895, more Japanese soldiers died from disease than perished on the battlefield. Therefore, the colonial government soon found it necessary to improve health conditions in the new colony in order to transform it into an "inhabitable land" for the empire (Chen 1992; Oda 1974). The Japanese considered the church hospitals insufficient for their purposes, and so they imposed their own health program on the

Figure 3.   Dr. Mackay (first on the right) and his Taiwanese assistants (Source: Guoli Taiwan Daxue Yixueyuan Fushe Yiyuan, Taiwan)

island.[20] As early as 1896, the government promulgated a series of health-related rules and regulations, including the Official Organization of the Pharmacy of the Taiwanese Governor-General *(Taiwan Sōtokufu seiyakujo kansei)*, Regulations of the Medical Occupation in Taiwan *(Taiwan igyō kisoku)*, Rules for the Prevention of Contagious Diseases *(Densenbyō yobō kisoku)*, the Opium Law of Taiwan *(Taiwan ahen rei)*, and Regulations of the Taiwan Central Hygiene Association *(Taiwan chūō eiseikai kisoku;* from Taiwan Sōtokofu, *Taiwan Sōtokufu minsei jimu seiseki teiyō* [hereafter *MJST*], vol. 2 [1896], pp. 240–58). These rules and regulations addressed various aspects of public health, from disease prevention to opium prohibition. In contrast to the church hospitals, whose service only covered three

20. The Japanese colonial government utilized the church hospitals for its own medical project in the initial years, but tried gradually to marginalize them. After around 1930, medical assistants trained in the church hospitals were allowed to practice medicine only in rural areas where no cosmopolitan physicians were present (Li 1989).

sites (Tainan, Danshui, and Zhanghua), the government's health program was meant to affect life throughout the island.

When Gotō Shimpei—himself a medical doctor—assumed the position of civilian administrator in Taiwan, he further developed health plans for the colony. Most notably, he built the first island-wide water supply and sewage system, formalized the harbor immunization system and other immunization measures, established the system of "police physicians" and "public physicians,"[21] and successfully implemented a gradual policy of prohibition of opium. Subsequent colonial officials built upon Gotō's groundwork. By 1920, state regulation of the medical profession was well established; a medical school and several hospitals regularly served the Taiwanese; the sanitary conditions of private residents, slaughterhouses, graveyards, public bath-houses, parks, and other public gathering places were supervised by the police and public physicians; and major epidemic diseases, such as pestilence, malaria, and cholera, were brought under control (Xie 1989; Ide [1937] 1988; Li 1952).

From 1921 to 1936, the Japanese continued to upgrade medical services and health conditions in Taiwan. Since the state had already extensively institutionalized the health system, it now attended to the dissemination of general medical knowledge and "modern" sanitary attitudes among the Taiwanese public. However, World War II interrupted such efforts. In the year before the outbreak of the war, Governor Kobayashi formally declared a policy of developing Taiwan as Japan's base for southward advancement. During the war, most of Taiwan's medical resources were absorbed by research teams investigating tropical medicine and, later, by Japanese forces of occupation in China, Manchuria, and Southeast Asia (Xie 1989).[22] Overall, the Japanese created a visibly healthier environment in Taiwan during the colonial period. This achievement, seen as an important benchmark in the modernization of the island, pleased the government, the educated Taiwanese, and eventually also the general Taiwanese population

21. Chapter 3 provides a detailed explanation of the roles of the "police physicians" and "public physicians," as well as other measures taken by the state to regulate the practice of medicine.

22. The US Navy also observed that "that number of qualified physicians . . . has been largely reduced as a result of the dispatch of doctors to 'Manchukuo' [Manchuria] and China" (Office of the Chief of Naval Operations 1944, p. 13). In order to replace these doctors, the governor-general passed a new regulation in 1941 which allowed the Practicing Physicians in Restricted Localities to obtain the status of Practicing Physicians through a state-administered examination (Li 1952, p. 66). Obviously, both the qualifications and the number of doctors serving the Taiwanese community were affected by the war.

(Chen 1992). As later chapters of this book illustrate, the Japanese government radically revised its descriptions of Taiwan within its imperial medical system during the years of colonial rule. From the Japanese perspective, Taiwan was transformed from a "sick zone" to a "healthy land," and finally to a "central base for tropical medicine." In this sense, improvements in health conditions in Taiwan appeared to embody the success of Gotō's "scientific colonialism."

In contrast to efforts to institutionalize cosmopolitan medicine, the state systematically discouraged, or even suppressed, traditional Chinese medicine (Chen 1992). In 1901, the colonial government held an examination for practitioners of traditional medicine to obtain medical permits. This was the only time the government issued such permits during the entire colonial period. Accordingly, the number of licensed practitioners of traditional medicine decreased drastically—from 1,223 in 1901, to 97 in 1942. Many unlicensed practitioners secretly continued to see patients under the guise of Chinese drugstore ownership, but they risked fines and imprisonment if discovered by the police. Even licensed practitioners were permitted to practice only in certain areas. Unlike practitioners of cosmopolitan medicine, they worked under the supervision of local public physicians. Violation of state regulation led to suspension or cancellation of their licenses (*Taiwan Sōtokufu furei*, no. 47, published in *Taiwan Sōtokufu fuhō*, 1901).

Although some of these traditional doctors adjusted to the changes by encouraging their children to attend medical schools, most suffered the widening gap in income and social status between themselves and the new doctors trained in the colonial system. Their experiences in fact closely mirrored the situation of traditional doctors in Meiji Japan. Hence, when traditional doctors in Japan founded the Eastern Medicine Association (Tōyō Idō Kai) in 1927, their colleagues in Taiwan were soon inspired to take similar action and founded the Taiwan branch of the EMA in 1928. Members of this organization published their own magazine and offered lectures in order to revive popular interest in traditional medicine. However, the Taiwan branch was forcibly disbanded in 1933. The short-lived struggle of these doctors failed to earn them recognition as members of the medical profession (Chen 1992).

TAIWANESE CONSCIOUSNESS AND CIVIL SOCIETY

Modern infrastructures, formalized education, and other modernization efforts ministered at a "natural" pace, in short the practice of "scientific colonialism," were combined with measures of control and co-optation to establish a strong and singular political and social order in Taiwan. The Japanese government unified and homogenized the society of Taiwan to a great extent, and thereby facilitated the development of a Taiwanese consciousness. As Ng argues, "The residents of Taiwan did not develop a 'Taiwanese consciousness' until the Japanese Era" (Ng 1989, p. 40). Ng points out that a Taiwanese consciousness among Han immigrants first developed in response to the recognition of the Japanese as obvious outsiders; it grew in the course of guerrilla wars waged against the Japanese; and it finally matured through constant social interaction, which was facilitated by the island-wide roads and communication networks built by the Japanese (ibid.). Other researchers also note that a formalized Japanese education provided a common language and thereby facilitated associational activities among educated Taiwanese of Fujian and Guangdong ancestries (Chen 1992, chapter 5). Taiwanese consciousness signaled the beginning of an imagined community among the Taiwanese people. By 1920, when military rule ceded to a civilian government, the space of that imagined community, at least on the surface, was protected as well as limited by the law. One can argue that Taiwan developed a nascent civil society during the first twenty-five years of colonial rule.

In the increasingly liberal atmosphere of the 1920s, this nascent civil society nurtured new forms of social action which might be recognized as modern social movements. In contrast to early anti-Japanese uprisings, which were typically patronized by local Han landlords or aboriginal tribal heads, and appealed to limited ethnic groups, these new movements were meant to mobilize the entire Taiwanese populace, and they developed as autonomous associations. These modern social movements fell into two large categories—those aiming for the full development of civil society and those suspicious of the capitalist and imperialist elements of civil society. The former included the campaign against Law No. 63, the Home Rule Movement, and the Campaign for the Attainment of Local Autonomy; the latter included the Taiwanese Communist Party and other leftist groups. The most influential of these organizations, the Cultural Association (Taiwan Bunka Kyōkai), interestingly enough, accommodated both trends.

Both trends in civil mobilization developed from Taiwanese student organizations in Tokyo in the early 1920s. As liberal and socialist thought grew increasingly popular among Japanese intellectuals after World War I, these ideas began to influence Taiwanese students in Japan and inspired them to form political organizations such as the New People's Society (Shinminkai) and Taiwan Youth Association (Taiwan Seinenkai). In 1920, with the support of a wealthy Taiwanese merchant-landlord, Lin Xiantang, the New People's Society organized to repeal the controversial Law No. 63, which gave the governor-general of Taiwan legislative and administrative powers unconstrained by the Meiji Constitution. The Taiwanese criticized Law No. 63 as unconstitutional and discriminatory, as it denied Taiwanese certain rights accorded to "true" Japanese citizens. After their campaign failed, the New People's Society shifted tactics from the quest for equality to an emphasis on difference. In 1921, they collected signatures in Taiwan and Japan for a petition to establish a Taiwanese parliament. From 1922 to 1934, fourteen such petitions were presented to the Diet in Tokyo.[23] Although all the petitions were rejected, the Home Rule movement lasted longest of all social movements in colonial Taiwan.

In 1921, several graduates from Taipei Medical School founded the Taiwan Cultural Association in Taipei. The Cultural Association declared itself to be dedicated to the cultural self-improvement of the Taiwanese. But its activities actually spanned a wide range: it functioned as an island base for the Home Rule movement, planned several series of public lectures, and sponsored newspapers, study groups, and other cultural activities (Cai et al. 1983, chapter 6). In 1927, the believers in socialist revolution took control of the Cultural Association and began to actively sponsor labor and peasant protests; the liberals split off to found the Taiwan People's Party (Taiwan Minshūtō) which continued to promote a liberal, reformist platform until its disbanding in 1931. In 1930, tensions between the radicals and the liberals also split the People's Party; those members who insisted on a reformist agenda left the party and founded their own League for the Attainment of Local Autonomy (Taiwan Chihōjichi Renmei), which lasted until 1936.

In 1928, a group of left-wing Taiwanese in Shanghai established the Taiwanese Communist Party. The members of the party were heavily influenced by Chinese and Japanese communists, although their activities in Taiwan received little support from either side (Lu 1989). State oppression and insufficient mobilization capability hastened the collapse of the Taiwanese Communist Party in 1932 (ibid.).

In addition to differing on the question of liberal reform vs. socialist revolution, these movements also differed on their nationalist agendas. Since Taiwanese were not allowed to openly embrace a non-Japanese national identity, their nationalist sentiments had to be expressed implicitly. More-

23. For a detailed analysis of the history of these petitions, see Zhou 1989. See also Wakabayashi 1983, part 1.

over, these implicit expressions of nationalism often promoted more of a mixed identity—Japanese, Taiwanese, and Chinese—than they did any singular identity. For example, the Home Rule movement struggled to preserve Taiwan as a distinct administrative unit within the Japanese Empire. Their petitions emphasized the need to design a Taiwanese parliament, based on the special historical and geographical backgrounds of the island. But as its 1921 petition shows, the movement legitimized itself on the grounds of the Japanese constitution and thereby also acknowledged the legitimacy of the Japanese rule. Tsurumi has translated parts of this important document:

PREFACE

We humbly submit that the Great Empire of Japan is a constitutional monarchy and that *Taiwan is an integral part of the Empire.* Therefore . . . it should go without saying that the administration of Taiwan should also be based upon the principles of constitutional government. . . .

At this important juncture in time, the Empire, which is charged with maintaining peace in the Orient, must pursue friendship with foreign nations and cultivate within the country a cooperation which will solidify the national foundations. Therefore in regard to administration of the new territory, Taiwan, it is imperative that the aspirations of the people, part of a worldwide trend of emerging thought, be recognized and that the races be treated equally in accord with normal standards of constitutional government. A parliament of Taiwan made up of members publicly elected by the residents of Taiwan should be established. Through it the people of Taiwan would be permitted to enjoy the Emperor's sacred pronouncement regarding equal treatment and to benefit from the blessing of constitutional government. *It is most urgent that, through the measure described above, the Taiwanese be allowed to perform their special geographical and historical mission as loyal subjects.*

If their desire is not fulfilled and the present system continues, or if civil rights are suppressed and the civil will suffocated, there is no guarantee that these new subjects will not come to question the rule of the Imperial Japan. For the sake of our nation we the undersigned petitioners are gravely concerned. It will be fortunate if the wishes of the undersigned petitioners are adopted and a parliament of Taiwan is established with powers to participate in the formulation of special laws for Taiwan and in enactment of the budget for Taiwan. . . . This will not only bring happiness to the people of Taiwan; it will also be a singularly great achievement in Imperial Japan's history of governing new territories. This is why we are submitting this petition. We humbly request that the petition be given serious attention.

PETITION

As stated above, we beg to request that a parliament of Taiwan made up of members publicly elected by the residents of Taiwan be established, and that a law be enacted to give this parliament powers to participate in the enactment of special laws and a budget for Taiwan.

The above petition is submitted by the undersigned through the good offices of Ebara Soroku, Member of the House of Peers, and Tagawa Daikichirō, Member of the House of Representatives.

January 1921

(Tsurumi 1977, pp. 186–87; my emphases)

The petition opened with an acknowledgment that Taiwan was an integral part of the Japanese Empire, and yet it ended with a call for a separate parliament. Thus it combined a quest for full Japanese *citizenship* with Taiwanese *nationality*, a strategy which invited critique from both sides. The Japanese state denounced the movement as an independence movement in disguise, while the more radical Taiwanese criticized it as a compromise with the oppressor (Zhou 1989).

The Cultural Association was equally ambivalent. Although it unequivocally proclaimed the distinct nature of Taiwanese culture vis-à-vis Japanese culture, it was hesitant to draw a clear line between Chinese and Taiwanese. "The Taiwanese Cultural Association sponsored summer school and night school courses in Chinese literature, language, history, and geography. . . . On the other hand, . . . the association's plays and operas were in Taiwanese dialects, as were the popular public lectures that drew upon the experiences of those who attended them" (Tsurumi 1977, pp. 197–98). Indeed, Cultural Association activists tended to aspire to the Chinese tradition, although they expressed the themes of this "great tradition" in forms inflected by Taiwanese cultural practice.

The Taiwanese Communist Party and the League for the Attainment of Local Autonomy took clearer stands. The Communist Party aimed to build an independent socialist nation in Taiwan. Even their Chinese supporters encouraged this effort, considering the Taiwanese as a minority people oppressed by the Japanese imperialists rather than as a subpopulation of the Chinese (Lu 1992, chapter 7). The league, on the other extreme, aimed for nothing more than the extension of Japan's system of local government to Taiwan (Wu 1986). Whether this was a practical strategy or an ideological preference, the members of the league never challenged the assumption that Taiwan was culturally and politically an integral part of Japan. These two movements, however, were comparatively less important to Taiwan's anticolonial activities than were the more ambivalent Home Rule movement and the Cultural Association.

ANTICOLONIAL ELITES: WHY DOCTORS?

Despite the differences in their political platforms and nationalist agendas, these movements were mainly movements of the educated elites, sometimes with the support of the landlords. Yanaihara (1929) identified these dissidents as the "middle class and intellectuals"; Wakabayashi (1983), as "native landlords and nationalist intellectuals"; and Zhou (1989), as "the emerging intellectuals." Tsurumi nicely summarizes the role of Taiwanese educated elites in anticolonialism:

> Conservative or radical Taiwanese anticolonialism was a product of Japanese education. Modern Japan no longer held mysteries for the Taiwanese. Their rulers, by school, teachers, and the printed world, had thoroughly acquainted them with a society once alien but now understood only too well. If educated Taiwanese accepted the premises upon which this society stood, they soon discovered that they, who in competition had proved themselves capable of first-class performance, were treated as second-class citizens. This discovery turned many intellectuals into anticolonialists. (Tsurumi 1977, p. 211)

Taking these observations as a point of departure, I wish to accentuate the double role of these Japanese-trained Taiwanese elites. It is true that Taiwanese anticolonialism was largely a movement of intellectuals. But on the other hand, the Japanese-manufactured Taiwanese elite also cooperated with the colonial system.

The co-opted native elites, as discussed earlier, included both gentry/landlords and educated elites, and, with the passage of time, the latter significantly outnumbered the former. Native elites were trained to facilitate the colonial system, but as an ironic outcome of colonial education, they sometimes used their power in ways not anticipated by the state. In colonial Taiwan, these educated natives manifested a significant yet ambivalent social power.

These people were mainly doctors, teachers, and common school graduates. Japanese-trained Taiwanese doctors and teachers, who emerged as the first and the major professional groups in Taiwan, were more influential than common school graduates. Of the two groups, doctors achieved higher status in both the colonial and the anticolonial domains. From the beginning, doctors were simultaneously more integrated into, and more autonomous from, the colonial system than were teachers. Doctors were more integrated in the sense that they benefited more from the system: they received more years of education, higher incomes after graduation, and a more elite status than did teachers (Chen 1992; Wu 1992). They were more autonomous in the sense that they were subject to less control. While all teachers worked as government employees under the close supervision of Japanese superiors, many doctors opted for the relatively autonomous career of private practitioners. Similarly, doctors received more positive evaluations than did teachers from both the Japanese and Taiwanese. The Japanese valued native doctors' contributions to the improvement of public health in Taiwan,[24] and, as I explain in the following chapter, the Taiwanese also praised Taiwanese doctors' leadership in antisystemic activities (see also Chen 1992). In contrast, the governor-general considered that Taiwanese teachers lacked enthusiasm in promoting the goal of colonial education, while the Taiwanese public complained that these teachers showed little courage in sponsoring activities organized in the Taiwanese public sphere (Wu 1983).

In short, Taiwanese doctors were presented more heroically in both colonial and anticolonial activities than were other educated elites. Their paradoxical position probably best characterized the ambiguous and contradictory nature of the social power of native elites in colonial Taiwan.[25] As members of a mature profession, doctors distinguished themselves in one important way: they were much more clearly located in a developed insti-

24. For example, Governor Uchida Kakichi (1923–1924) gave a very positive evaluation of native physicians in a speech given at the twenty-fifth anniversary of the medical school. Even for a speech on such an occasion, his praise of native physicians seemed unusual. He noted that these doctors "contribute to the public health everywhere on the island, and furthermore, some of them work diligently in far and foreign places such as South Manchuria, southern China, and the South Seas" (Senmon Gakkō Kōyūkai 1924, p. 7). See also chapter 7 in Oda 1974 for similar evaluations of Taiwanese medical students.

25. Taiwan is not the only case that testifies to the ambiguous role of colonial medicine. Although the specific dynamics are quite different in British India and British Malaya, medicine was also perceived as a means both to impose imperial rule over the native body and to improve the welfare of the colony. See David Arnold, *Colonizing the Body: State Medicine and Epidemic Disease in Nineteenth-Century India* (Berkeley: University of California Press, 1993); Lenore Manderson, *Sickness and the State: Health and Illness in Colonial Malaya, 1870–1940* (Cambridge: Cambridge University Press, 1996). Arnold makes a convincing point on the ambiguous role of the practitioners of colonial medicine: "Doctors—Indian as well as European—had their own evangelizing agendas and were confident that their practical successes would bring increasing recognition of the superior efficacy of Western medicine and the benefits of colonial rule. . . . But Western medicine also set up opposing currents. . . . Outright resistance might be one expression of this, but so were varying degrees of accommodation and appropriation" (pp. 288–89).

tutional base than were teachers or other educated natives. The doctors' institutional base granted them material resources, organizational autonomy, and a distinct culture with which to challenge the colonial system. While all intellectuals were exposed to the dominant narratives of modernism and anticolonialism at the time, the doctors' modernist and anticolonial thoughts and deeds were grounded in specific professional practices. At the same time, however, doctors were invested in defending and further developing this institutional base, which was part and parcel of the colonial system. How then did they negotiate between these conflicting forces? The following chapters take up this question with an analysis of the changing structural locations and ambivalent social identities of doctors in three time periods.

3 National Physicians (1920–1931)

In colonial Taiwan, colonialism and professionalism were both set in motion by the Japanese colonial state and developed in close mutual interaction. The very interaction of these two social processes engendered structural conditions which—though powerful—were multiple, incoherent, and often contradictory; thus, its social consequences cannot easily be assumed or predicted. This chapter analyzes one such unintended outcome—the development of liberal anticolonialism among Taiwanese physicians in the 1920s.

I first delineate the specific structural conjunction that resulted from the intersection of various dimensions of the medical profession (organizational autonomy, professional culture, and market position) and various dimensions of Taiwanese ethnicity in colonial Taiwan (community networks that sustained ethnic solidarity, an often contested "ethnic culture," and ethnic inequality). I examine this structural conjunction in the context of a strong colonial state which constantly attempted to exercise regulatory power and establish cultural hegemony. As noted in chapter 1, not all of the dimensions just described were equally important in shaping the structural conjunction at all times; my discussion preferences historical context over "consistency in variables."

Then I document the important involvement of doctors in the liberal anticolonial movements of the nascent Taiwanese civil society, which crucially shaped their interpretation of the structural tensions that surrounded them. In the third section of this chapter, I trace how doctors became a self-conscious social group, forged for themselves a meaningful understanding of their environment, and struggled to formulate and present a socially salient public identity that did not come readily from their structural location. In the process, these doctors—initially trained by the Japanese as a hegemonic strategy—became mobilized on behalf of their ethnic community, though not without constraints, to mutate the state's colonial project.

THE PHYSICIANS' "IN-BETWEENNESS": STRUCTURAL CONTRADICTIONS

Although cosmopolitan medicine was single-handedly institutionalized in Taiwan by the Japanese colonial regime to serve as a tool both in civilizing the colonial subjects and in legitimizing the colonial regime, the implementation of these plans brought together multiple social domains and fused them in new and unpredictable ways. As the state trained and employed Taiwanese physicians to help carry out health projects, they were gradually incorporated into the professional community of medicine. The state tried to control them; the medical community was meant to assimilate them. While both attempts succeeded to some extent, doctors' social identities remained grounded in their Taiwanese community. Gotō's project of "medical missionaries," therefore, quite unintentionally situated its Taiwanese agents in between domains of the state, the medical profession, and their own ethnic community.

Three sets of structural contradictions become particularly salient when considering Taiwanese doctors' in-between position. First, the regulatory power of the state and the organizational autonomy of the medical profession were often in competition. Second, within the medical community, professional *organizations* institutionalized ethnic inequalities between the Japanese and Taiwanese, whereas the professional *culture* tended to challenge these inequalities. Third, within the Taiwanese community, Taiwanese physicians shared a cultural tradition and a sense of solidarity with their ethnic group, but were sometimes distanced from this group by their professional culture and class position.

The Profession vs. the State: Organizational Autonomy and State Regulation

As the medical project was central to the design of scientific colonialism, the colonial regime attempted to uphold direct control over the medical system in the colony and to cultivate its efficiency and instrumentality. The state did this specifically through the implementation of two systems during the first few years of the colonial period: the system of the "police physicians" and "public physicians," and the system of medical education and licensing. In the former the state directly assigned and supervised physicians' tasks; in the latter it regulated physicians through education, licensing, and examinations.

In 1897, the Japanese government added the position of "police physician" to local governments in Taiwan. Police physicians were state agents who carried out health policies in local communities. In addition, they oversaw a wide variety of health-related affairs, ranging from administration of public health to the practice of medical jurisprudence (Li 1952, pp. 57–60). A law was passed in 1909 to establish the police physicians as a mandatory part of local government staff.[1] The police physicians resembled the colonial police in many aspects; these two groups shared similar titles (i.e., "police" and "police physicians"), the tasks of regulating the colony, and the same official communication networks.

Just prior to this, in 1896, the colonial state promulgated the Rules and Regulations for Public Physicians in Taiwan. Eighty public physicians were recruited from Japan (though the original goal was to recruit 150) and underwent three months of special training in basic Taiwanese and immunization procedures for the most life-threatening diseases in Taiwan at the time, such as malaria, cholera, and bubonic plague. While they were not state employees, public physicians received state subsidies and were appointed by the state to practice medicine in designated areas of Taiwan. They took charge of general local sanitation, immunization, and corpse examination, and served as the state's agents in the regulation of pharmacology and Chinese medicine (Xie 1989, pp. 53–55; Oda 1974, p. 52; see also Li 1952).

In addition to assigning police physicians and public physicians to work in designated areas, the colonial regime recognized that private physicians would be indispensable to the thorough implementation of its medical policies in the colony.[2] Most private physicians in Taiwan graduated from the Medical Training Institute of Taipei Hospital,[3] which was established in 1897 by the governor-general of Taiwan to provide basic training in cosmopolitan

1. The positions of "police physicians" were changed to those of "sanitary technicians" in 1944.
2. See Taiwan Kyōikukai 1939, pp. 926–27.
3. In 1899, the name of the institute was changed to Taiwan Sōtokufu Igakkō (the Medical School of the Governor-General of Taiwan). In 1918, the school began to admit Japanese students, but it kept them segregated from Taiwanese students. In 1919, the Taiwan Medical School was upgraded to a college, called the Taiwan Sōtokufu Igaku Senmon Gakkō (the Governor-General's Medical College of Taiwan), and in 1922, it adopted the policy of "integrated education" for the two ethnic groups. In the same year, it finally acquired equal status to the medical colleges in Japan, and was changed to Taiwan Sōtokufu Taihoku Igaku Senmon Gakkō (the Medical College of the Governor-General of Taipei; see Li 1953, p. 328; Chen 1992, p. 29). Despite these name changes, I refer to this school as the Medical School or Taipei Medical School throughout this book.

medicine to the Taiwanese. Graduates from the Medical School were licensed to practice throughout the island.[4]

Upon the founding of the Taipei Medical School, the governor-general, Kodama Gentarō, his chief civilian administrator, Gotō Shimpei, and other colonial officials agreed that education should remain instrumental to the political designs of the regime. As Tsurumi puts it, "irresistible Taiwanese demands for higher education were to be channeled into professional studies, which would produce the kind of trained natives the colony required" (1977, p. 214). After founding the Medical School, colonial officials explicitly warned the government in Japan about the danger of the Medical School becoming a source of political empowerment for the natives, as had been observed in India, Indonesia, Algeria, and the Philippines (Wu 1992, pp. 97–98; Chen 1992, p. 27). In response to these warnings, the colonial state designed a policy to selectively recruit students for the Medical School (Tsurumi 1977). Clearly, the medical profession was established to function as an effective and subordinate tool of colonial administrators. On the one hand, the colonial regime diligently recruited, trained, and funded the staff for its broad-based health system, including police physicians, public physicians, and medical school graduates. On the other hand, the state retained the authority to coordinate the occupational division of labor.

However, the subordination of professional authority to political authority did not remain as uncontroversial as the state had expected. As the medical profession expanded, it inevitably cultivated its own internal logic. The continual development and improvement of the field became a driving impetus within the medical profession and, gradually, the betterment of medical practice and education was prioritized over the fulfillment of state policy. Perhaps the first notable sign of this trend lies in the discrepancies between the policies of the colonial state and the agendas of various state-appointed Japanese leaders in the Taiwanese medical community. For example, despite the state's explicit intent to provide only a limited education to the colonized, the first president of the Taipei Medical School, Dr. Yamaguchi, declared as early as 1899 that the simplified curriculum at the Taipei Medical School was a temporary measure and that, in due course, the train-

4. In addition to regular private physicians, the governor-general of Taiwan also recognized the "practicing physicians in restricted locations." The term "practicing physicians in restricted locations" applied to doctors who obtained their licenses through a state-administered examination instead of a regular medical course. They were allowed to practice only in specific, usually remote, areas (Li 1952, pp. 64–66).

ing program at the Medical School would be upgraded (Senmon Gakkō Kōyūkai 1924, pp. 16–20). Dr. Yamaguchi was remembered to have shown the same commitment in his own actions. When he visited Tokyo in the same year, he bought a great number of books in various fields and planned to ship them to Taiwan for the library of a Taiwanese university that he believed should soon be built. Such words and actions put his own career at risk and, in a dramatic turn of events, Dr. Yamaguchi received a telegram that abruptly terminated his appointment on the eve of his scheduled return trip to Taiwan (Ohzuru 1995, p. 9; see also Chen 1992 p. 28).

Likewise, Drs. Horiuchi and Yoshida at the Medical School attempted to address the issue of ethnic segregation faced by their students. Taipei Hospital, the only state-run hospital in Taipei at the time, exclusively admitted Japanese patients and refused to provide internship opportunities for Taiwanese medical students. Alternatively, Horiuchi and Yoshida located two charity units for Taiwanese patients to provide internships as part of their students' training. These professors were fondly remembered for their personal commitment, as they walked many miles with their interns to these places every day (Guoli Taiwan Daxue Yixueyuan Fushe Yiyuan 1995, p. 16). Meanwhile, the second president of the Medical School, Takagi Tomoeda, opposed the regime's policy of ethnic segregation and bargained with Taipei Hospital to gain internships for his Taiwanese medical students (Senmon Gakkō Kōyūkai 1924, p. 78). After these attempts failed, he successfully requested that the Japanese Red Cross consider establishing a branch hospital in Taipei and allowing his Taiwanese students to complete internships there (Du 1989). While none of these Japanese doctors appeared to be particularly concerned with improving the *political* conditions in the colony, they were adamant about raising the standards of the *professional* training in their field—a manifestation of developing professional autonomy in the medical community during this time.

Furthermore, as health care gradually moved beyond the initial stage of institutionalization, its Taiwanese agents started to enjoy a certain degree of professional autonomy. During the 1900s and the 1910s, the state turned its attention to immunization efforts, distribution of health care, and the dissemination of general medical knowledge in remote towns and villages. In this effort, the Japanese found that the language, rules, and in fact the very "otherness" of Japanese doctors at public hospitals often alienated and even discouraged Taiwanese patients from seeking treatment.[5] In order for cos-

5. Fan Yanqiu's (1993) work on Yilan Hospital is an excellent case study which illustrates this point with rich data and examples.

Table 2. Private Physicians in Taiwan, 1909–1942

Year	Number of Doctors at Public Hospitals and Clinics	Number of Private Physicians	Number of Public Physicians	Total Number of Physicians	Percentage of Private Physicians
1909	120	154	77	351	44%
1911	107	197	84	388	51
1913	118	251	89	458	55
1915	155	329	94	578	57
1917	108	399	103	610	65
1919	155	462	104	721	64
1921	173	542	101	816	66
1923	180	570	132	882	65
1925	154	649	169	972	67
1927	207	717	188	1,112	64
1929	171	805	209	1,185	68
1931	200	897	225	1,322	68
1933	208	1,017	241	1,466	69
1935	323	1,103	248	1,674	66
1937	333	1,240	272	1,845	67
1939	411	1,382	279	2,018	68
1941	422	1,513	293	2,228	68
1942	492	1,665	284	2,441	68

SOURCE: Chen 1992, p. 39

mopolitan medicine to thoroughly penetrate the colony, they discovered, it had to be practiced in more familiar ways by more familiar people. The state therefore enlisted Taiwanese graduates of the Medical School to serve on these medical missions and later encouraged them to open their own clinics. In fact, the state had to rely on these clinics as an important supplement to the public health care system. In 1911, the percentage of private Taiwanese physicians began to exceed that of state-employed doctors, and this situation continued throughout the colonial period. As the number of private physicians increased over time (see table 2), they came to constitute a (relatively) autonomous social force.

In short, by the 1910s the medical profession in Taiwan had gained some degree of authority to coordinate its own internal division of labor and, in this sense, it achieved a measure of organizational autonomy from the state. The professional authority of the medical field, as we will see later, was soon to compete with, keep in check, and even challenge the colonial political authority that had promoted its creation.

Tensions within the Medical Community

Japanese "scientific colonialism" was articulated and justified through a "diffusionist model," which, not surprisingly, situated the metropole at the center of all modernizing forces. In this model, the colonizers occupied the position of benign mentors, and the colonized filled the role of eager pupils, united in the goal of modernizing Taiwan. The medical system accommodated colonial hegemony very well. In his speech at the first graduation ceremony at the Taipei Medical School in 1902, Gotō Shimpei made an explicit analogy between teacher-student relationships at the Medical School and relations of colonial hegemony in Taiwan:

> Since Taiwan became the territory of the Japanese Empire, the Empire has been kindly exposing the Taiwanese people to modern civilization. You graduates are the especially fortunate ones among the three million Taiwanese; you have learned about, and are now ready to practice, the most advanced knowledge and skills. Does this not bring your ultimate happiness and honor? You have received a special favor from the Japanese state and the governor-general of Taiwan. (Senmon Gakkō Kōyūkai 1924, p. 25)

The organizational structure of the Taipei Medical School and hospitals embodied this master-apprentice "ideal." At the Taipei Medical School, prior to 1919, all professors were Japanese, and all students were Taiwanese. After their graduation, at hospitals and in state-headed health projects, Taiwanese physicians found themselves continually playing the role of disciples, led by Japanese physicians or policymakers.[6] At public hospitals, Taiwanese physicians were almost exclusively placed in low-ranking positions, as assistants to their Japanese colleagues (Fan 1993).

In spite of this context of paternalistic and hierarchical relationships between Japanese and Taiwanese, there was a prevalent, liberal, humanist professional culture, emanating from Japanese professors and being gradu-

6. For example, Dr. Lin Yushu, who graduated from the Medical School and later worked for a state-headed medical project, comments in his memoirs on the similarities between the mentorship he received at school and the mentorship he was placed under at work (Lin 1935).

ally cultivated among their Taiwanese students. From the start, the presidents of the Taipei Medical School all appeared to be liberal thinkers (Du 1989). Their pursuit of professional autonomy, as illustrated earlier, also signaled a relatively liberal attitude in that they were at least nonchalant and at best critical toward the ethnic hierarchy upheld by the colonial state. But perhaps the most telling example is President Takagi's role as an enthusiastic advocate of humanist thinking. He is favorably remembered for ignoring the common school rules regarding language in the colony and allowing his students to speak Taiwanese at school (ibid.). His famous edict—"Become a human before you become a doctor"—was quoted repeatedly by his Taiwanese students and was very influential (Du 1989; Chen 1992).[7]

Surprisingly, the hierarchical power structure and liberal professional culture actually coexisted for quite some time in the medical community. Taiwanese students seemed to accept the power vested in their mentors and admired their liberal and humanist orientation. Numerous accounts illustrate how favorably Taiwanese medical students at this time regarded their Japanese teachers (e.g., Chen 1992; Du 1989). Similar depictions of the Japanese professors at Taipei Medical School were reiterated and reinforced in several important forums that contributed to the making of the profession's collective memory. At a conference among "eighty-something doctors," held by a medical journal, *Hope (Yiwang)*, in 1978, several participants emphasized that the teaching "become a human before you become a doctor" guided them throughout their medical careers ("Gaoling yishi zuotanhui" 1978). Their words appear all the more significant since they were uttered under an authoritarian regime that took a strong anti-Japanese stand in postwar Taiwan. In 1995, marking its centennial anniversary, National Taiwan University Hospital (formerly Taipei Hospital) published two volumes of collected essays. Authored by the editorial committee as well as a great number of individual doctors who had affiliations with the hospital, these essays detailed their histories and memories. The revisiting

---

7. Obviously, there existed numerous competing theories of liberalism. However, the Japanese doctors and their Taiwanese students did not appear to be particularly conversant in these theoretical debates. Consistent with the European Enlightenment tradition, their liberalism subscribed to a general ideal of universal freedom, equality, and fulfillment that was transcendent of any primordial social divisions. Philosophical and historical studies have yielded to the realization that "even in the best situations [the liberal ideal] has been only partially realized" (Rockefeller 1994, p. 87). Colonial Taiwan certainly does not come close to being one of the "best situations," yet the Japanese and Taiwanese doctors at the time did not seem to have developed serious critiques of the liberal ideal.

of institutional memory this time was more celebrated, attracted an impressive number of contributors, and took place in a freer, post-democratization Taiwan. Despite all these changes, the same theme emerged. A 1932 Taiwanese graduate of the Medical School put it succinctly in his comment that he and his classmates had always "respectfully thought of Dr. Horiuchi Tsuguo [the third President at the Taipei Medical School] as a kindhearted father figure" (Zeng 1995, p. 269).

The words of individual doctors converge with the collective memory of the profession. A Taiwanese physician fondly recalled another "good" Japanese mentor in his autobiography:

> In 1919 I started to work at Tainan Hospital. The President at the hospital then was Dr. Akashi, one of the Japanese I respected. . . . He never was discriminatory toward Taiwanese. . . . [According to the regulations in the hospitals at the time, as a medical assistant], my duties were limited to copying prescriptions, carrying out examinations, and checking patients' medical records. Not being involved in the treatment of patients accounted for my lack of interest in my work. In the end, Dr. Akashi went along with my request and charged me with the responsibility of primary care for a number of patients. My job began to involve office practice, provided that there were patients who wished to see me. [Dr. Akashi's decision] was made with unprecedented insight, but numerous complaints about this came from the Japanese staff. (Han 1966, p. 25)

Like many other Taiwanese physicians faced with institutionalized ethnic inequality, Dr. Han eventually left the public hospital to start his own clinic. But these private physicians did not directly challenge the discriminatory organization of public hospitals.

After 1919 things started to change. Ironically, when the governor-general did at last attempt to create an ethnically integrated system of education, this only served to trigger discontent among these liberal but otherwise respectful students. The colonial government issued the Command for Integrated Education (*Kyōgaku-rei*) in 1919, which loosened its political grip on medical education.[8] The Integration Rescript of 1922 further extended the practice of ethnically integrated education to other levels of schooling. Although the new policy was intended to improve education for the Taiwanese, it was often used by colonial officials to serve the interests of

---

8. The Medical School was originally supervised by the Police Bureau. With the reform, the Medical School was now placed under the supervision of the Internal Affairs Bureau (Taiwan Kyōikukai 1939, pp. 926–28).

Japanese residents in Taiwan.[9] This situation intensified the contradiction between liberal culture and ethnic inequalities in the medical community. Taiwanese students began to argue that while school authorities had formalized an ethnically integrated education, they had not provided for the equal treatment of both ethnic groups.

For example, in 1924, the Medical School promised to change its segregated educational system. As a result, the preparatory course for Taiwanese students was extended from four to five years, and future graduates of the five-year preparatory course were promised admission to the Medical School without entrance exams, as was the case with Japanese students on the island. However, as the graduation date for students of the new preparatory course approached, the college suddenly decided that Taiwanese graduates would, after all, have to pass the old entrance examination. Though all the graduates of the preparatory course passed the entrance exam, students expressed serious discontent and severely criticized the Medical School (see *Taiwan minpō*, hereafter *MP*, vol. 2, no. 6, p. 12). Similarly, Taiwanese physicians publicly voiced critiques of unequal treatment. For instance, they openly denounced the ethnic distribution of promotions, pay raises, and allocations of internships (see *MP*, no. 261, p. 4; *MP*, no. 408, p. 13).

Other examples also document the jarring noises of discontent produced by a community that accommodated both a practice of ethnic inequality and a liberal trend of thought. A Taiwanese 1930 Medical School graduate recalls, "The School provided two separated dormitories, one for us and one for the Japanese students, who differed from us in their language, habits, etc. . . . The two sides had conflicts from time to time, although in general we got along OK" (He 1995, p. 76). A Japanese graduate from the same school in the same year added another dimension to the story (perhaps with some misgivings) that focused on their president's liberal corrective to such conflicts. According to him, "Under the leadership of President Horiuchi, when any conflicts occurred between Japanese and Taiwanese students, it was surely us Japanese that would be punished" (Sugatani 1995, p. 262).

In short, in the 1920s, the medical community was increasingly affected by contradictory trends. On the one hand, ethnic inequalities and de facto

9. The integration policy was not closely observed at the level of elementary education. In Taiwan, Japanese children still received a better elementary education than did their Taiwanese counterparts. Since they were trained differently at an early stage, ethnic integration in higher education actually disadvantaged the Taiwanese. Formerly all-Taiwanese facilities were now open to Japanese students, and thus Taiwanese students faced stiff competition for these slots. For a detailed discussion, see Tsurumi 1977, pp. 91–106.

segregation continued to pattern life in the medical community. On the other hand, the ideal of equality undercut this structure. By the 1920s, the relationship of Taiwanese physicians to their Japanese supervisors was fraught with ambiguity. To Taiwanese medical students and doctors, their Japanese counterparts simultaneously embodied two identities, oppressor and mentor—a paradox never resolved throughout the colonial period.

Tensions within the Taiwanese Community

As Yanaihara Tadao points out in his classic *Taiwan under Imperialism* (*Teikokushugika no Taiwan*), "Class antagonisms and ethnic conflicts in [colonial] Taiwan were rival forces which nevertheless were intertwined with one another" (Yanaihara 1929, p. 117). Because of the market position of the medical profession, Taiwanese physicians, perhaps more than other social groups, lived the contradiction of these two forces.

While doctors and non-elite Taiwanese faced the Japanese as a common oppressor and united at distinct points in their resistance to colonial rule, physicians were often viewed by non-elites as the "typical native bourgeoisie." As they occupied a privileged market position, low-income people often had to plead with them to reduce their charges for medical care. In 1908, for example, a private Taiwanese physician's monthly income ranged from 200 to 500 Japanese yen, while teachers—the other major group of educated native elites—earned just 12 to 45 Japanese yen per month (Chen 1992). Doctors clearly formed a distinct privileged class in the colonized population.

The history of the formation of a professional strata in colonial Taiwan reinforced the class position of the medical elite. The governor-general strategically targeted the children of local gentry and landlords in recruitment efforts for the Medical School and the normal school, the two elite educational institutions (see chapter 2). By the 1920s, children of the old elite emerged as a new professional social elite, as teachers and especially doctors. The elite family background of many physicians often accorded them additional resources and social status, which further enhanced their market position. Therefore, under the colonial system, Taiwanese physicians simultaneously shared a sense of solidarity with the non-elite Taiwanese community and occupied a class position that was often in conflict with the interests of that community.

Furthermore, the social formation of this group reinforced the contradictions that emerged between their professional culture and ethnic traditions. Coming from families of local gentry or landlords, many physicians were deeply immersed in traditional Chinese culture since, in the early colonial

Figure 4. Liu Juchuan in 1910. Liu (left) wore a pigtail and Chinese-style robe before he entered medical school. (Source: Guoli Taiwan Daxue Yixueyuan Fushe Yiyuan, Taiwan)

period, native elite families continued to favor the Chinese private schools (*shobō*) over the Japanese "barbarian schools" (Wu 1992, p. 315).[10] Thus, in addition to their training in colonial institutes, many young physicians in the 1920s had at least some experience in the *shobō* and learned many things about traditional Chinese culture, such as poetry writing (Cheng 1992; Tsurumi 1977, p. 168). These physicians were also among the most "modernized" residents of Taiwan. With their training in the sciences and their exposure to modernist discourses in post-Meiji Japan, many doctors became critical of several traditions of Taiwanese society, which they denounced as reactionary and backward (Chen 1992).

Upon entering the Medical School, many Taiwanese students transformed their clothing and physical appearance, in addition to developing a liberal philosophy. Instead of pigtail and robe, they now wore short hair and a

---

10. According to *Taiwan kyōiku enkakushi* [A Record of the Development of Education in Taiwan], the Chinese private schools functioned parallel to the Japanese common schools *(kōgakkō)* for at least the first decade of colonial rule. The total number of students at the common schools, 23,178, exceeded that of the private schools, 21,661, for the first time in 1904 (Taiwan Kyōikukai 1939, pp. 408–10). By 1923, the Chinese private schools were clearly on the wane (Tsurumi, p. 124).

Figure 5. Liu Juchuan in 1913. Liu (far left) now wore short hair and a Japanese-style uniform as a student at Taipei Medical School. (Source: Guoli Taiwan Daxue Yixueyuan Fushe Yiyuan, Taiwan)

Japanese-style uniform (see figures 4 and 5). Their views on rituals and traditions underwent similar changes. Dr. Han, along with many of his peers, rebelled against old Taiwanese customs and held a creative, and eye-opening, wedding ceremony in 1926. Against the prevailing custom of arranged marriages at the time, Dr. Han and his bride (who was supposed to remain submissive and silent during a traditional wedding) wrote and read aloud to the wedding guests their vows, which featured the spirit of free love and individual choice·

> The two of us have befriended each other freely for four years and ten months since June 26, 1921. The many tests we encountered did not change our mind. Today, we agree to marry each other on this sacred occasion. From this day on, we hope to shoulder our share of responsibilities [within the family], to love and to cherish each other, for ever and ever. As husband and wife, we hope to build a wonderful family and to further dedicate ourselves to improving an imperfect society—so that we can fulfill our responsibilities as humans. Such is our vow. With earnest sincerity we professed it in your presence. (Han 1966, p. 39)

Needless to say, their "modern" spirit was considered new and unusual, but ultimately earned praise from the newspaper *Taiwan shinminpō* a few years later (ibid.).

In short, although they inherited a traditional culture, these doctors also developed a liberal and modernist orientation, which resulted in a mixed cultural relationship with their Taiwanese community. In fact, they had an ambiguous relationship to the larger Taiwanese community in general. They were united under common systems of oppression, but at the same time they developed contradictory market interests and cultural traditions.

ENTERING CIVIL SOCIETY

Thus far I have sketched the ways in which a relational configuration of the colonial state, the medical profession, and Taiwanese ethnicity took shape in the first half of the colonial period. With the emergence of a nascent civil society in the 1920s (see chapter 2), these interacting structural forces began to play out in a broader public domain which surpassed the bounds of the medical system and local communities. The mobilization of liberal anticolonialism in this nascent civil society encouraged many doctors to embrace the liberal aspects of their in-between position and to become major players in many anticolonial activities.[11]

Among the various social movement organizations in Taiwan during the 1920s, the Taiwan Cultural Association (Taiwan Bunka Kyōkai) stood out as the central locomotive of Taiwanese cultural and political activities (see chapter 2). Established by a few Taiwanese physicians, with financial support from several landlords, the Cultural Association proclaimed the education of the masses to be its formal goal. Through education, the association hoped to modernize Taiwanese society and improve its international status. Despite the resonance of these goals with the policies of the colonial regime, the colonial police viewed the Cultural Association as an anticolonial, antigovernment organization, and closely monitored its activities (see Taiwan Zongdufu 1988; hereafter *KE*).

11. My discussion concurs with Chen's study (1992) of Taiwanese physicians' social status, which was probably the first major contribution to this topic. His research revealed a significant finding: in disputes between liberal nationalists and left-wing radicals within Taiwanese anticolonial organizations in the late 1920s, physicians were generally inclined to identify with the liberals. However, Chen treats physicians as a homogeneous social category, and he assumes that their political attitudes reflected the expression of a bourgeois modernist mentality. He did not examine the contradictory structural forces surrounding these doctors, and hence misses the complexity involved in the evolution of physicians as a group.

Table 3. Occupations of the Core Members
in the Cultural Association

Occupation	Percentage (N)
Landlord	28.84 (15)
Physician	26.92 (14)
Journalist	13.46 (7)
Small-business owner	9.61 (5)
Lawyer or teacher	5.77 (3)
Other	15.38 (8)
Total	*52*

SOURCE: Lin 1993, pp. 77–79

As documented by police records, physicians constituted a significant portion of the organizers of the Cultural Association. According to these records, there were fourteen physicians among the fifty-two core members of the Cultural Association. Table 3 shows that—in comparison to other groups, such as journalists, small business owners, lawyers, or teachers— physicians and landlords were statistically overrepresented in the Cultural Association. While landlords were the largest group, physicians took the lead in most activities of the Cultural Association, such as organizing public lectures, writing journal articles, and negotiating with the police.

Physicians consistently made up about 30 percent of the rank-and-file of the Cultural Association, until the internal split between liberal and radical wings in 1927 (Chen 1992, p. 136). By the end of 1931, among the 1,138 native physicians in Taiwan, at least 116 of them had been leading activists in anticolonial activities (Chen 1992, p. 143). Furthermore, the police record showed that the most active physicians usually participated in several political or cultural organizations in addition to the Cultural Association. They played an important role in both the liberal reformist organizations and the agencies of the emergent public discourse, such as journals and study groups (see *KE*). Their membership across these two types of organization—the political and the cultural—was evidence of the direct linkage between the emergence of a liberal civil society and the rise of anticolonialism.

A much larger group of doctors were most likely involved as supporters, if not leaders. While the police did not keep track of less prominent participants, other sources suggest a picture of general, active participation among doctors. Anecdotal accounts indicate that many doctors made financial donations, and several others participated as speakers for the Cultural Association and similar organizations (Chen 1992, p. 152). The story of Dr. Lin Kunyuan provides a typical example. Although his name was never mentioned in any newspaper or police record, he discusses his 1929 arrest and subsequent release in his autobiography. Dr. Lin, then a student at Taipei Medical School, was invited to speak at a local gathering in his hometown during a summer vacation. This speech was interrupted by on-site police who arrested him because he criticized the ethnic inequalities in education and lamented the Taiwanese people's sufferings. His comments included a metaphorical argument that "the Taiwanese rooster cries in a special voice—one that's so loud that you can probably hear it in China" (Lin 1978, p. 44). Lin was only released after another Taiwanese doctor pleaded with the police that Lin's words were meant as intellectual comments with no political consequences.

The Cultural Association recruited doctors like Lin by mobilizing community networks and appealing to cultural orientations. Since Dr. Jiang Weishui was one of the founders of the Cultural Association, the organization enjoyed a close connection to the Taiwanese students and graduates of the Medical School. According to police records, "Under Jiang Weishui's influence, the students and graduates of the Medical School had become a central force within the [Cultural] Association" (*KE* vol. 1, p. 227). The police were concerned with frequent student agitation concerning ethnic inequalities at the Medical School, and noted in their secret records that the Medical School was "where the infiltration of the Cultural Association was most thorough" (p. 231).

In addition to mobilizing community networks, the Cultural Association's promotion of "the people's well-being" connected with the cultural orientations of many doctors. The Chinese cultural heritage that many Taiwanese doctors had in common contained a long tradition of connecting politics and medicine, both regarded as means to promote the public welfare. Medicine had long occupied a privileged position as a socially beneficial occupation for the learned man. In the words of an ancient Chinese intellectual-politician, "Man shall be inspired to be either a great statesman or an excellent doctor." This was a familiar saying to the educated, including these Taiwanese physicians, such as Dr. Han, who quoted this famous saying when asked to explain his motivation for entering the Medical School during his entrance exam (Han 1966).

This cultural tendency was reinforced, and somewhat modified, by the liberal and modernist ideas that were introduced with cosmopolitan medicine. While their Chinese heritage provided a cultural frame for Taiwanese physicians to make the connections between their roles as doctors and activists, their exposure to liberalism and science influenced them to become promoters of modernization in Taiwan. The efforts of the Cultural Association to fulfill its professed goal of "improving cultural standards" contributed to the modernization project. For example, the Cultural Association sponsored the only non-state-affiliated newspaper, *Taiwan minpō*;[12] organized reading groups, and, most important (and most problematic for the state), planned an intensive series of island-wide public lectures. Physicians were active participants in these lectures, the discourse of which centered on the theme of modernization and drew heavily on their role as scientists and their exposure to Western and post-Meiji Japanese societies. Topics included "Glimpses of Foreign Countries," "Meiji Restoration and Japan," "The Ideal Cultural Life from a Medical Perspective," and many others that covered general medical knowledge and advocated the importance of science and democracy (see Lin 1993; Cai et al. 1983).

While many physicians seemed to orient their talks toward disseminating new information and promoting modern sciences, some spoke on very provocative topics, such as "Politics in Taiwan—Where Public Opinion Doesn't Matter." Dr. Han, for example, boldly picked topics like "Taiwan under Authoritarian Rule," "Perspectives on Reforming Taiwan," "Paths to Liberation Movements," "Mistakes of the Age and Colonialism" (Zhuang 1995, p. 87). The police found these public lectures threatening, regardless of topic:

> These public lectures are the most serious problem with the Cultural Association. Since the level of education in contemporary Taiwan is fairly

---

12. In 1920, a group of Taiwanese students in Tokyo (most of whom belonged to the New People's Society) founded the journal *Taiwan seinen*. *Taiwan seinen* was renamed *Taiwan* in 1922. In 1923, the founding members of the journal established a publishing company in Taiwan, but the journal continued to be published in Tokyo. In the same year, *Taiwan* transformed itself from a journal into a newspaper called *Taiwan minpō*, which is abbreviated as *MP* in my discussion.

But even if *MP* called itself a newspaper, it only appeared biweekly in the beginning, and later, every ten days. Starting in 1925, *MP* was published once a week. During these years, its readership in Taiwan continued to grow, but its headquarters were still located in Tokyo. Although the core members of *MP* had many times negotiated with the governor-general, the latter did not approve the plan for *MP* to move to Taiwan until 1926. Starting in August 1927, *MP* was formally published from its offices in Taiwan. The move significantly enlarged its readership. In 1930, *MP* was renamed *Taiwan shinminpō*, in anticipation of becoming a daily newspaper. With the governor-general's final approval, *Taiwan shinminpō* (hereafter, *SMP*) published its first issue as a daily on April 15, 1932.

For a detailed discussion of this history, see Cai et al. 1983.

low, [the Cultural Association] can hardly rely on written materials to advocate their political agenda. So the public lectures become the major means for them to gain public support. . . . Local members of the Cultural Association invite speakers [from its headquarters in Taipei] whenever there is a chance. They mobilize local people to welcome the speakers, but it is really a form of demonstration. (*KE*, as quoted in Lin 1993, p. 117)

Although it is impossible to recover the content of the majority of these lectures, the few examples preserved by the police records seem to support this point. In "Glimpses of Foreign Countries," for example, Dr. Wang "introduced" to the Taiwanese people the story of the German occupation of two French provinces, Alsace and Lorraine. He then concluded that "the Germans forced the people in these two provinces to use German instead of their own language, French. As a result, their cultural development was impeded during German occupation. It seems that we Taiwanese should think about what this story means" (Chen 1992, p. 155). Obviously, the talk carried political content which its title did not suggest.

The relatively autonomous professional practices of doctors shaped their contribution to the Cultural Association and Taiwanese civil society in general. As an attempt to deliver health care to the underprivileged, the Cultural Association sponsored community clinics that provided medical care at low cost. Under the influence of the Cultural Association, many physicians who ran private clinics also offered *shifei juan*, which were essentially tokens for discounted medical services. Poverty was a glaring feature of the general population in the colony. Lack of medical knowledge and a widespread mistrust of cosmopolitan medicine further blocked the poor from receiving proper medical care. In this context, community clinics, *shifei juan*, and similar devices that increased the accessibility of cosmopolitan medicine were considered by both the Cultural Association and the physicians themselves as a self-protective mechanism of the Taiwanese society.

Beyond these organized activities, doctors were also politicized in their daily practice. Perhaps characteristic of professional practices under a colonial regime, a doctor's objective judgment could often constitute a critique of and even a challenge to the state's daily practices of power. Most notably, a doctor's scientific and neutral documentation of a patient's physical condition could, on certain occasions, become a record of police violence. The colonial police penetrated every corner of Taiwanese society and functioned as important patrolling agents of the state. They were notorious for abusing Taiwanese suspects, but physicians were able to "measure" and document police violence scientifically. If a physician issued a documented diagnosis to a suspect who had been victimized by police, the suspect could then bring the case to higher authorities. More frequently, physicians were called in to mediate between the police and a suspect who had been abused, and they would withhold a documented diagnosis in return for compensation for the suspect. Many such instances were reported in the opposition newspaper, the *Taiwan minpō*.[13]

Doctors were mobilized through their networks within the Taiwanese community and their cultural orientations, which were rooted in both their Chinese heritage and their education in liberalism and science. Their relatively autonomous professional practices further shaped their contribution to the Taiwanese civil society that began to grow and flourish during the 1920s. Their involvement in anticolonial activities and other aspects of civil society created opportunities for doctors as a group of professionals to reflect upon and articulate a group identity. While individual doctors might not have entered civil society as self-conscious members of the Taiwanese medical community, in the process of their civic participation they gradually became aware of themselves as a distinct social group and started to develop a group identity.

"NATIONAL PHYSICIANS": CONSTRUCTING IDENTITY NARRATIVES

Structural location of doctors was a powerful and influential factor in their group formation, but it could only condition rather than dictate their *identities*. Similarly, their mobilization in the nascent civil society brought about crucial contexts in which the group became self-conscious, but the physicians had to experience and interpret their environment and in so doing formulate an identity recognizable to themselves and others. The structural environment became fully meaningful to these doctors only when they were substantially integrated into their personal and group life. While there could be diverse ways in which individual doctors constructed their own identities by relating themselves to these structural tensions as well as a great number of other conditions in their personal lives, my focus here is on the formation of a *group* identity. Continuing my attempt to trace the intersections of two macro social trends, namely, professionalization and colonization, the following discussion describes the narratives through which doctors recognized themselves as a collective and formulated their collective identity.

13. For example, see *MP* no. 120, p. 13; *MP* no. 188; *MP* no. 389, p. 8; see also Chen 1992.

A Compound Identity: Ethnic Professionals

Doctors' group identity was, from the beginning, a compound category, in which physicians attempted to combine their ethnic and professional roles. In the early 1920s, some members of the Taiwanese medical community began to publicly describe themselves as "Taiwanese physicians" or "national physicians" (*minzoku ishi*)—a label that served to differentiate them from Japanese physicians. Under the influence of the Cultural Association, in several cities, Taiwanese doctors split from preexisting local medical associations, which accommodated both Japanese and Taiwanese doctors, and formed independent Taiwanese medical associations (*KE* vol. 2, p. 173). In 1925, a group of Taipei Medical School graduates who were pursuing higher degrees in Japan held a formal gathering and, representing themselves as a collective of "Taiwanese physicians," initiated contact with the Japanese medical community (*MP* no. 84, p. 13). In 1927, more than forty Taiwanese physicians and medical students in Tokyo, together with a few others in Kyoto, established a new organization, the New East Asian Medical Association (Shintōa Igakkai), which formally declared that its members should "perform the duty of a Taiwanese physician" (*MP* no. 149, p. 5). The formation of such organizations signaled the birth of a self-conscious social group.

These doctors saw themselves not only as physicians who were Taiwanese, but as "physicians for the Taiwanese nation." In addition to offering free and low-cost medical services to the poor, numerous Taiwanese physicians volunteered to write articles on health issues for the opposition newspaper, or gave public lectures on medical topics. Incorporating these experiences into their group identity, local medical associations often stated in their charters that they assumed the responsibility of improving health conditions for the Taiwanese community at large.

Furthermore, as many doctors came to believe in the connection between physical and societal diseases, some medical associations explicitly drew an analogy between themselves and Dr. Sun Yat-sen, the physician "national father" of the Republic of China. They declared that "to live up to the role of Taiwanese physicians, one needs to cure the physical *and* the social diseases of the nation" (*MP* no. 179, p. 4). A famous example nicely illustrates how this analogy was drawn between physical and social diseases. Dr. Jiang Weishui, a founding member of the Cultural Association, wrote a social critique of Taiwan in the form of a medical diagnosis. His document, entitled "Clinical Diagnosis," was first published in a Cultural Association newsletter (*Bunka Kyōkai kaihō*) in 1921. A few sections from the "diagnosis" are worth quoting at length:

NAME: Taiwan Island

SEX: Male

SYMPTOMS: Immoral . . . impoverished spiritual life, . . . superstitious, reactionary, unsanitary

CAUSES: Intellectual Malnutrition . . .

PRESCRIPTION:

Basic Education	maximum dose
Supplementary Education	maximum dose
Pre-school Education	maximum dose
Libraries	maximum dose
Reading Groups	maximum dose

(Jiang, as quoted in Lin 1993, pp. 98–99)

This interesting document became very important in the history of anti-colonialism in Taiwan and was cited on many occasions. No other document articulated more explicitly the analogy drawn between physical and social diseases in the Taiwanese doctors' modernist critique of colonialism. Other doctors continued to elaborate on the theme of this document, thus firmly establishing in the public imagination the basic analogy between their medical and social responsibilities.[14]

By the second half of the 1920s, the general public in Taiwan had also widely accepted the implications behind the label of "national physicians." For example, a survey of articles in the *Taiwan minpō*, the only opposition newspaper at the time, shows that the newspaper devoted an unusually large amount of space to the professional activities of Taiwanese doctors. It published frequent reports on the establishment of new clinics, the conferment of medical degrees to Taiwanese students, and so on. Essentially these matters were considered community news. The Taiwanese public saw their doctors as public figures worthy of great respect and attention.

Challenging State Power

Once Taiwanese doctors articulated an identity as "national physicians" and were recognized as such, they began to use this formulation to reason through other structural contradictions that they faced. In particular, this new identity significantly affected their position between the colonial state and their ethnic community.

14. It is noteworthy that this "diagnosis" focuses on the issue of "spiritual impoverishment" but marginalizes the problem of poverty. This oversight seems to suggest the class-bound nature of doctors' vision for their social activism, which became more explicit during the campaign for reduction of medical fees, as discussed later in this chapter.

As noted before, individual doctors medically documented police violence to hold them responsible, at least to some extent, for their abuse of institutional power. Such encounters helped to further consolidate the nascent group consciousness of Taiwanese physicians and facilitate mobilization, at the collective level, of their professional autonomy and knowledge to challenge the state's abusive acts. In particular, when the police or legal authorities rejected a documented diagnosis, local Taiwanese medical groups were quick to act in defense of the legitimacy of their professional knowledge. For example, a Taiwanese physician was once arrested after the police decided that one of his diagnoses was invalid. Though this physician was eventually released, local physicians were collectively mobilized to express their discontent (see *MP* no. 389, p. 8).

Events surrounding the spread of typhoid in 1928 provide another example of collective effort on the part of Taiwanese doctors to criticize the colonial police and more broadly the monitoring state. In the cities of Taipei and Tainan, native physicians complained about the inadequacy of state plans to control the spread of the disease. They focused their complaints on the *militancy* with which the police sought to improve local health conditions and the unkind attitude with which Japanese physicians treated native patients at state-run hospitals. They pointed out that these two problems increased mistrust of medical institutions and discouraged people from obtaining appropriate treatment for typhoid (see *MP* no. 225, pp. 11–12; *MP* no. 238, p. 3). In response, native physicians demanded larger roles in state-run hospitals and sought to organize separate medical clinics where native patients could receive culturally sensitive and friendly treatment.[15]

On other occasions, the task of "measuring" police violence led many physicians to join other social groups in publicizing human rights issues in Taiwan. For instance, a 1928 report in *Taiwan minpō* stated that, according to the results of an autopsy, a certain suspect had been strangled to death while in detention. But the report in the government-controlled *Taiwan News* (*Taiwan shinbun*) indicated that no traces of torture or physical mistreatment were discerned. Upon reading the report in *Taiwan News*, the two physicians who performed the autopsy immediately made a request to the appropriate authority to repeat the autopsy. A year later, the same two

---

15. In general, the physicians' critique of the medical system resonated with the discourse of the opposition newspaper. Several accounts there criticized state bureaucrats or the police for being authoritarian and culturally insensitive (*MP* no. 82, p. 5; *MP* no. 95, p. 10). Likewise, state-run hospitals were criticized for being overly bureaucratized, inefficient, and ethnically and economically discriminatory (*MP* no. 142, p. 4; *MP* no. 160, p. 7; *MP* no. 161, pp. 10–11; *MP* no. 275).

physicians carried out another autopsy in a possible case of police violence. Convinced that there was evidence of the violation of human rights, they forwarded their concerns to the Taipei Legal Association (Taihoku Bengoshi-kai). They also had their case reported in the opposition newspaper, which subsequently motivated the People's Party (the Taiwan Minshūtō)—a short-lived Taiwanese opposition party—to plan several public lectures on police violence and human rights (*MP* no. 246, p. 10).

In this agitated civil society, an incident called the Opium Dispute took place at the end of the 1920s and decisively marked the transformation of individual confrontations with police violence into a form of collective action. Opium prohibition was a major goal of the colonial regime from the beginning of its rule. In 1929, the governor-general relaxed the prohibition measures in a revised opium policy, declaring that the new policy would be more practical and humane (Ryū 1983, pp. 159–60). But since the Japanese government had a monopoly on opium sales, the People's Party suspected that the government simply wanted Taiwanese to continue to smoke opium so that it could benefit financially. The People's Party accordingly protested the new opium policy for over a year, not only by filing formal petitions with the regime, but through communication with several international organizations. This probably facilitated the regime's decision to ban the party (ibid., pp. 170–71).

Taiwanese doctors saw the Opium Dispute as a crisis for the national health of Taiwan. In support of the People's Party, island-wide Taiwanese medical associations submitted written protests to the governor-general and the head of the colonial police bureau.[16] Their written protests were prepared with abundant citations from the medical literature, which created a "scientific" framework for this issue (*MP* no. 296, p. 12; *MP* no. 298, p. 10; *MP* no. 300, p. 10; *MP* no. 302, p. 11). These physicians invoked professional expertise as a legitimate tool for evaluating the "humaneness" of the new opium policy. Their scientific evaluations raised powerful challenges to the state (Ryū 1983, p. 162). The Japanese medical community, in contrast, remained silent throughout the event.

A contemporary Taiwanese intellectual and activist, Xie Chunmu, wrote in 1930 that "the medical associations announced their oppositions [against the new opium policy] from an expert's position and thoroughly embarrassed the state" (quoted in Ryū 1983, p. 211). Xie recorded the "sugges-

---

16. Such written proposals were submitted by almost all the local Taiwanese medical associations, including the local associations in Gaoxiong, Tainan, Taipei, Pingdong, Jiayi, and Zhanghua (see Xie 1930).

tions" that the local Tainan Medical Association presented to the governor-general, which were typical of these petitions:

1. The issue of new permit [for the purchase of opium] should be strictly limited to the cases where rehabilitation efforts, according to medical judgments, will put the patient's life in danger.
2. All current holders of opium permits should be subjected to medical examinations. Those patients whose addiction is diagnosed to be treatable should be placed in a rehabilitation center by force.
3. The government should establish state-managed opium smoking houses. All opium smoking activities should be confined to such places and nowhere else. If permit holders smoke opium outside of these government-run opium smoking houses, they should be punished [by the law] for illegal opium smoking.
4. Private opium dealers should be completely banned. Opium should only be sold and purchased at these government-run opium smoking houses. (quoted in Ryū 1983, p. 162)

The Jiayi Medical Association submitted a similar petition and went further to point out that the state needed to intensify its effort to "educate and civilize" Taiwan and promote an anti-opium consciousness. The association asked the state to explain why discussion of opium as a "social evil" had been taken out of new editions of school textbooks. Whether expressing a political strategy or an honest opinion, the Jiayi Medical Association strategically used the modernization framework to make its argument. Since modernization was precisely what the colonial state used to legitimize its rule in Taiwan, the state was put in a difficult position by the association's sharp words (Ryū 1983).

The efforts of doctors and the People's Party notwithstanding, the new opium policy was eventually implemented. The protestors, however, did have an important impact. First, they communicated their concerns in a telegram to the League of Nations, which in response sent investigators to Taiwan between February 19 and March 2 in 1930 (Ryū 1983). This stirred up great anxieties in the Japanese governments, both in Taiwan and Tokyo, which intensified the debate in the public sphere and eventually helped pressure the regime to implement plans for the treatment of opium addicts. More importantly, the critical discourse developed by doctors and the People's Party was widely circulated in the media and was greatly influential. In the eyes of the new generation, smoking opium was seen as the result of state manipulation rather than merely the continuation of a traditional habit (ibid.). This discourse may have been more effective than state policies in combating opium addiction.

In the course of taking action against the Opium Policy, Taiwanese doctors debated and in turn further consolidated their identity. Should they act in accordance with state regulation and respect the state's policies on opium? Or could they act as autonomous professionals and defend their ethnic community in ways they saw fit? While doctors were torn between these two positions and debate was heated, eventually most Taiwanese medical associations concluded that they had a responsibility to defend the nation's health, even at the risk of state sanctions. These discussions and actions further clarified the political implications of their identity as national physicians.[17] The Taiwanese medical community had by this point imagined—and enacted—its role as the guardian of the national health against opium and a suspicious colonial state. Indeed, during the Opium Dispute, physicians combined their professional autonomy and knowledge with an alternative political legitimacy in the form of opposition organizations in order to protect their ethnic community.

Furthermore, they came to confront the dual cultural heritages they carried as offspring of the old gentry class and new members of the modern scientific community. Since opium smoking was a common habit among wealthy gentry and landlords up to the initial years of the colonial period, doctors were potentially dealing with their own fathers or older brothers in their mobilization against this behavior. A concrete example arose in the Pingdong Medical Association. One member tried to persuade the association to withhold its critique of the new opium policy because his own father was an opium dealer and addict. This issue stimulated lengthy discussion and forced association members to take a stand. In the end, most members disagreed with the opium addict's son and collectively asserted their role as modern reformers (*MP* no. 303, p. 11). Similar discussions at various local medical associations further reinforced the modernist orientation of the "national physicians'" collective identity.

There were, however, aspects of this collective identity that were called into question and left unresolved. Most notably, the relationships between the Taiwanese and the Japanese medical communities in Taiwan remained important but difficult to define. As described above, Japanese doctors were both mentors and oppressors in the eyes of many Taiwanese doctors, and the ambiguity in this relationship remained unresolved throughout the colonial

17. The state did punish the most active physicians in this event. In many instances, these physicians were harassed by the police through unfounded charges of malpractice, unauthorized supervision of their clinics, or suspension of their licenses; see *MP* nos. 7, 142, 184.

period. During the Opium Dispute, Taiwanese medical associations appeared confused and awkward when confronted with appeals to interethnic professional ties by Japanese colleagues/mentors. For example, after several visits made by Dr. Horiuchi, the Japanese principal of the Taipei Medical School, the Taipei Medical Association decided to withdraw the association's "propositions" on the opium problem. As illustrated earlier in this chapter, Dr. Horiuchi was held in very high esteem by most Taiwanese physicians (many of whom were his former students), and his involvement placed an emotional obligation on many members of the Taipei Medical Association (the chair included) to soften their stand somewhat. At the same time, other members of the Taipei Medical Association disapproved of and criticized their chair's "malleable stand," and some even threatened to break away from the association (*MP* no. 300, p. 10).[18]

As demonstrated by their involvement with the Opium Dispute, the mobilization of Taiwanese doctors in civil society provided a context for them to "narrativize," or experience, connect, and interpret, many key dimensions of their surrounding relational configuration. They developed a clear political consciousness as a group of "national physicians" and aligned themselves with the nation against the state. Their internal discussions in the medical associations often adopted a modernist framework and thus further reinforced their modernist orientation. The group was, however, less successful in articulating a coherent relationship with their Japanese colleagues.

Defending the Professional Market

Shortly after this modernist and politically conscious group came to the defense of its ethnic community during the Opium Dispute, the members of the profession were confronted with another challenge. It became essential to relate their identity as national physicians to the contradiction between their ethnic solidarity and class differences with the Taiwanese community. As the medical profession and the Taiwanese public debated this issue, doctors came to collectively embrace their market privilege, thus inscribing a class dimension into their collective identity.

---

18. The Taipei Medical Association's inability to collectively develop a coherent interethnic professional relationship is similar to the internal conflicts within the Taiwan Dental Association. In 1930, Taiwanese dentists raised concerns of ethnic inequality and threatened to form an independent organization. But their Japanese seniors and friends persuaded them to honor their personal ties and refrain from radical action. In the end, as with the Taipei Medical Association during the Opium Dispute, Taiwanese dentists abandoned their plan for an independent association (*MP* nos. 339, 355, 359).

During the depression of the late 1920s, as the economic gap between physicians and their low-income patients widened, doctors were increasingly awkward in negotiating their ambiguous position as "charitable elite." They were a group that both had attained a privileged market position and provided low-cost medical service on a voluntary basis. Various peasant, worker, and community organizations began to point out the inadequacy of voluntary charity work and demanded more systematic reforms in the distribution of health care. These groups questioned the basic concept of the commodification of health care and, no longer grateful for doctors' charity work, asked the profession to collectively curtail its pursuit of market interests. Such voices brought great pressures to compel the national physicians to face the class contradiction between themselves and their "nation."

A 1926 article in the newspaper *Taiwan minpō* pleaded with "a hope in our National hands [*guosho xianshen*]" and critically reminded doctors that "medicine was a humanist practice [*renshu*] and yet today's doctors had been pre-occupied with their own benefits" (*MP* no. 120, p. 10). In 1930, an island-wide campaign for reduction of medical fees took place in the depths of the depression. A *Taiwan minpō* article articulated a public expectation that national physicians should protect the interests of their ethnic community, especially after their collective mobilization during the Opium Dispute. The editors urged, after reporting Gaoxiong Medical Association's failure to pass the motion for reduction of medical fees: "Gaoxiong Medical Association was the first [among Taiwanese medical associations] to issue their formal written protest against the new opium policy this spring. Wouldn't it be nice if they would be the pioneer again in this campaign for the reduction of medical fees?" (*MP* no. 333, p. 8). A 1930 news article further discussed the nature of health care:

> In a society dominated by capitalist organizations, market profits have become an important goal for many practicing physicians. But society still views medicine as a career in public welfare. . . . Medicine as a profession enjoys such high esteem and respect by the general public precisely because society views medicine as a career in public welfare. Have today's practicing physicians forgotten their natural duty? They are so reluctant to lower medical fees that we really cannot see any signs of sincerity [about their natural duty]. (*MP* no. 324, p. 2)

Similarly, a number of working-class and peasant organizations appealed to the "social responsibility and conscientiousness" of Taiwanese physicians, requesting a profession-wide reduction in medical charges (*MP* nos. 120, 220, 237, 334, 335, 337).

Many individual doctors responded to such requests by issuing more *shifei juan,* or low-cost medical coupons. Alternatively, some doctors, with the help of charity organizations, established nonprofit community hospitals (Chen 1992). The profession as a collective, however, was hesitant to institutionalize fee reductions. In contrast to their proactive stand in the Opium Dispute, all Taiwanese medical associations refused to impose systemwide fee reductions, even though they seemed to encourage individual doctors to lower their fees as they saw fit. The public, which had praised and appreciated such measures at one point, now viewed them as merely a device to pacify public discontent rather than a useful solution to the problem of health care distribution. A 1931 newspaper article issued a sharp criticism of medical coupons, arguing that "these coupons were a form of charity and had absolutely nothing to do with our demand for general fee reduction. It was just a measure to calm down an angry public" (*SMP* no. 277, p. 4). While the public seemed to welcome the establishment of new community clinics, their comments were sometimes meant as much as a critique of the medical profession as praise for individual doctors and charitable organizations (*SMP* nos. 328, 338, 348, 362). For example, one report about a new nonprofit clinic in Keelung was printed under the title "Because the Medical Association refused to lower their fees, a nonprofit hospital will be opened" (*SMP* no. 336, p. 3). Another report described these nonprofit clinics as a "by-product of [the fee reduction] campaign." The report questioned, "The Xinchu Medical Association have agreed to lower their medical fees more than a month ago. Why haven't they done anything just yet? Are they going to quietly sneak out of this one? ... Of course the new Philanthropy Hospital that came about under such circumstances will be greatly welcomed by the majority of us" (*SMP* no. 341, p. 3).

Ultimately, this debate demonstrated that medical associations and the campaign for fee reduction held different visions of an ideal health care system. While the campaign envisioned a distributive system that was based on need, the medical associations were principally committed to the existing, market-based distributive system. With a collective identity as national physicians, doctors had made themselves accountable for the general well-being of their ethnic communities and felt obligated to answer to the demands of the campaign. But they were only willing to go so far as to modify the market with individual acts of charity and dismissed the idea of reforming the entire health care distribution system.

A contrast between two newspaper articles in 1930 illustrates this basic difference. In an interview with the newspaper, the head of the Taipei Medical Association emphasized Taiwanese physicians' sympathy for the poor. He stated that "the medical charges set by our Association are usually

20 percent lower than those set by Japanese practitioners on the island. We have always been concerned about the well-being of the poor and have tried to provide special treatment for them" (*SMP* no. 335, p. 2). In the second article, the People's Party explicitly criticized "special treatment" for the poor, which often took the form of low-cost medical tokens, on which physicians prided themselves. They pointed out that doctors tended to respond to societal demand for fee reductions by issuing more medical tokens, which created many problems: (1) they usually became a marker of poverty and shame; (2) thus most people were reluctant to rely on them for medical treatment; (3) the recipients of the "special treatment" usually received discriminatory treatment from physicians; and (4) physicians often demonstrated a condescending attitude toward these patients (*SMP* no. 340, p. 2).

Most medical associations disagreed with these criticisms. They reasoned that despite their strong commitment to the well-being of their coethnics, they were entitled to a reasonable profit. The fundamental difference between the logic of social needs and that of the market remained unresolved through negotiation efforts (*SMP* no. 324, p. 2; *SMP* no. 336, p. 3; *SMP* no. 341, p. 3; *SMP* no. 337, p. 9; *SMP*, no. 377, p. 4). Although these doctors did sacrifice their profits to some degree, and compromised with the poor much more than their Japanese colleagues, they were perceived as having failed to live up to the public's expectation of them as national physicians (see also *MP* nos. 174, 371, 383). While they did defend their ethnic community by participating in various anticolonial activities, these national physicians seemed equally adamant in protecting their professional market. In the process, both doctors and the general public came to perceive the national physicians as a distinct class.

SCIENTIFIC COLONIALISTS, NATIONAL PHYSICIANS: PROFESSIONAL POWERS AND HYBRID IDENTITIES

This chapter provides an analysis of the in-between location and identity of Taiwanese physicians during the 1920s. I have analyzed the structural contradictions surrounding these doctors, documented their liberal anticolonial mobilization in civil society, and traced the ways in which they, by interpreting and acting upon their environment, developed a group identity as "national physicians." As a non-Western, colonial case, the story of the national physicians brings a comparative perspective to the recent sociological debate about the social formation of professions; as a history of group formation situated at the intersection of colonialism and professionalism, their story illustrates a central ambiguity in Japan's "scientific colonialism."

Since the publication of two monumental works in the 1970s, Freidson's

(1970) *Professional Dominance* and Larson's (1977) *The Rise of Profession-alism*, American sociologists' understandings of professions have largely progressed under the overarching question about the relationships of the professions, state, and market. Freidson locates the origin of professional power in the attainment of professional autonomy, or control over work, through state licensure and credentialism. Professional power manifests itself in the expanding professional "market shelters," where a profession monopolizes supply and the substance of demand within its jurisdiction. In response to his critics, Freidson (2001) acknowledges the "unpleasant truth" that such state-sanctioned market monopoly lies at the crux of the institutions of professionalism. Yet he views professionalism as a valuable solution to certain organizational problems in complex societies and finds the reasonable position to lie not in damning the principle but in protecting its appropriate practice from abuse.

Larson (1977) distrusts the abstract neutrality of professionalism. Situating the phenomenon of expert authority in the historical stream of capitalist development, Larson emphasizes the market incentives in the conversion of knowledge to property and the role of professionalism in the justification of the bourgeois ideology of meritocracy. Meanwhile, professions constitute themselves as agents of the state, define our needs, and, in a Foucauldian sense, develop a "penetrating technology of power" as a new form of discipline (Larson 1984).

The dialogue between Freidson and Larson has shaped the framework of debate in the past two decades. Scholars continue to articulate the subtlety of professions' relationship to the state and the market. For example, Halliday (1987) departs from the monopoly thesis to investigate professions' contribution to state structure. He believes that "the centrality of monopoly to the professional enterprise has a developmental dimension" (p. 350). As a profession becomes established, its collective actions are seen as less geared toward maintaining monopoly and more centered on shaping political policies. Abbott (1988) debunks the very concept of professionalization, shifting the focus from individual professions to professions as a system. In effect, his concept of jurisdictional competition may not differ fundamentally from that of monopoly; it broadens Larson's analysis by showing that a profession bargains with not only the state but also other occupations (Macdonald 1995). Through a comparative study of the United States, Britain, France, Italy, and Germany, Krause (1996) observes a converging trend in the death of professions' "guild power." Krause's sweeping conclusion presents a stronger version of several earlier critiques of Freidson's professional dominance thesis.

Out of the debates grows an increasing awareness of historical contingency. Balzer states it succinctly: "Professionalization is not the single thread running through the fabric of modern society. . . . It must be viewed in the broader context of social history or it distorts more than it reviews" (1996, p. 5; see also Larson 1990; McClelland 1991; Burrage 1990). This historical awareness eventually challenges us to move beyond the framework of state-market-professions, for if we scrutinize professions' varying patterns of embeddness in capitalism and state formation, then why ignore their intersections with other social processes? With this realization, what are previously viewed as informal mechanisms of exclusion, such as race, ethnicity, and gender (Freidson 1986), become recognized as threads of social fabric shaping patterns of professionalization.

Brint's (1994) survey of U.S. professionals gestures in this direction, as he observes that professionals' attitudes come from their demographic backgrounds as much as the inherent values of their professions. Professionals possess the values they do because they "are more likely to be relatively young, highly educated, urban, and nonreligious" (Brint 1994, p. 102).[19] Through her analysis of occupational closure strategies, Witz (1992) studies how professionalization intersects with patriarchy and cautions against the assumption "that exclusion on the ground of gender and race is an 'informal' element of credentialing. . . . Rather, . . . gendered exclusionary mechanisms were embedded in the formal credentialing process" (p. 195). Davies (1996) further points out that, beyond the discussion of exclusion, sociologists need to better understand the particular forms of inclusion for women in the professional world.

Taking this argument one step further, we ought to examine the intersections of professions with other macro-social processes (such as racism and colonialism) as well as broaden our consideration of the dimensions of such intersections. To these ends, I argue that the professions should be conceptualized not only as a status category but also as sites of identity formation. The emphasis on intersection leads to the question of how professionals straddle two or more institutional locations. Here, the role of race or gender may partially—but only partially—manifest itself as the exclusionary mechanisms that Witz (1992) discusses. At a different level, race and gender interact with professions as competing institutionalized identities,

19. Brint explains this in detail: "The most consistent predictors of social conservatism were advanced age, lower levels of education, high levels of religiosity, and residence in the South. Other anchoring variables—residence in small towns and suburbs, marriage and child rearing, membership in the dominant gender and racial groups—all showed the expected associations with conservative views. Of the employment-related variables, lower incomes, human services occupations, and location in the manufacturing and trade sectors were associated with conservative views, while the more intellectual social and cultural professions were associated with greater liberalism" (1994, p. 99).

which agents of the professional projects are challenged to reconcile and integrate. Race/gender and professions, then, are mutually constitutive, each shaped by the other in an interactive process.

In this sense, as a case of the intersection between ethnicity and the profession, the story of the national physicians bears great theoretical importance. The case accentuates the in-between position of ethnic professionals by demonstrating that neither ethnic nor professional culture, interests, or organizations played a more dominant part in the formation of this social group. Rather, in the course of their social formation, these doctors' modernist professional culture was mixed with a Chinese tradition that closely associated medicine and politics; their pursuit of market interests was qualified by a sense of ethnic solidity with their consumers; and their organizational autonomy served alternately to protect their professional market and to assist in the anticolonialism of their ethnic community. Ultimately, a meaningful collective identity came about as their collective imagination enabled them to discern coherence in these experiences of the in-between, and to incorporate elements of their choosing into an identity narrative as national physicians. As a case of ethnic professionals' in-betweenness, these doctors illustrate how our studies of the social formation of a profession, placed in specific historical context, can be fully fruitful only when an analysis of its structural location is coupled with an analysis of group identity.

Placed in the colonial context, the national physicians also offer a good case for better understanding the potential for anticolonial resistance at the site of structural in-betweenness.[20] Instead of insisting on locating anticolonial resistance only outside the colonial system (e.g., Chatterjee 1993), many scholars consider how internal tensions could be turned against the system. For example, the importance of Indian doctors in anticolonial movements has been acknowledged (Arnold 1993). At a more abstract level, forms of resistance are documented in studies about processes of the mutual though unequal transformation of the metropole and the colony (see Sahlins 1989). Many colonial and postcolonial scholars have pointed out that the colonial hybrid is often creative and disruptive. The contradictions it embodies stimulate new imaginings of identity and destabilize old categories in the colonial regimes (Bhabha 1994; see also Cooper and Stoler 1989).

20. I have elaborated elsewhere a different dimension of the story of the national physicians. Focusing on their experiences as a case of social movement, I discuss the interaction between the political opportunity structure and identity formation. The physicians' activism also provides a case in point to illustrate how global processes affect social movements within states. See Ming-cheng Lo, "Confronting Contradictions and Negotiating Identities: Taiwanese Doctors' Anti-Colonialism in the 1920s," in *Globalizations and Social Movements,* ed. John A. Guidry, Michael D. Kennedy, and Mayer N. Zald (Ann Arbor: University of Michigan Press, 2000).

Despite Japanese pride in racial homogeneity, Japanese colonialism bred many hybrids. As one such example, the story of the national physicians is illustrative of a central logic of Japanese colonialism and yet subversive to its original plans. The very basis of the profession's power—that is, the early institutionalization of medicine, the size of the Taiwanese medical community, and its high degree of professionalism—was part of Japan's plan to bring modernity to the colony in the most effective and natural manner. As discussed earlier, Japanese colonialism emphasized the similarities between the colonizers and the colonized without collapsing their hierarchical distinctions and thus brewed a more ambiguous self/other distinction than did Western colonialisms, whose Orientalist dichotomy is well represented in Said's famous thesis and its numerous variants (see Dirks 1992). When these ambiguous ethnic ideologies were wedded to the policies of scientific colonialism, whose central rationale was to deliver science to the colonies with the utmost "naturalness," the Japanese colonial administration was led by its own logic to cultivate effective, self-dependent, and therefore potentially subversive, native agents. The growth of the Taiwanese medical profession during this period indicates the Japanese administrators' effort to colonize by selectively "Japanizing" and empowering some groups of the colonized, granting them a certain institutional basis and inadvertently creating a contradictory structural location for them. The success of Japan's ambiguous ethnic policies and scientific colonialism gave rise to the formation of native professionals, in this case Taiwanese doctors, who served as agents for the state as well as defenders (though with a market self-interest) of the Taiwanese ethnic community.

Japanese colonizers were a "hybrid" category themselves, in the sense that they tried to imitate Western colonizers in order to effectively resist them (Robertson 1995; Tanaka 1993). The Taiwanese physicians used a similar strategy, empowering themselves vis-à-vis Japanese rule exactly by internalizing certain institutional and cultural aspects of Japanese colonization. Japanese imperialism represented neither a mere reproduction of Western hegemony nor complete control of its own colonies, but a hybridization process. In this sense, the hybrid is more a multitude than a single category. (How can we collapse the Taiwanese doctors and their Japanese colonizers into the same category?) Instead of imposing a teleological reading on the development of the in-between identity, our challenge is to trace and theorize its changing potential and tensions. To this end, I now turn to an analysis of the demobilization of "national physicians" in the 1930s.

4   The Years of Public
Demobilization (1931–1936)

The previous chapter traced the process through which Taiwanese physicians confronted the structural contradictions in their social location and gradually constructed a collective identity as "national physicians." My analysis highlights the in-betweenness of these ethnic professionals, documenting the interactive dimension in their social formation as well as their political potential as a hybrid category within Japanese colonialism. However, the developmental trajectory of the Taiwanese medical community changed radically after the Manchuria Incident of 1931 (described below). Taiwanese doctors were distanced from their ethnic community and increasingly incorporated into the Japanese imperial medical system. The narrative of national physicians was silenced in the professional as well as the public arena.

Centered on an investigation of the changing dynamics of the in-between position and identity of Taiwanese doctors, this chapter discusses the social transformation of the Taiwanese medical profession in the first half of the 1930s. I start with a delineation of the radical increase in state regulation and oppression in the colony and move on to explain how the colonial state solidified its grip on the native civil society by recategorizing its discourses and activities. In the context of this new state/society relationship, ties between the ethnic and the professional communities were largely replaced by a closer relationship between the profession and the state. The narrative of national physicians became a lost legacy during these years, altering the meanings of doctors' hybrid identity.

THE TYRANNY OF THE STATE

The Manchuria Incident ushered in an era of militarization in Japan which subsequently escalated the tyranny of the state in the colonies. The incident, which occurred in 1931, was a product of emerging political climates in China and Japan in the late 1920s. Because of its long-standing territorial ambitions, Japan supported the Chinese warlord, Zhang Zuolin, in Manchuria. But toward the end of the 1920s, Chiang Kai-shek began a series of campaigns to establish his authority in China, and challenged Japan's position in Manchuria and other areas north of the Great Wall. Meanwhile, Zhang Zuolin's son, who succeeded him after Zhang's murder in 1928, increased his opposition to Japanese influence in Manchuria. The Tokyo government and the Kwantung Army hoped to shift the tide of these new developments (Beasely 1990; Hunter 1984).

Changes in the political climate at home further aggravated their concerns. The world economic crisis around 1930 seriously hampered the Japanese economy. The collapse of the American stock market and a slump in global trade had a devastating effect on the Japanese business and agricultural sectors. These economic problems destabilized the political climate in Japan, and the political instability in both Japan and Manchuria eventually stirred the Kwantung Army into unauthorized military action. Officers in the Kwantung Army conceived of a plan for the occupation of key points in Manchuria. In order to have legitimate cause for their military advancement, they "manufactured" an incident on the South Manchuria railway: On September 18, 1931, a bomb exploded on the railway outside Mukden. "In response," the Kwantung Army immediately seized the city, and by the next morning they began the occupation of southern Manchuria.

The Manchuria Incident hastened the pace of militarization in Japan. The Kwantung Army continued to conduct military actions without authorization from the government in Tokyo and, as they were not sanctioned or stopped, they expanded their scale of action. As Hunter explained,

> The government in Tokyo was powerless to stop the fighting and, faced with a fait accompli, announced that its policy was nonexpansion of the conflict. However, government instructions were largely ignored by field officers on the grounds of operational necessity, and at each advance the government was increasingly forced to act as an apologist for the military's acts. By early 1932, almost the whole of the three provinces of eastern Manchuria had been occupied with the backing of the War Ministry and General Staff in Tokyo. In February 1932 the puppet "independent" state of Manchukuo was established. China appealed to the League of Nations, and Japan's failure to withdraw her troops led to the establishment of the Lytton Commission and Japan's subsequent withdrawal from the league. . . . Japan continued to make small advances and clashed frequently with Chinese troops up until the outbreak of full-scale war in 1937. (1984, pp. 120–21)

In addition to the expansion of military action in China, the army's unauthorized moves increased the influence of the military in Japanese domestic politics. The military often imposed its position on the cabinet through assassinations and threats, and the weakened party leadership was unable to command the loyalty of other segments of the ruling elite, namely, the armed forces and the bureaucracy. Instead of party cabinets, cabinets emerged with a proportion of party representatives, whose numbers decreased over the years. The rise of a left-wing group in the Diet failed to alter events in any substantial way. "One proposition that has been almost universally accepted by historians is that after 1930 the influence of the military in Japanese politics increased to the point of dominance" (Beasely 1990, p. 177).

In short, the political situation in Manchuria, which appeared especially urgent in the context of domestic and international economic crisis, encouraged the expansion of unauthorized military action in Manchuria and other parts of China. The Manchuria Incident thus served as a prelude to the rise of the military in Japan and the weakening of Japanese party cabinets. Militarization of the Japanese state and nation escalated continuously during the period between the seizure of Manchuria in 1931 and the outbreak of the war in China in 1937.

Parallel to political changes in Tokyo, the Japanese colonial state grew increasingly regulatory and dominating. Modifying Gotō's policy of slow, "scientific" Japanization, the state now attempted to forcefully speed up the integration of the colonies into the Japanese Empire. In 1933 the government passed a law to legitimize the status of interethnic adoption and marriage between Japanese and Taiwanese (Ng 1989). In 1935 the colonial state held the first direct local elections in Taiwan and brought the system of the island, at least superficially, to resemble that of Japan. Alongside this attempt at integration, the state ceased to tolerate the autonomous social movements and organizations of the 1920s. The People's Party was banned in February of 1931, and numerous members of left-wing organizations were arrested later that year. These arrests, together with internal conflicts within these organizations, caused the complete disintegration of left-wing organizations in Taiwan (Lu 1989). In December 1931, the Cultural Association also collapsed after the police arrested most of its leaders (Ng 1989, p. 145; Yang 1988, p. 154). Within one year, the colonial state had demobilized all powerful oppositional organizations in Taiwan.

The state justified its repressive measures as responses to the radicalization of these organizations. For example, the colonial police maintained in an open statement that the People's Party was banned because it had deteriorated from a reformist organization which sought to advance the welfare of the island to a radical and dangerous group which openly attacked the mother country and encouraged left-wing, militant nationalism.[1] The radicalization of the party, the police argued, threatened the social order and interethnic harmony of Taiwan, and therefore the state was compelled to intervene. Peattie observes convincingly, however, that the militarization of the state and not the radicalization of these organizations was the main reason behind the increase of state repression:

> The decade of the 1920s, still open to the wind of Taishō liberalism, had seen a good deal of discussion and debate on colonial affairs. As late as the autumn of 1930, when controversy erupted in the Diet over responsibility for the Musha Rebellion in Taiwan, it was possible to debate the nature and purpose of Japanese colonial policy. But after 1931, amid the growing sense of national crisis and militancy, Japanese colonial thought assumed a doctrinaire orthodoxy which supported a policy of exploitation, regimentation, and forced-draft assimilation in Japan's overseas possessions. The pale wash of liberal reform and modest accommodation to the interests of Japan's colonial people during the earlier decade was soon dissolved in the acid of aggressive nationalism and military necessity. (1984, p. 119)

The colonial state under the "pale wash of liberal reform" of the 1920s was comparatively restrained in its exercise of regulatory power. But with political developments in Tokyo after the Manchuria Incident, the colonial state in Taiwan flamboyantly exercised its regulatory power and, on meeting resistance, unapologetically resorted to repressive measures.

A TRUNCATED AND DISJOINTED CIVIL SOCIETY

The regulatory and repressive hand of the state continued to reach into Taiwanese civil society even after it had destroyed the formal social movement organizations. In addition to overt repression, the colonial state intervened with the organizational and discursive realms within Taiwanese civil society. Specifically, Taiwanese civil society was forcibly split into two small, narrowly defined, and easily supervisable domains: the cultural and the political spheres. The cultural sphere was circumscribed by a narrow definition of culture which emerged in the early 1930s. The political sphere was directly monitored by the state. The fuzzy space of "the social," which used

---

1. The police cited the People's Party's critiques of the Japanese government during the Opium Dispute and other incidents (Jian 1991).

to accommodate a wide range of concerns, was lost in this reframing of Taiwanese civil society. In this way, the state imposed its schema of control on the Taiwanese people, effectively depriving them of agency to set the parameters of public communicative actions.

The Literary Circles

The cultural sphere in 1930s Taiwan was transformed both by state intervention and by its own internal dynamics. In the 1920s, "culture" in Taiwanese civil society was defined broadly. From public lectures on health care to reading groups on the Chinese classics, all activities involved in the circulation of ideas were considered cultural. The central organization for oppositional movements, after all, called itself the Cultural Association. Literature, which was to be recognized in the 1930s as the major "real" cultural enterprise, was but one among many activities. During this relatively relaxed period of the 1920s, a group of Taiwanese writers initiated the "new literature movement," which is often considered by literary historians as the foundation of modern Taiwanese literature. While the old-generation scholar-gentry in Taiwan had immersed themselves in the writings of classical Chinese, the "new literature" writers believed in the value and power of "everyday language" and began to publish short stories in colloquial Taiwanese.[2] These early creators of Taiwanese literature did not at first establish a distinct literary circle, but rather participated with other educated elites in the broadly defined "cultural" sphere. Most of their works appeared in the Taiwanese-run newspaper *Taiwan minpō*, together with nonliterary writings.

By the 1930s, however, intensified state repression had stifled most cultural activities in Taiwanese civil society. Because it lacked explicitly political overtones, the new literature movement escaped repression longer and, therefore, gained new importance to many Taiwanese intellectuals (see Ye 1987; Fix 1993). Literature became the only major form of free public communication that could accommodate the many concerns and voices of the Taiwanese. "In the early 1930s an incipient literary movement emerged within Taiwanese intellectual circles to become a serious critique of Japanese rule" (Fix 1993, p. 251).

2. Through the birth of this "new literature," many Chinese writers who emerged after the May Fourth Movement were introduced to Taiwan, and these works were reprinted in *Taiwan minpō* in the late 1920s. The modernist and anti-colonial overtones of the May Fourth Movement were inspiring to many Taiwanese writers in the 1920s. For discussions of Taiwanese literature in the 1920s, see Ye 1987, Li 1979, and Lin Ruiming 1996.

Under these changing circumstances, Taiwanese literary circles began to organize themselves more actively. The Taiwan Literary Arts Writers Association was founded in 1931. Various important literary journals appeared in subsequent years. For instance, *Forumosa* was first published by a Taiwanese group in Tokyo in 1931. *Nanyin* was founded in 1932 in close connection with the League for the Attainment of Local Autonomy. After the first island-wide conference in literature and arts, *Taiwan wenyi* was founded in 1934, as was *Xianfa budui*. A famous leftist writer, Yang Kui, broke away from *Taiwan wenyi* and started *Taiwan xinwenxue* in 1935. From the establishment of the Taiwan Literary Arts Writers Association in 1931 until the governor-general's ban on non-Japanese publications in 1937, the literary circles in Taiwan grew rapidly.

The literary history of these journals is complex and merits a detailed analysis in itself. But given my focus on the differentiation of Taiwanese civil society, their ideological and organizational features deserve special attention. Consistent with the spirit of the new literature movement in the 1920s, as well as the way many Taiwanese intellectuals defined the role of literature in the 1930s, many writers during these years turned to "local literature." The writers of the "local literature" camp aspired to realism and aimed to represent the pains and worries of Taiwanese people in their works. Their writings provided an alternative outlet for social and political critique and also attracted a growing readership.

However, the growth of the literary sphere also encouraged greater internal specialization. Even while the writers of "local literature" advocated representation of broad social concerns, their groups were becoming exclusively literary in nature. Writers gradually reached the consensus that they should work to produce "good literature" and not merely use literature to serve politics, despite their ideological positions on class issues, national identity, or the liberal tradition.[3] As Fix (1993) succinctly states, "A literary agenda [became] separate from the political movement." He explains that

> in 1934, the literary movement in Taiwan experienced a critical turning point. With the emergence of two associations, the Taiwan Literary Association and the Taiwan Literary League, and the activities and periodicals each promoted, the literary movement finally "came to its own." An island-wide organization, a literary agenda separate from the political movement, and a vibrant new surge of publication activities offer evidence of a peak in the new Taiwanese literature movement. (pp. 276–77)

---

3. For a discussion of these debates, see Fix 1993.

In the increasingly specialized literary sphere, literature might be informed by politics, but literary writers claimed autonomy from the political sphere. A recent, ten-volume publication in Taiwan that surveys Taiwanese literary activities in the colonial period also supports Fix's observation;[4] the world of Taiwanese writers was closed to nonspecialists. For example, in contrast to their high rates of participation in the Cultural Association, only one or two physicians became active in the literary sphere.[5] Most members of the literary sphere were teachers, writers, or literary and art critics by training.

In a sense, the formulation of a specialized and autonomous literary sphere, both in terms of organizations and agendas, inevitably qualified its "publicness." As the only surviving aspect of the 1920s cultural sphere in the era of heavy state intervention, the literary sphere for a while seemed committed to the task of representing the general concerns of the public. But eventually, it turned its attention exclusively to literary issues and welcomed only writers and their patrons. Unlike the Cultural Association of the 1920s, these literary groups or journals were accessible to a relatively narrow public.

The Political Sphere

In the 1920s, a lively political sphere developed within Taiwanese civil society. Debates brewed among various segments of civil society throughout this decade, and discussions of social issues gradually coalesced into political discourses and strategies for influencing state policies. The establishment of the People's Party in 1927 illustrates the attempt to institutionalize such a political sphere. However, the story of the differentiation of *l'homme* and *citoyen* did not take the same course in Taiwan as in Europe. In the 1930s, after the state crushed the People's Party and other social movement organizations (SMOs), the nascent political sphere in Taiwan was basically destroyed.[6] The colonial state then "manufactured" a political sphere which was at the same time easy to supervise and administra-

4. The collection, entitled *Taiwan zuojia quanji (Riju shidai)* [A complete collection of Taiwanese writers—the Japanese period], vols. 1–10, is the first part of a multivolume collection of Taiwanese literature from various periods.

5. Two well-recognized physician-writers were Lai He and Wu Xinrong.

6. The League for Attainment of Local Autonomy survived until 1936. But this organization was conservative and ineffective. Historians differed on whether it had been co-opted or it was strategically self-restrained, but they generally believed that it had little impact on either the Japanese authority or the Taiwanese people (see Mukōyama 1987; Cai et al. 1983; Wu 1986).

tively more integrated with the mother country. One way the state achieved this was by engineering elections for local councils, which were introduced in 1935.[7]

The first popular election of local councils in Taiwan was touted as an answer to long-standing demands for local self-government in Taiwan, yet it was extensively controlled by the regime. Since the reform of the administrative system in 1920, the Cultural Association, *Taiwan minpō*, and other Taiwanese organizations and groups continuously criticized the system in Taiwan as "pseudo-self-government."[8] In 1935, the colonial government finally introduced the first popular elections, but limited voting privileges to members of the male population who made yearly payments of five Japanese yen or more in local taxes (Li 1986). Thus, the state eliminated the vast majority of poorer, and therefore Taiwanese, voters (E. Chen 1984). To further ensure Japanese dominance, the government manipulated the election by dividing seats into the categories of "government-selected" and "popularly elected." The openings in the former category were directly filled by the government, and those in the latter decided by votes. By this schema, the government appointed 60 out of 161 council members. Furthermore, according to Chen Yisong, a Taiwanese lawyer who was a popularly elected city council member in Taipei, the government required that candidates give their campaign speeches in Japanese (Chen 1994). Restricted suffrage, the assignment of seats, and other state interventions served to truncate the "publicness" of these elections.

Wu's detailed analysis (1992) of the backgrounds of council members-elect reveals that the majority of the seats in the "government-selected" category were assigned to co-opted elites, while the openings in the "popularly elected" category were captured by former leaders of social movements.

---

7. Edward Chen explains how the new political climate in Japan after the Manchuria Incident sped the attempt to integrate the colonies administratively and legally. He notes the tensions between Japanese residents in the colonies and the government on the issue of integration: "Holding virtual monopoly of higher positions in the colonial government and managerial and skilled positions in colonial finance and industry, they opposed integration, fearing that it would eventually wipe out the political and economic advantages they enjoyed" (1984, p. 273). The compromise between the fear and the need to integrate often became "a thinly disguised form of racial discrimination," for example, with the elections of local councils in Taiwan and Korea (ibid.).

8. In hopes of moving the government to institute local elections, the *Taiwan shinminpō* even conducted a mock election in 1930. It was noted that many of those elected from the mock election actually became elected in local councils in the post-1945 elections, after the Japanese left (Li 1986).

This observation confirms the idea that the government had good reason to fear actual popular elections as former leaders in the opposition would undoubtedly have dominated local offices.

The state's "preventive measures" stalled the development of Taiwanese political culture. A review of the make-up of the members-elect further reveals constraints on the "publicness" of the election. As table 4 indicates, the business sector supplied about half of the members-elect. Physicians, the most highly paid professionals in the colonial period, ranked second in number among the elected. It seems, therefore, that the election results were highly dependent on the financial resources of the candidates. Just as in the European version of the story about the differentiation of *l'homme* and *citoyen*, political processes in Taiwan favored the "haves" over the "have-nots." But in the Taiwanese case, the colonial government directly manipulated elections by assigning seats to co-opted elites and restricting the language used in the campaign. These two mechanisms together excluded much of the Taiwanese public from the political game.

The "publicness" of politics was jeopardized not only by the exclusionary mechanisms built into the political system, but also by the domestication of its discourses. By channeling former social movement leaders into the elections, the state was forcing them to formulate and express their concerns in a language that was provided and controlled by the state. (After all, candidates were required to deliver their speeches only in Japanese.) By participating, these Taiwanese willingly or unwilling legitimized the political system which they wished to challenge.

From the diaries and memoirs of some Taiwanese candidates, it is clear that many of these candidates felt constrained and were frustrated by this heavy state intervention. But they chose to participate in the elections, since they were the only political route available to them. For instance, Chen Yisong, a lawyer member-elect in Taipei in 1935, recorded in his autobiography that, although disappointed and frustrated by the restricted suffrage, he was excited about the "first election in the history of Taiwan" and hoped to continue his oppositional struggles against Japanese authority through the election (Chen 1994, pp. 170–71). His experiences in politics seemed to increase his willingness to accept the political system of his time. He recalled that the election was "clean, orderly," and much better than the postwar elections held by the Chinese Kuomintang government which served "privileges and money at the expense of law and justice" (ibid., pp. 176–78).

Within a few years, then, the colonial state had effectively truncated Taiwanese civil society and caused it to become disjointed. Both remaining public spheres, the literary and the political, were reduced in size and power.

Table 4. Occupations of the Council Members-Elect in 1935

	Shūkai (P)	Shūkai (G)	Shikai (P)	Shikai (G)	Total (N)
Businessman	52.5%	50%	37.7%	45.2%	44.7% (72)
Physician*	17.5%	27.8%	27.9%	21.4%	23.6% (38)
Teacher*	20%	16.7%	8.2%	9.5%	12.4% (20)
Lawyer	5%	0%	8.2%	4.8%	5.6% (9)
Other	5%	5.6%	18%	19%	13.7% (22)
N	40	18	61	42	161

SOURCE: Wu 1992, pp. 235–40

NOTE: Shūkai means County Council; Shikai means City Council; P indicates "popularly elected"; G indicates "appointed by the government."

*Most of the physicians and teachers among the council members-elect in this election had multiple roles in addition to their professional ones. Many of them held positions in the old local councils or the *hokō* system. Still others were entrepreneurs, or "capital bearers." In this table, I have categorized members by their primary role, which I assumed to be the first one listed under their names.

While the Cultural Association attracted a large and potentially unlimited membership, the numbers of literary writers, readers, and council members were limited either by specialty or fixed openings. Within such limits, the mobilizing capacities of literary organizations or political campaigns differed qualitatively from those of the SMOs in the 1920s. Furthermore, by dividing Taiwanese civil society into these two spheres, the state greatly diminished the fuzzy space of the "social," where the parameters of public discourse might adapt to the changing concerns of diverse segments of the public. In its truncated and disjointed form, civil society no longer accommodated the production of reflexive and creative interpretations of social experience.

The destructive transformation of civil society changed the lives of former activists. Lin Jiwen's 1991 study traces the changing paths taken by core members of the Cultural Association and proposes the following interesting findings: Between 1930 and 1935, the regime forced core members of the Cultural Association out of political activity, but it allowed them to safely withdraw to the realm of their economic and professional activities (pp. 62–64). Accordingly, many of these former activists became increasingly involved in business (ibid.). This trend continued into the years of World War II (1937–1945). Lin's analysis of the social positions of former key activists offers another piece of evidence about the "depoliticization" of their roles.

The diaries and memoir of a physician-writer, Dr. Wu Xinrong, provide a glimpse into the life changes experienced by a former political figure at this juncture. Dr. Wu explains that when he was arrested in Tokyo in 1929 because of his affiliation with the Taiwan Youth Association (Taiwan Seinenkai), his diaries were used by the police as evidence against him. After his release, he decided to stop writing the diaries (Wu 1981, pp. 1–2). He resumed writing in 1933, when, as he declares, he was "no longer an actual activist or a member of any organization" (ibid.). Placed in the context of the time, Wu's statement of 1933 appears as a conscious and significant declaration of the depoliticization of his life.

Similarly, Dr. Han Shiquan, an important activist in the Cultural Association and the People's Party in the 1920s, describes in his memoirs how he decided to withdraw from politics into medicine:

> My efforts to improve my medical skills and knowledge continued after I graduated from medical school. However, occupied with the daily routines in the hospital as well as the political activities in local areas, I didn't really have a chance to make much progress. At this time, the death of my son made me feel that I was indeed incapable [of saving people's lives]. Moreover, with the dismissal of the People's Party, reformist efforts among the Taiwanese were deprived of a center. I therefore decided to go to study in Japan. (Han 1966, pp. 46–47)

DOCTORS' CHANGING "IN-BETWEEN" POSITION

Along with these macro changes, new structural and cultural relationships developed between the medical and ethnic communities in the colony as well as between these two domains and the state, shaping new dynamics in the relational configuration surrounding doctors as a social group. In these years of public demobilization, the medical community not only severed its ties to civil society, as did many other social groups, but also developed closer state connections, an improved professional market, and deeper class tensions in relation to the Taiwanese ethnic community. More specifically, as the Taiwanese medical community became increasingly incorporated into the expanding imperial medical system, its relative professional autonomy gradually declined. Meanwhile, as an integral part of a very resourceful imperial medical system, the Taiwanese medical community developed an expanding professional market. At the same time, its relationship with the Taiwanese ethnic community continued to evolve; the elevated market position of doctors further intensified their class contradictions with other Taiwanese. A close examination of these changing relationships will clarify the new dynamics of the relational configuration in which doctors were located.

The Expanding Japanese Medical Empire—Shifting Boundaries

The medical profession in Taiwan was drawn into an expanding imperial medical system and, in the process, gradually compromised the relative organizational autonomy that it had achieved in the first two decades of the colonial period. As the Japanese imperial medical system expanded, the Taiwanese medical profession was gradually incorporated, on a voluntary basis at this stage, into a team of "medical missionaries" who, as Gotō's design of scientific colonialism instructed, spread Japanese "civilization" through medical services and helped to establish Japanese hegemony in Asia. In this process, the Taiwanese medical profession attained increasingly important status in the imperial medical system and grew increasingly dependent on the state to shape the direction and growth of the profession. To accentuate the imperialist nature of the Japanese medical system in its empire, I describe this system as a "medical empire."

A careful examination of changing immunization laws on the borders between Taiwan, Japan, China, and Southeast Asia reveals a telling trend in the expansion of the Japanese medical empire as well as Taiwan's shifting location within it. As discussed earlier, when first annexed in 1895, Taiwan was regarded as a disease-stricken area that posed a danger to the health of the Japanese people and was quarantined to block the outflow of contagion. For example, in 1899 the Japanese government issued the Harbor Immunization Regulation, which, theoretically, applied to both Taiwan and Japan (Li 1953). However, the traffic from Taiwan to Japan was subject to much stricter medical surveillance than traffic in the other direction. Taiwan was placed in the same category as China and India with respect to the regulation of cargo entering Japan. This meant that immunization bureaus in Japan were notified that they should carefully investigate and record all cases of contagious disease found among passengers on ships coming from Taiwan (*MJST* vol. 5 [1899], p. 97). In 1905, however, because of the Russo-Japanese War, many on-board doctors were allocated to ships sailing to Russia. As a result, the passengers of some ships going from Taiwan to Japan did not undergo correct immunization procedures, and the Japanese complained that these passengers "managed to carry diseases into Japan." The governor-general accordingly called for further precautions (*MJST* vol. 11 [1905], p. 135).

Japan, on the other hand, was unquestioningly regarded as a "healthy land." In contrast to the detailed measures regulating traffic from Taiwan to

Japan, only loose regulations applied to traffic in the other direction. In the case of "infected ships" bound to Taiwan, the Japanese government required only that the names, situations, and places of epidemics in Japan be "reported" to the Immunization Bureau in Taiwan; no pronouncement of specific actions was recorded (MJST vol. 6 [1900], pp. 108–9).

Gradually, as immunization authorities began to view Taiwan as also a "healthy land," they relaxed their patrol at the border between Taiwan and Japan. In 1911, the governor-general of Taiwan decided that examinations of passengers on ships sailing from Taiwan to Japan could be suspended, because public health conditions in Taiwan had improved, and the danger that Taiwanese ships would carry pathogens to Japan no longer existed (MJST vol. 17 [1911], pp. 373–74). In 1922, immunization regulations at the Japan-Taiwan border recognized both sides as "equally healthy."

China, India, and Southeast Asia, however, remained designated as "sick zones"—the new frontier of dangerous disease from which the medical empire needed protection. So, from 1919 onward, new immunization bureaus were added to harbors on Taiwan. The crews and passengers of ships sailing from cities in southern China were subjected to mandatory medical examinations at these posts. Bureau staff examined such passengers for major signs of poor health and potentially contagious diseases that might have led to epidemics in Taiwan. Several outbreaks of bubonic plague on China's southeast coast had spread to Taiwan in the early twentieth century, leading to a major epidemic. Consequently, a 1921 law prohibited the importation of certain items from any harbor south of Shanghai (Li 1953).

The "sick zones" of India, southern China, and Southeast Asia were not only to be quarantined; they were to be "cured"—a euphemism for "conquered." Taiwan was to become the base for the project to cure/conquer these areas, contributing money and medical resources toward the colonization of the new frontier. Thus, as the Japanese medical empire expanded, Taiwan moved from the periphery toward the center, and Taiwan's importance to the Japanese medical empire became more widely acknowledged. In an article published in the Taiwan Times (Taiwan jihō), a government-controlled publication, Taiwan was described as "guarding the gateway to our sanitary conditions"; in particular, it was seen as guarding against the threat of epidemic diseases originating in China, India, and Southeast Asia (Kiribayashi 1932, pp. 34–35).

The Taiwanese "Medical Missionaries"

With the incorporation of the Taiwanese medical community into the expanding Japanese medical empire, a growing state directorship influencing the profession's course of development emerged. Initially, Japanese "medical missionaries" in Taiwan treated their Taiwanese colleagues as an inferior group for them to civilize and patronize but also to keep segregated. Twenty years after cosmopolitan medicine had been institutionalized in Taiwan, the Japanese doctors still collectively objected to proposals for interethnic medical associations because "Taiwanese doctors differ from us [Japanese doctors] in living standards and levels of education" (*Taiwan igakkai zasshi* [*Journal of the Medical Association of Formosa*], hereafter *TIGZ*, no. 164 [1917], p. 595).

With Taiwan as a base for the expansion of the Japanese medical empire, however, Taiwanese doctors were recruited as new members of the team of "medical missionaries" in China and Southeast Asia. The so-called "*hakuai byōin* project" illustrated this trend. The Japanese established *hakuai byōin*, or "philanthropic hospitals," in southern China from 1918, and in Southeast Asia from 1921. These hospitals were ostensibly cofounded by China and Japan, but were actually run by the Japanese. Consistent with Gotō's original plan for the "medical missionaries," the goal of these philanthropic hospitals was to increase "Sino-Japanese amity" and to offer good medical services to local Japanese and Taiwanese residents (see Taiwan Sōtokufu, *Taiwan Sōtokufu jimu seiseki teiyō*, hereafter *JST*, vol. 25 [1919], p. 662; see also *JST* vols. 26–43 [1920–1937]). The physicians sent from Taiwan to these hospitals on the Chinese mainland further specified their mission as "guiding the development of medicine and public health in the Republic [of China]" (*TIGZ* no. 290 [May 1929], p. 533). A 1931 article by one Dr. Shimojō in the *Taiwan Times*, a semi-official publication, evaluates the effects of this medical "mission." After reviewing the profiles of the four philanthropic hospitals in southern China, Dr. Shimojō observes, "[By 1931], the number of patients had increased three to eight times since the opening of these hospitals. Insofar as 90 percent of these patients are Chinese, we can rest assured that our medical skills have won the general trust of the local residents" (1931, p. 48).

The medical resources in Taiwan were channeled by the state to support these imperial medical projects. At least until 1937, funds for these hospitals were generously provided by the governor-general in Taiwan.[9] These hospitals were also staffed mainly by doctors trained in Taiwan. For example, all

9. The philanthropic hospitals were established in Xiamen in 1918, Guangdong and Fuzhou in 1919, and Shantou in 1924. The governor-general of Taiwan recorded financial support to these hospitals in a yearly publication (see *JST* 1919–1937). Starting with 1921, the government-general also began to provide financial support to hospitals in Southeast Asia (see *JST* 1921, p. 718).

of the seven physicians assigned to the Xiamen Philanthropic Hospital—
two Japanese and five Taiwanese—were based in Taiwan. As a co-optive
strategy, the state granted these new Taiwanese medical missionaries a
more equal status. Whereas in Taiwan, Taiwanese and Japanese physicians
did not receive equal pay for equal work, in China they were both considered "Japanese" and paid according to the same scale (although ethnically
Japanese doctors still tended to occupy higher positions).[10]

The establishment of the Faculty of Medicine at Taipei Imperial
University further illustrates the changing relationship between the state
and the Taiwanese medical community. Taipei Imperial University was
established in 1928, primarily to accommodate the increasing numbers of
Taiwanese-born Japanese students (*wansei*) on the island (Wu 1992). Unlike
other imperial universities in Japan, the Taipei Imperial did not have a
Faculty of Medicine when it was opened; the governor-general of Taiwan
believed that the Taipei Medical School was sufficient to train native medical practitioners, since it was not in Japanese interests to provide the
Taiwanese with more advanced knowledge (ibid.). But as Japanese designs
on southern China and Southeast Asia grew, so too did an awareness of the
importance of tropical medicine, and the Faculty of Medicine was finally
added to Taipei Imperial University in 1936. From the beginning, the purposes and directions of the faculty at the most important training institution
for the profession in Taiwan were specified and determined by the state.

In contrast to the confrontation between the colonial state and several
Japanese presidents at the Taipei Medical School that took place in the initial years of the colonial period, the Japanese leaders in the medical profession now seemed to concur with, or at least defer to, the state's directorship
about the shape of professional training. Dr. Oda, one of the first Japanese
professors of the Faculty of Medicine at Taipei Imperial University, recalled
that "in addition to the advancement of civilization in Taiwan, the development of [Japan's] activities in southern China and Southeast Asia was
becoming increasingly important. This finally led to the realization of the
plan for establishing the Faculty of Medicine at the Taipei Imperial University in Showa 11th year" (1974, p. 123). Dr. Oda was in agreement with the
official rationale behind the establishment of the Faculty of Medicine:
"When I went to Taipei for my new job, the level of Sino-Japanese conflict

---

10. Obviously, this brief discussion does not address the complex dimensions of
the history of the philanthropy hospitals, nor does it intend to do so. My purpose
here is to trace the expansion of Japan's power via medicine in China. For excellent
case studies of these hospitals, see Nakamura (1988, 1989, 1990, 1991).

was escalating. The threat of malaria was a big obstacle to the victory of the Japanese army in China. . . . Coming to Taiwan made me realize how little I really knew about malaria. To be able to participate in the research and teaching of tropical medicine, I realized that I should begin with the study of malaria" (1964, pp. 91–92).[11]

The newly founded medical faculty trained many Taiwanese "medical missionaries" to be dispatched to China and Southeast Asia. In the memoirs of many Japanese and Taiwanese doctors, the wartime experience on medical missions to the South constitutes an important topic. Although complete data on these activities are unavailable, the records of the Faculty of Medicine at Taipei Imperial University provide a glimpse of them. According to a publication by the Alumni Association of the Faculty of Medicine in 1978, medical research or service groups from Taipei Imperial University were sent to southern China or Southeast Asia in the following years: 1938, 1939, 1941, 1942, 1943, 1944. Many of these activities were consigned by the military (Tōneikai 1978). This trend continued well into the last period of the colonial era, cultivating the Taiwanese medical community as increasingly important, resourceful, and state-dependent.

Moving Upward in the Pyramid

Under these circumstances, the profession's market also developed related changes. Although authorities still carefully saw to it that the Taiwanese remained subordinate to Japanese physicians, colonial authorities now opened many new training and career opportunities to Taiwanese physicians. Thus, as Taiwanese doctors continued to enjoy an enviable market position, they further developed favorable career opportunities within the profession and enjoyed an improving internal market. This contained professional expansion is documented in two groups of evidence: the changing profile of contributors to the *Journal of the Medical Association of Formosa* and the structure of the student population at the Faculty of Medicine at Taipei Imperial University.

The level of participation of Taiwanese physicians in the professional journal provides an index of the change in career opportunities for Taiwanese physicians and medical students. The tables of contents of the *Journal of the Medical Association of Formosa* from 1902 to 1942 indicate a steady increase in Taiwanese authorship over time (see table 5 and

---

11. Another professor, Dr. Mori Oto, commented upon his departure for Taipei Imperial University that his work should "center on the research in tropical diseases." See *Teikoku daigaku shinbun (Imperial University News)*, February 3, 1936.

Table 5. Percentage of Taiwanese Contributors to the *Journal of the Medical Association of Formosa*

	Number of Taiwanese Contributors	Total Number of Contributors	Percentage of Taiwanese Contributors
1908	14	70	20.0%
1909	0	32	0
1911	12	74	16.2
1912	12	80	15.0
1915	14	99	14.1
1916	3	83	3.6
1917	2	45	4.4
1918	3	69	4.3
1919	5	77	6.5
1920	6	54	11.1
1923	3	47	6.4
1926	3	57	5.3
1927	6	63	9.5
1928	4	46	8.7
1929	7	76	9.2
1930	11	74	14.9
1931	13	119	10.9
1932	9	136	6.6
1933	24	175	13.7
1934	36	159	22.6
1935	28	172	16.3
1936	59	234	25.2
1937	37	165	22.4
1938	25	154	16.2
1939	21	145	14.5
1940	31	154	20.1
1941	45	151	29.8
1942	45	142	31.7
1944	57	175	32.6

SOURCE: *Taiwan igakkai zasshi (Journal of the Medical Association of Formosa)*, 1902–1944

NOTE: I include only scholarly articles in these numbers. Reports on professional activities and other miscellaneous writings are not counted in this table. Missing years in the table reflect incomplete or unavailable data.

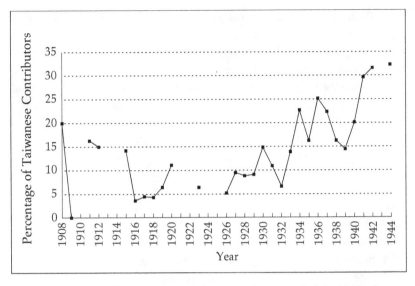

Chart 4. Percentage of Taiwanese Contributors to the *Journal of the Medical Association of Formosa* (Source: *Taiwan igakkai zasshi [Journal of the Medical Association of Formosa, 1902–1944]*)

chart 4). The proportion of Taiwanese contributors remained above 13 percent after 1930, except for the years of 1931 and 1932. After 1940, it rose to more than 30 percent. Nevertheless, Taiwanese still represented less than one-third of the total number of contributors over the entire colonial period. By 1942, in contrast, among graduates from Taipei Medical School and the Faculty of Medicine at Taipei Imperial University, the number of Taiwanese (1,661) was about three times the number of Japanese (598). These numbers reflect the pyramid structure of the medical community in Taiwan: a small number of Japanese physicians and medical students occupied top positions, while the vast number of Taiwanese remained in subordinate and inferior positions. Even though limited openings at the top of the pyramid were made available to the Taiwanese in the early to mid-1930s, the overall structure of the profession did not change.

The opportunities for medical education available to the Taiwanese, usually a faithful predictor for their later career opportunities, were also constrained by the pyramid structure. The opening of the Faculty of Medicine at Taipei Imperial University provides a good example. For Taiwanese youth who wanted a career in medicine, the new faculty represented a significant upgrade in the educational opportunities available in their homeland. Taipei Medical School, the only medical school in Taiwan before 1936, was only a "specialized college" and did not provide a university education. The new Faculty of Medicine represented the first chance for Taiwanese medical students to receive a university-level education inside Taiwan. The quality of this education also seemed promising. According to both the memoirs of contemporary Japanese professors and the newspapers published by the Tokyo Imperial University at the time, several professors from other Imperial Universities— supposedly the first-rate education and research institutes in Japan—were recruited to teach at the new Faculty of Medicine in Taipei.[12] The opportunity to receive good medical training from an Imperial University proved to be very attractive to Taiwanese students. As Wu's analysis shows, of the Taiwanese graduates of Taipei Higher School (Taihoku Kōtōgakkō), from its establishment in 1928 until the end of Japanese colonization in 1945, 60.6 percent went into medicine. Before 1936, the majority of these students went to medical schools in Japan; after 1936, more than 50 percent went to the Faculty of Medicine at Taipei Imperial University (Wu 1992, pp. 108–9).

On the other hand, however, such an opportunity was not given to Taiwanese students without restrictions. Tsurumi observes that "of the 40 medical students admitted to the university in 1936, only 16 were Taiwanese; out of the 265 students who remained in the medical college, 136 were native islanders" (1977, p. 124). This situation was due to the overall discriminatory structure of colonial education:

> The problem for Taiwanese applicants to Taihoku [the Taipei Imperial University] was that Japanese were favored—not officially, of course— in entrance selections, and since the number of places was small to begin with, only a few could ever hope to get in. For the Taiwanese who had no means of getting to Japan, where he knew he could enter a university much more easily, familiar frustrations mounted. This situation remained essentially unchanged until the end of Japanese rule. (ibid.)

The opening of the Faculty of Medicine did not change the pyramidal structure of the internal professional market. It enlarged the structure and, at the same time, opened up limited positions for the Taiwanese at the top of the pyramid. As in the case of professional journals, however, the Japanese were still favored. This "pyramid" represented the delicate balance between the upward mobility of Taiwanese doctors and their containment in the imperial medical system. Taiwanese physicians were rewarded with an improving internal market for their contribution to the medical empire, while they "safely" remained in subordinate positions.

12. See Oda 1974. See also *Teikoku daigaku shinbun (Imperial University News)*, May 6, 1935, p. 6, and June 3, 1935, p. 6.

Physicians: Native Bourgeoisie

With all the changes in the state, civil society, and the medical community, new relationships developed between Taiwanese doctors and their ethnic community. While in the past, Taiwanese doctors had used their professional knowledge and autonomy to serve their ethnic community, the new "medical missionaries" now allowed these same attributes to be claimed by the empire. The only constant feature of their role in the ethnic community seemed to be their class position. Taking into consideration the economic structure of Taiwan, their class position was further consolidated during this time.

Physicians consolidated their class position through two avenues. First, income from medical practice continued to be high and enviable by the standards of the colonized population (Chen 1992). More important, it was increasingly common for doctors to invest in outside businesses, for example, credit unions or manufacturing industries. In colonial Taiwan, it was not uncommon for doctors to inherit sizable fortunes, as many of them came from elite families. Many physicians invested the wealth they inherited or accumulated through their professional practices in business (Chen 1992). Medical practice and business investments did not make the physicians economically competitive with Taiwanese merchant-landlords or Japanese capitalists, but by the 1930s these activities did consolidate their position as a recognized class of native bourgeoisie. Their class position appeared especially attractive to the Taiwanese public (and therefore continued to motivate young students to vie for entry to medical school) in the context of the flow of native capital in the colonial period, which I will briefly survey.

Prior to the Japanese invasion, local capital-bearers in Taiwan merged to form a merchant-landlord class and accumulated great fortunes over the generations (see chapter 2). Tu Zhaoyan's voluminous study of the Taiwanese economy during the colonial period describes the changes in the merchant-landlord class across four periods:

1. 1895–1905: In this period, the native capital-bearers were resistant to the alien regime, but were soon pacified and integrated into the new social order.

2. 1905–1914: Japanese capitalism, which based itself on the sugar industry, quickly expanded into Taiwan during this time. Unable to resist the tide, local capital-bearers had to subordinate themselves to Japanese capitalists.

3. 1915–1931: Local capital-bearers were basically still under the control of Japanese capitalists and remained a subordinate group. But

internal differentiation within this group began to take place. Some local capital-bearers cooperated with the Japanese ruling power and further refined their roles as collaborators-entrepreneurs. Others cooperated with nationalist movements and aimed for political reforms. This gradual polarization became explicitly manifest during this period. For local capital-bearers, it was a period of turbulence and disintegration. (This was also the period in which, of the half century of its reign, Japanese colonial rule underwent the most drastic changes.)

4. 1931–1945: Due to worldwide depression in the early 1930s, the prices of agricultural products—rice and sugar, in particular— dropped precipitously in what amounted to a serious blow to the local merchant-landlord class. Furthermore, in the second half of the 1930s, the emerging forces of Japanese monopoly capitalism, which centered on the weapons industry, and the increasing regulation of the economy by the state both put great pressures on local capital-bearers and reduced the economic space accessible to them. This period witnessed the fading of the power of Taiwanese capital-bearers. (Tu [1991?] pp. 367–68)

In short, native capital in Taiwan was increasingly absorbed by the Japanese throughout these four periods. Some Taiwanese capital-bearers were able to fund nationalist movements for a short time (during the 1915–1931 period), but they were subordinated to the Japanese after 1931. Their economic power declined further as Japanese imperialism continued to expand. Since the most powerful capitalists in colonial Taiwan were all Japanese, and as the only influential native capitalist class was in decline, the economic success of the physicians represented the standard to which the general Taiwanese population aspired. Although the physicians' medical practice and business investments influenced the Taiwanese economy very little, medicine came to represent a very significant avenue for upward mobility for two reasons. First, it was far more realistic for a young Taiwanese to plan to accumulate wealth through medical practice and investment than to try to rank himself among the landlord-merchants, whose fortunes were almost exclusively inherited. Second, opportunities for small-business investment were very attractive in the context of the declining strength of local capitalists.

In a sense, the physicians' involvement in small businesses produced a subtle change in their class position. Their privileged class position in the 1920s was largely due to professional status. But now their position was buttressed by their role as capital-bearers. Whereas formerly their only strategy for preserving their class position was to maintain control over scarce skills, they now also wielded capital. Thus, the economic gap between physicians and the general Taiwanese population grew wider and more insurmountable. Doctors had securely achieved the position of native bourgeoisie in Taiwan.

"MEDICINE IS MY WIFE; LITERATURE, MY MISTRESS": SILENCED AND COMPARTMENTALIZED IDENTITY NARRATIVES

In the course of these structural transformations, doctors' identity narratives as "national physicians" disintegrated. Unlike those of the 1920s, professional and public discourses rarely elaborated on the identity of the physicians. The narrative of "national physicians" appeared silenced or perhaps forgotten.

Several issues of *Jiayi [Kagi] igakkai zasshi,* the association magazines of the Jiayi Medical Association (whose participation in the Opium Dispute was discussed in chapter 3) have been preserved from this period and serve to illustrate this change in the identity narrative of Taiwanese doctors. In contrast to the active discussion of doctors' social identities in the 1920s, these association magazines recorded almost no discussion of this sort. In the four issues of the magazine that are available (published respectively in March 1934, September 1934, June 1935, and October 1935), only one article touched on the issue of doctors' identities.

Published in September 1934, the only piece that broke the silence noted and lamented the doctors' loss of legacy. The article, entitled "Contemporary Views on Medicine," described this legacy as the "right of medicine," or a special trust and respect that doctors wielded in their role as the community caretakers. The author explained that "as time goes by, the general public seems to have gradually lost the trust they used to place in doctors. Instead, they now tend to view doctors the same as merchants. . . . As a result, the profession's mission of a humanist practice seems to have failed, 'the right of medicine' (*iken*) was undermined accordingly, and the public lost its trust in doctors" (p. 22). But even this public discussion of doctors' social roles did not suggest an agenda to restore all aspects of their lost legacy. In contrast to the specific connection between medicine and the nation that many medical associations and doctors had claimed in the past, this article cast the ideal of the community caretaker in a depoliticized and unelaborated metaphor with a religious overtone:

It is modern civilization and sciences that accorded us the power to cure patients and save lives and, as a result, led people to trust us as they did the living Buddha. . . . We are obligated to revive our medical ethics and . . . reflect critically upon the rampant individualism [in our profession], . . . so that we may again hope to serve as the living Buddha for tens of thousands of families. (p. 24)

Although a sense of moral commitment emerged in this metaphor of identity as the "living Buddha for tens of thousands of families," much of the old memories regarding the profession's specific ties to the Taiwanese ethnic community and its involvement in politics was muted.

In this muted identity narrative, some fragments of the legacy of doctors' multiple social participation were still manifest. But their presence signaled the compartmentalized roles played by doctors, rather than a well-integrated identity once constructed by and used to powerfully represent this community. In the *Jiayi igakkai zasshi,* for example, there was an active interest in creative writing among this group. Each issue of the magazine typically contained two or three pieces of creative writing, usually in the forms of short essays and Chinese poetry, in addition to the more standard categories of academic reports (on average, five pieces per issue) and reports on new professional regulations passed in Japan or Taiwan (with no comments of their own). Although literary interest became a feature of professional publications, it was never made relevant to their role of doctors. If such attempts were made, these literary-minded doctors might have been interested in comparing themselves with Lu Xun, the famous Chinese physician-writer from the same period whose work had been published often in *Taiwan minpō* during the 1920s. (One is reminded here of the analogy once drawn by Taiwanese medical associations between Dr. Sun Yat-sen and the national physicians during the earlier period.)

The experiences of individual doctors were consistent with this group-level pattern. For example, in his diary during the years before the outbreak of the war, Dr. Wu Xinrong, the physician-writer discussed earlier in this chapter, spent many pages describing his activities and conversations with his literary friends. He also closely tracked the numbers of patients at his clinic, drew up plans for improving and expanding his medical practice, and, occasionally, mentioned his activities at the Medical Association. Nevertheless, he never drew connections between these spheres of activity, and he let these different dimensions of his life fall into two parallel narratives (see Wu 1981). Although Dr. Wu had once used the phrase the "Taiwanese Lu Xun" to honor Dr. Lai He, an editor at the *Taiwan minpō* during the 1920s and a well-recognized physician-writer, Dr. Wu did not elaborate on the literature-medicine linkage beyond Dr. Lai's individual case. That Dr. Wu himself would rather keep the two in separate tracks was revealed in his famous saying: "Medicine is my wife; literature, my mistress."

During the years between the Manchuria Incident and the outbreak of the second Sino-Japanese War, the state demobilized most social movements in Taiwanese civil society. But unique to the physicians, their profession was increasingly mobilized by the state to facilitate the development of colonial medicine. The professional autonomy of the Taiwanese medical community gave way to state regulation in shaping its goal and directions, while the ties between the profession and the state cultivated an expanding professional market. Meanwhile, new economic trends further consolidated the class differences between doctors and the general Taiwanese population. The cultural ties between the medical profession and the Taiwanese community were weakened. The new relationships among the state and the ethnic and medical communities constituted a significantly different configuration; the medical community developed stronger ties with the state as it lost many of its old connections with the Taiwanese ethnic community. Situated in this new set of relational configurations, the profession did not develop a salient collective identity narrative; it only left muted and fragmented discourses.

In light of my efforts to contextualize professional formation in its intersection with other social categories, these new developments represent a process in which the profession was uprooted from its ethnic community. The evidential traces of state manipulation in this transition show that the "de-ethnicization" of the profession is a highly political product. While the structural conjunctions that accounted for the demobilization and "de-ethnicization" of doctors were specific to this historical period, this history suggests a general lesson for the need to denaturalize and problematize the "non-ethnic" (and "asexual" for that matter) images of professions. We need to recognize that in its social formation, a profession often undergoes the process of becoming rooted in and uprooted from particular ethnic, racial, or class communities. Only with a fuller understanding of these processes will we achieve a more complex historical sociology of the professions.[13]

13. Andrew Abbot's (1988) study points in a similar direction. Abbott proposes that we study the interaction of different professions rather than insist on a single-profession focus, so that we may better understand the formation of the system of professions. In a later article in which he surveys the field, Abbott notes that his proposal of an interactive perspective has not been duly heeded by recent studies (Abbot 1993). My perspective suggests that we extend Abbott's approach and study processes of the interaction between professionalization and other social processes.

The cogency of Dr. Jiang Weishui's "Clinical Diagnosis," which served to structure and bridge many doctors' social and medical concerns, therefore, dissolved in this new and confusing era. Instead, Dr. Wu's famous saying better summarizes doctors' fragmented identities in this period: "Medicine is my wife; literature, my mistress." During this era of public demobilization, the hybrid identity of doctors ultimately became unstable and enigmatic, and was thus infused with the air of something vaguely illicit. These changes suggest how unwise it would be to make general assumptions about the potential for creativity and resistance in the hybrid. From their anticolonialism to their demobilization, the evolving in-betweenness of doctors cautions us against the postcolonial celebration of the colonial hybrid. Instead, the contrast of these two different "hybrid" identities poses a question: How are we to theorize the different forms of hybrid power?

5 Medical Modernists (1937–1945)

The outbreak of the second Sino-Japanese War in 1937 ushered in the Kōminka Era in colonial Taiwan, which initiated a new phase of interaction between colonialism and professionalization. The Kōminka Era, or a period of state-led intensive assimilation, constituted a time when Japanese colonizers consciously undermined ethnic boundaries within the empire. In this context, the colonial state sought the thorough incorporation of the Taiwanese medical profession into its imperial medical system, deploying it as a tool of imperial expansion in China and Southeast Asia. The state's efforts at intensive Japanization of both ethnic and medical communities radically transformed the structural location and hybrid identity of Taiwanese doctors.

This chapter analyzes these changes in the relational configuration that surrounded doctors during this time, and develops a detailed discussion of how doctors experienced and related themselves to the new structural environment. Medical doctors and students from this time developed what can be described as a "medical modernist" identity. Constructing a perspective grounded in their professional experiences, they dismissed the particularities of their Taiwanese ethnicity and embraced what was perceived as the universality of humanism and rationality. The relevance of ethnicity did not, however, fade away so easily, and the modernist narrative was, therefore, strained and, at times, disturbed by bracketed categories. This intriguing and previously neglected history holds important implications for ethnic relations within Japanese imperialism and, more generally, for the location of culture in ethnic formation.

"KŌMINKA": INTENSIVE, STATE-LED ASSIMILATION

The period of forced assimilation introduced drastic changes in the relationships between the Taiwanese ethnic community and the Japanese colonial state, but to better understand these changes, a brief discussion of Japan's earlier assimilation ideology is necessary. Even in its initial stages, the assimilation policy in the Japanese Colonial Empire was marked by the peculiarities and ambiguities of Japan's colonialism (Peattie 1984; Robertson 1995). As an Asian empire colonizing people who were perceived as racially and ethnically related, Japan reasoned that the colonized were "not quite Japanese but perhaps capable of becoming Japanese" (Tsurumi 1984, p. 279). Furthermore, assimilation ultimately "defined a process whereby, as a strategy of colonial domination and control, *the Japanese nation assumed a protean character capable of absorbing, re-appropriating, and thus neutralizing cultural difference*" (Robertson 1995, p. 972; my emphasis). This "protean Japaneseness" was supposed to easily absorb, and be absorbed by, colonial subjects who racially and culturally resembled the Japanese. "Japaneseness" was expected to eventually spread throughout Asia. However, the process of "becoming Japanese" is, as Robertson puts it, "fundamentally ambiguous and contradictory" (1995, p. 972). While this assimilationist ideology was practiced widely in Japan's colonies, it nevertheless failed to penetrate deeply into indigenous societies. The Japanization process only served to "reinforce the physical identities of indigenous populations with their rulers" (Peattie 1984, p. 41). This consequence of assimilation efforts created serious issues for Japanese authority concerning internal differences in the empire; in order to maintain the purity of Japaneseness, the colonizers needed to protect themselves against "contamination" by the colonized.

Tensions between the drive for expansion and the need to preserve the purity of "Japaneseness" became particularly acute after the beginning of World War II in Asia. "Wartime pressures demanded the mobilization of all colonial resources and manpower. Yet, without the colonial subjects' wholehearted loyalty toward the mother country such mobilization would be incomplete" (Chou 1996, p. 42). In order to radically deepen the effects of Japanization among colonial subjects without sacrificing its breadth, the Japanese colonial government launched the Kōminka Movement, a series of intensive assimilation campaigns, in its two biggest colonies: Taiwan and Korea.[1]

In Taiwan, the Japanese government took various measures to thoroughly regulate and restructure indigenous ethnicity. *Kōminka* programs—which included a national-language movement, a program of name-changing, and

---

1. *Kōminka* literally means "imperialization" (of colonial subjects). For a comparison of the different effects of the Kōminka Movements in Taiwan and Korea, see Chou 1996.

reforms of native religious and social customs—aimed to undermine the salience of Taiwanese culture. The fourth program in the Kōminka Movement was a military recruitment campaign, an indicator of the wartime purpose behind assimilation efforts. Under these *kōminka* programs, the Taiwanese were "persuaded" to speak only Japanese on all occasions, adopt Japanese-style names, and convert to Shintoism. These cultural traits, such as naming patterns, language, and religious activities, were precisely the medium and manifestation of the Taiwanese ethnic identity. With *kōminka*, the state aggressively attempted to eradicate and regulate the culture, and therefore the ethnic identity, of the Taiwanese community.

Along with these efforts, the Japanese state also tried to close the gap of ethnic inequality. For example, Taiwanese families who were proven to speak only Japanese at home were "awarded" plaques bearing the inscription "the family of national language" (*kokugo katei*). Equipped with this title, members of these families had "better chances . . . to enter supposedly good schools, or priority for employment in government or public organizations" (Chou 1996, pp. 52–53). Toward the end of the war, Japan implemented other policies to officially upgrade the status of these Taiwanese. For example, Japanese government employees in Taiwan regularly received 40 to 60 percent of their base salaries as bonus compensation; during this time Taiwanese employees also began to receive an additional 30 percent of their salaries. In 1945, a few months before Japan's defeat, the central government in Tokyo passed a series of laws which granted Taiwanese and Koreans the right to participate in congressional elections (Ng 1989, pp. 187–88).

These attempts at complete regulation of Taiwanese ethnicity were varied in their effects. Scholars found that "the religious reforms met the coldest reception; the name-changing program was also unpopular among Taiwanese, at least in the beginning. With regard to the 'national language' movement, the rapid growth of the population of 'national-language speakers' during the Kōminka Era seems to suggest a certain degree of success. Finally, the volunteer program, targeted at young people, seems to have aroused enthusiasm among them" (Chou 1996, p. 67). In comparison,

> Korean responses to each of the *kōminka* programs largely followed the same pattern, but the Koreans often showed more resistance and less compliance than the Taiwanese in each case. Scholars in the field of Japanese colonial history have long noticed that the colonial experiences of Taiwan and Korea differed in that the interactions between the ruler and the ruled in Korea were much more violent and stormy than those in Taiwan. The study of the *kōminka* movement helps substantiate this impression. (ibid.)

In general, the *kōminka* programs significantly redefined the relationship between the colonial state and the Taiwanese community. Whereas in the past the state had merely imposed its rule on the ethnic community, it now aimed to transform the very identity of the ethnic community, absorbing it into the Japanese nation and effacing its distinctive characteristics.

WARTIME MEDICINE: SERVANT OF THE STATE

The Complete Politicization of Medicine

As discussed in chapter 4, during the years leading up to the highly politically charged Kōminka Era, the Taiwanese medical community gradually assumed center stage in Japan's East Asian medical project. By the 1930s, Taiwan was both the police and the pioneer at the frontier of this medical empire. Later, as Japan's interest in acquiring tropical colonies increased and was actualized with the building of the Greater East-Asia Co-Prosperity Sphere, Taiwan's importance was further magnified. In his published work, Dr. Shimojō Himakazu, a Japanese medical doctor at the Tropical Medicine Research Center (Nettai Igaku Kenkyūjo) in Taiwan, explained how the tropical conditions in Taiwan contributed to the refinement of knowledge on tropical ecology and population dynamics, which in turn informed imperial policies toward Japanese immigrant communities in Southeast Asia. Referred to by Dr. Shimojō as "the only tropical area *within our country*" (*waga kuni;* 1942, p. 67; my emphasis), Taiwan was no longer an exotic "other," but rather an important and integral part of the Japanese Empire. As Taiwan's "difference" was found to be useful to Japan's colonial project in southern China and Southeast Asia, it evolved from a problem to a resource.

Gradually, the Taiwanese medical community became a base for medical missions in the new southern colonies. Not just responsible for curing sick bodies, it also had to "cure" colonial bodies by spreading Japanese medical ideology to these places. In a *Taiwan Times* article on "tropical hygiene" published in 1942, Morishita Kaoru, a professor of medicine at Taipei Imperial University, proposed the establishment of an administrative center in Taiwan to oversee the so-called Welfare Community of the Co-Prosperity Sphere (Kyōeiken Kōsei Burokku). He advised that "although Tokyo would be a good place, Taiwan seems a more practical option. . . . Taiwan is positioned at the center of the Greater East Asia Co-Prosperity Sphere, and features both a Japanese worldview and tropical characteristics" (1942b, p. 54).

In another *Times* article published in 1942, Dr. Morishita commented on the increasing politicization of medicine since the beginning of the war. The central role of Taiwan in the *medical* aspect of empire management had, according to Dr. Morishita, lent itself to the increasing importance of Taiwan in the *political* aspect of empire building (1942a). Similarly, the editors of a collection of essays on tropical medicine, published in Tokyo during 1942, declared that Taipei Imperial University was the "foundation for Japan's advancement in the South." As if to back up this claim with empirical evidence, eight of the eleven articles in the edited volume were written by medical doctors in Taiwan, seven of whom were professors at Taipei Imperial University. From these writings emerged a formula linking Taiwan's medical and political importance in the colonial empire: "Taiwan = center for research of tropical medicine = basis for Japan's southward advancement" (see Taiheiyō Kyōkai 1942).[2]

As the war continued, the politicization of medicine escalated through a series of policies that extended state control over the entire medical community in Taiwan. The Japanese government announced the Law for National Mobilization (*Kokka sōdōinhō*) on April 1, 1938, and a series of related laws and regulations were put into practice in the empire over the ensuing years. The medical community in Taiwan was gradually but thoroughly brought under the umbrella of "national mobilization." Dr. Li, a Taiwanese physician and scholar of medical history, provided a detailed discussion of the regulation of medical practitioners during this period (Li 1949). The regulation affected various aspects of the life of medical practitioners:

1. *The requirement for self-report (enacted in 1938).* This law required all medical doctors, dentists, pharmacists, and nurses to register with the government as eligible candidates for any wartime medical projects. In 1941, the government enacted two related laws which specified the procedures for conscription of medical practitioners.

2. *The establishment of Taiwan Medical Service Group* (Taiwan Hōkō Ishidan) *in 1941.* This group was reorganized and split into two groups in 1943: the Taiwan Medical Association and the Taiwan Dentist Association. These groups, like many other service (*hōkō*) groups in wartime Japan, were meant to serve as channels through which the state could control and mobilize social resources for the war effort. In Taiwan, this was the first time during the colonial period that Taiwanese and Japanese doctors were ordered by the

2. For a detailed discussion of Japan's "southward advancement," see "Part 3: Japan's Wartime Empire and Southeast Asia," in Duus, Myers, and Peattie 1996.

state to organize interethnic medical associations, to be managed predominantly by the Japanese side of the membership. Taiwanese physicians, whether private practitioners or state employees, were now subject to supervision and regulation by these interethnic, Japanese-controlled associations.

3. *The dispatch of medical practitioners to Southeast Asia.* Starting in 1943, large numbers of Taiwanese doctors were sent to Southeast Asia as translators as well as military doctors.

4. *The formation of medical air-defense groups.* Formed in 1944, these groups were on call after air raids to provide island-wide medical service. [3]

The governor-general's yearly publication *Outlines and Summaries of the Administration of Civil Affairs* also documented these measures of mobilization. In addition, the *Outlines and Summaries* discussed three other aspects of mobilization (see *JST* vols. 43–47 [1937–41]). First, the governor-general advised immunization authorities at entry ports to Taiwan to become stricter in their practice after the start of the war. This change was described as a measure necessary to block the flow of disease and the threat of chemical warfare from China. Second, the governor-general followed Tokyo's policy and launched a campaign to "improve national health." Local health bureaus were charged with the responsibility of developing workshops and programs to implement the "national policy of cultivating the people's physical strength on the home front" (see also "Kokka sōdōin ka no kenkō shūkan," 1939, pp. 187–88). Third, the governor-general continued to support the activities of philanthropic hospitals in China and Southeast Asia, but with an explicitly military purpose. These hospitals were to assist the Japanese army not only by maintaining health conditions on the front, but also by pacifying local residents with medical services.

As the war brought about and indeed justified these laws and regulations, the governor-general was able to establish total control over the Taiwanese medical community. The complete politicization of medicine greatly diminished the relative autonomy and organizational capacity that the profession had achieved in the first half of the colonial period. Medicine was finally reclaimed by the colonial state.

3. For the original text of the law, see *Taiwan igakkai zasshi (TIGZ)* 38, no. 9 (1938), pp. 154–55.

Changing Discourse on the Health of the Nation

The redefinition of the "health of the nation" further completed state mobilization of medicine. As Taiwan became fully integrated into the Japanese medical empire, native physicians were gradually silenced by state bureaucrats on questions regarding the "health of the nation." Historical documents reveal an amazing contrast in the discourse on "health" in Taiwan between the 1920s and the 1940s. In the 1920s, when Taiwanese were still marked as different and inferior, native physicians were more free to define the health of the island. With relative autonomy, Taiwanese physicians in the 1920s developed a collective self-identity as "national physicians," whose goal was to serve the Taiwanese people. They offered medical services and participated in reformist movements, promising to cure both physical and social diseases for Taiwan. By the 1940s, however, as the Taiwanese people acquired a sufficiently "Japanese look" and as tropical medicine in Taiwan facilitated the advance of the forces of Japanization in other regions, Taiwanese definitions of public health were supplanted by a discourse on the health of the Japanese Empire. The empire replaced the ethnic community as the social body served by medicine.

The equation of public health with the health of the empire profoundly altered the ideological framework for thinking about ethnicity in Taiwanese society. The aforementioned "formula" (Taiwan = center for research of tropical medicine = basis for Japan's southward advancement), served to define Taiwan as an integral part of the Japanese Empire and also effectively severed Taiwan's racial and ethnic connections to China. China was both the site of the enemy and the source of disease, against which Taiwan needed to defend itself. The governor-general's annual report for 1941 drew a telling analogy between the invasion of enemies and the invasion of diseases from China:

> As the Sino-Japanese conflict intensifies, our island is becoming increasingly important both economically and militarily. Accordingly, the traffic between our island and southern China is busier than ever and is having a serious impact on the island's health conditions. In response, we have attempted to improve health policies and facilities in Taiwan, . . . and this year we managed to *prevent the invasion of such malicious diseases as cholera and pestilence.* (*JST* vol. 47 [1941], pp. 620–21; my emphasis; see also *JST* vols. 45–46 [1939, 1940])

By severing Taiwan's ties with China, the colonial government sought to forge a new image of the Taiwanese as "our people." During the war, Japanese authorities in Taiwan repeatedly referred to the Taiwanese as "our people," in contrast to the prewar terminology *hontōjin,* or "people from this island." These official wartime discourses swiftly, and perhaps intentionally, elided the boundaries between the colonizers and the colonized, equating Taiwanese and "our people" without qualification.[4]

An emergent discourse about the "health of the nation" in the empire during this time also transformed the meanings of womanhood. Official wartime propaganda on the "health of the nation" emphasized the need for robust manpower, which rendered reproductive activities a central theme in the new medical discourse. As "concerns over falling population growth rates and the poor physique of army conscripts spurred the government to pronatalist policies" (Uno 1993, pp. 299–300), the state turned its attention to the fertility of mothers and the health of babies. The political repression of Japan's birth control movement (1938) was followed by the passing of the National Eugenics Law (1940), which represented a more aggressive effort to medically monitor motherhood and reproductive activities (p. 300). In both Japan and Taiwan, women were officially mobilized to serve the nation as active, fertile child-bearers.[5]

The medicalization of the female body at home went hand in hand with the recruitment of female caretakers on the war front. When the military began to recruit Taiwanese men to serve as military porters in July 1937, it also recruited Taiwanese women to serve as war nurses. In the language of the period, if Taiwanese youth aspired to become cherry blossoms, Taiwanese women wished to become "*yamato* flowers," or good and worthy Japanese women (Chou 1991). These war nurses were considered "women of the wartime nations" *(gunkoku no fujin),* who ensured the health of the nation

---

4. However, despite the state's enthusiastic pronouncement of the Taiwanese as "our people," some Japanese were worried about internal "contamination." These Japanese were concerned that protracted residency in Taiwan as a result of colonization might alter the Japanese physique. As Dr. Soda expressed in a 1937 *Taiwan Times* article, "Japanese who live in Taiwan are experiencing two major bodily changes: they are becoming slimmer and are losing weight. . . . Although we cannot conclude that slim, light bodies are necessarily weaker, we know that at least among members of the same race, such body structures are prone to diseases like tuberculosis." He reaffirms his belief that "our national fate is rooted in the maintenance and improvement of the human power of our people. . . . We need to achieve a thorough understanding of our people's physical strength, which we should improve." A survey of the table of contents of the *Journal of the Medical Association of Formosa* at this time also reveals a steady research interest in the physique of Japanese residents in Taiwan. Thus, despite the pan-Asian rhetoric of Japanese colonialism, there existed a persistent fear of the contamination of the Japanese body by the colonized.

5. The Japanese women in Taiwan were openly encouraged to influence their "younger sisters," namely their Taiwanese counterparts, and to help them understand their "noble mission" as child-bearers for the nation (Hong 1995, pp. 65–66).

by treating front-line soldiers (see "Sokoku no hanayome," in *Taiwan Sōtokufu rinji jōhōbu buhō* [*Newsletters of the Temporary Information Department*], 1939, p. 1). They were described as the mothers and sisters of the nation's fighters, and they went to the front as "brides of the ancestral land" (ibid.).

Losing their voices in the discourse on the "health of the nation," native physicians were deprived of agency in defining the ethnicity and gender roles in Taiwanese society. As other studies on fascism also show, state appropriations of ethnicity and sex/gender often signal the erasure of the public/private distinction (Berezin 1996). This erasure, in the context of colonialism, further marks the moment of final penetration of colonial forces into the inner domain of indigenous life.

Internal Market within the Profession

Meanwhile, the politicization of medicine continued to expand career opportunities within the Taiwanese medical community. The state initiated and funded new medical projects, especially on tropical medicine, in order to facilitate Japanese expansion in southern China and Southeast Asia. New professors were recruited from Japan, and new research positions were added.

In addition to jobs related to tropical medicine, other opportunities were created for native physicians. As explained earlier, the Taiwanese medical community can be depicted with a pyramidal structure, with small numbers of Japanese occupying the top positions and huge numbers of Taiwanese occupying the bottom ones. With the passage of time, Taiwanese students and doctors moved slowly upward within the pyramid, but the war escalated this upward mobility for Taiwanese members of the medical community. After the military began to draft Japanese medical doctors and students in Taiwan, the vacancies they left were filled by their Taiwanese colleagues, who would not be formally drafted until early 1945.[6] A greater number of middle- and high-ranking positions in medical institutes became accessible to the Taiwanese, even though Japanese personnel maintained priority.

In my interviews with Taiwanese doctors, I learned that they were well aware of the changes in their professional opportunities during this time. For instance, I asked a Taiwanese physician, whom I will refer to as Dr. F, about his memories of his career during the war. He described himself and his Taiwanese colleagues as "substitutes" for the Japanese:

6. Taiwanese people were not subject to conscription until 1945. However, the military began to recruit Taiwanese as military porters as early as 1937. Taiwanese medical practitioners began to be sent to southern China or Southeast Asia as military doctors or translators in 1943.

DR. F: It was in the middle of the war. We were like substitutes. Sub-
           stitutes. Do you know what I mean? . . . The Japanese had all
           been drafted, and the Taiwanese didn't have to be drafted. . . .
           The Japanese all went to war, and the hospitals couldn't func-
           tion, so we became the substitutes. . . . So after I graduated, I
           joined the surgical department at Taipei Imperial University.
           In the past there had been hardly any Taiwanese surgeons,
           maybe one or two in every big city. The year [I joined the
           surgical department] was the start. But we didn't receive any
           salary. For the six or seven years I was at Taipei Imperial, I
           had no salary. It was called a "non-paying assistantship."

LO: Were there any assistants who were paid?

DR. F: Those positions with pay were all taken by the Japanese. . . .
           But anyway, in that year, about ten of us joined the surgical
           department, and we all had the opportunity to do research. . . .
           Our professor mentored more than ten Taiwanese students.
           Eventually about ten of them became Ph.D.'s! Ten of them!

LO: So you worked as unpaid assistants in the surgical
           department and did research under his mentorship at the
           same time?

DR. F: Right. It wasn't that easy usually. If it hadn't been for the fact
           that almost all the Japanese were drafted, how should we Tai-
           wanese have had such precious opportunities? (Life-F, for sim-
           ilar examples, see also Lin 1983; Lin, unpublished manuscript).[7]

Thus, Taiwanese medical doctors and students enjoyed increased research
opportunities because of the war, although better positions were still
reserved for the Japanese. Despite discrimination, the Taiwanese were able
to advance in the profession faster than before, and therefore they welcomed
the opportunity to be "substitutes."[8]

It's not accidental that my informant should choose to describe himself
and his Taiwanese classmates as "substitutes." They were, in the unspoken
spirit of *kōminka*, considered substitutes for "real Japanese." In the interview quoted above, it was clear that Dr. F understood well how the system
incorporated them. There is, however, another layer of meaning to "substi-

7. I conducted interviews with ten Taiwanese doctors to collect their life stories.
Quotations from these interviews are referenced as Life-[letter]. A detailed discussion of the interviewing process is provided in the appendix.

8. As Xie (1989) points out, public health conditions in Taiwan actually regressed
during the war because most Taiwanese medical resources were channeled to the
front. While the Taiwanese public had difficulty accessing good medical service during this time, according to my informants, this did not seem to affect the upward
mobility of Taiwanese medical doctors and students until the last year of war.

tutes." As Taiwanese students and doctors in the medical community were increasingly incorporated into the empire through their professional activities, their experiences inadvertently led to a process in which they substituted a professional identity for an ethnic one. As the next section demonstrates, their experiences in the medical community during this time display this—a struggle to ground their identity in their profession.

"PROTEAN MODERNITY": THE IDENTITY NARRATIVES OF "KŌMINKA DOCTORS"

As the Japanese state worked to impose total regulation over the Taiwanese ethnic community and to further integrate the medical profession with the imperial system, how did native physicians experience and articulate their identity? How, to be more specific, did they negotiate a social group identity as assimilated native doctors?

Although doctors seemed to maintain the strong group awareness that was developed in the previous periods, they left few traces of a collective identity during the Kōminka Era. As most of their voluntary associations (e.g., local medical associations) were dismantled, silenced, or incorporated into state-controlled organizations, the social space for the group to discuss, develop, and register narratives of a collective identity was radically diminished. The decline of such a social space, outside of individuals' subjective consciousness, where collective statements, symbols, and other cultural artifacts are communicated by and for the group, signals the disintegration of collective identity.

What history left for us to observe from this period, then, was doctors' collective identity *in the making*. The legacy of a strong group awareness from earlier periods led many doctors and medical students to continue to reflect upon the meaning of doctors' social roles by producing individual narratives and small group discussions. The common patterns in individual doctors' narratives and traces of identity formation that took place in small "submerged networks" indicate a process of collective identity construction which, because of the absence of collective agents to coalesce and stabilize these individual narratives, was never brought to completion.[9]

9. Some people might argue that if we had better access to the data from this highly regulated historical period, we would be able to reconstruct a better-formulated collective identity of the doctors. While I certainly agree about the scarcity of data, I am critical of the assumption that there was a well-formulated collective identity of the doctors waiting to be expressed. As illustrated in my discussion of the concepts of collective narrative and the role of a collective agency (e.g., formal organi-

In my attempt to address the difficulty of documenting the *kōminka* doctors' collective identity, I searched for informants who remembered situations in the medical profession between 1937 and 1945, and looked for common patterns in these doctors' narratives. When, in some cases, a common pattern failed to emerge, I acknowledged the discrepancy among the narratives and treated this as part of the process of identity formation. I was able to locate one important submerged network, Anzu (Apricot), uncovered some of its unpublished materials, and collected in-depth interviews with some of its members. The story of Anzu provides an important record of the attempts of Taiwanese medical students to articulate a collective narrative in the limited social space available to them.

The written and oral sources suggest that, much like their forerunners in the 1920s, Taiwanese medical students and practitioners in this period continued to embrace a modernist professional culture. But instead of serving as inspiration for the empowerment of their ethnic community, modernity was a justification for decentering ethnicity. Young Taiwanese medical doctors and students of this period embraced modernity's promise of progress toward universal truth and good. In so doing, they bypassed, albeit temporarily, the troublesome issue of ethnic identity.

These doctors uniformly described their field as ultimately modern (*gendaiteki*). In contrast to the divergent theoretical literature on the conditions and consequences of modernity, these doctors' narratives underline one common interpretation of "the modern." For them, "the modern" stood for an ideal situation in which human lives could be continually improved by rational thinking and action. These two major themes, rationality and humanism, structured their interpretations of their "modern" professional experiences.

In an illustrative example, Dr. Lin Tianyou's autobiography explains that he chose the field of medicine because it was "rational." He withdrew from Taipei Normal School, which would have prepared him for a teaching career, and enrolled in Taipei Medical School instead, because he realized that "in the colony, teachers were nothing more than the rulers' tool," whereas the

---

zations, submerged networks, community reputation entrepreneurs, etc.) in chapter 1, a collective identity of a group does not exist a priori. Rather, the making of collective identities depends on social networks and communicative channels. This view concurs with recent scholarship on social movements that stresses the interaction between identity formation and social movements. Instead of assuming that group interests are predetermined and group identities preformed, these scholars argue that the networks and activities of social movements contribute greatly to shaping the collective identity of the group (Melucci 1989, 1996; Mueller 1994).

field of medicine could accommodate his "orientation for the rational and objective analysis of things" (Lin 1983, p. 4). Lin's words indicate his belief that medicine was ultimately a rational discipline free from political manipulation.

Other doctors' words reveal that Dr. Lin's interpretation was a common one. It was a widely held belief among Taiwanese doctors at the time that their field was comparatively more rational than other parts of colonial society. Dr. Lin Yanqing, for example, commented on the profession's capacity to formulate demands for reforming the irrational aspects of the medical system: "Many professors were angry at the limits on Taiwanese applicants to Taipei Imperial University. . . . It was said that Professor Hosonoya of the Faculty of Medicine once openly reported this fact at the [Medical] Association in Japan, and that this troubled the governor-general of Taiwan" (Lin, unpublished manuscript). Likewise, in interviews and memoirs, doctors from this period commonly believed in the "humanist" nature of medical science. The saying of Dr. Takagi, a Japanese physician from earlier years, "Before becoming a doctor, become a human," was remembered by many as an important motto for the Taiwanese medical community. Young Taiwanese medical students viewed their Japanese mentors as rare individuals who held fast to humanism even in a colonial society during wartime. Dr. Zhang recalled in an interview how these humanist Japanese boldly expressed their antiwar sentiments: "There were plenty of them. . . . [Among my professors at Taipei Higher School and Taipei Imperial University], many of them unashamedly expressed their anti-war sentiment . . ." (Shozawa 1995a, p. 171).

Construed as a culture of rationality and humanism, modernity was generally accepted by Taiwanese doctors and medical students as the central defining feature of their community. This culture shaped their interpretation of Taiwanese tradition; it influenced their perspective on everything in their lives, from language to habits and lifestyles. They consequently grew critical of their own ethnic culture. For instance, Dr. F explicitly described Taiwanese tradition as backward while praising Japanese influences as modern. He identified doctors with the modern:

DR. F: Everything . . . education and society, everything was
          Japanized. That is to say, our environment had been much
          modernized by that time. That's why we could communicate
          with the Japanese. Otherwise, we would have been doing
          nothing but going to the temples every day, according to
          Taiwanese customs. "Inquiring about the gods' intentions,
          seeking for the [blessed] drugs." That's what Taiwanese were

best at. "Inquiring about the gods' intentions, seeking for the [blessed] drugs," do you know what that is?

LO: Yes . . . that you go to the temple and . . .

DR. F: [Interrupting Lo] Right! And you beg for the ash of the incense burned in front of the gods, and drink it with water! That was the level of Taiwanese culture in the past. Before they went to see a real doctor, they had to first ask for the gods' permission. (Life-F)

As this example shows, these doctors believed that Taiwanese tradition should be modernized by new sciences such as medicine. In my interviews, they tended to use "Japanese" and "modernist" interchangeably. Thus, they rarely saw reason to resist the influence of Japanese culture on Taiwan.

Furthermore, young Taiwanese medical doctors and students tended to *displace* the issue of ethnicity in their pursuit of modernity. These doctors believed that during the wartime period, rationality and humanism stood as central values of both Japanese and Taiwanese members of the medical community. Their common values united medical doctors and students across ethnic lines, at least from the perspective of the Taiwanese. For example, when asked whether Japanese doctors treated Taiwanese patients unkindly in state hospitals, Dr. F replied without hesitation: "Oh, that would be very rare. Basically, in a doctor's mind, ill people deserved all his attention and respect. . . . Japanese doctors were also very kind to Taiwanese patients" (Life-F). These doctors claimed that in their experience the spirit of humanism differed more by generation than by ethnicity. They often commented on the sharp contrast between the humanist values of their day, during the Japanese colonial period, and the commercial values of the medical community in the years after the Japanese left. Dr. H and his father practiced medicine in these two periods respectively. In my interview Dr. H remembered the doctor-patient relationship of his father's generation as a warm, human relationship, whereas he described the one of his generation as a commercial exchange (Life-H).[10]

In short, during this time, Taiwanese medical doctors and students were absorbed by "protean modernity." Their minds, informed by rationality and humanism, were convinced of the ideal of universal good and uninterested in the particularism of their ethnicity. The particularism of their ethnicity, to be sure, did not vanish from their lives; it was merely suppressed and displaced in their life narratives. The tensions between universalism and par-

10. For more examples, see "Yiren zhuanlan," a series of interviews with older physicians, in *Taiwan Medical Journal* vols. 23–29.

ticularism were not unique to these doctors' experiences. Studies of other cases suggest that "the basic zeal to erase differences meant that modernism was both troubled by the existence of variations and contained many, especially as new groups and ideas burst into the public scene" (Hart 1996, p. 35).[11] Before turning to these tensions within "protean modernity," I first explain the mechanisms through which these doctors came to identify themselves with "the modern."

Interethnic Professional Ties

Taiwanese medical doctors and students were absorbed into modernity through two principle mechanisms. The first, interethnic professional ties, emerged from their professional experiences. As changes within the Taiwanese medical community increased the opportunity for close interaction between Taiwanese and Japanese, preexisting interethnic professional ties grew stronger. These ties constituted a central category of experience for Taiwanese medical doctors and students.

Interethnic professional ties generated a certain respect and affection among native physicians for their Japanese mentors. Native physicians often remembered their Japanese mentors as the embodiment of positive norms and professional values in the medical community. Dr. Lin Tianyou vividly described his impression of his professors, all but one of them Japanese, in such a manner:

> The lights in [their] labs stay on till very late every night. Their work ethic can well serve as the model for all students. . . . Like Professor Yokogawa, for example, they don't care about professional degrees or professorships. They have higher goals; their goal is the truth. . . .
> I think that [Doctor Sawada] is truly a great figure in clinic medicine. Patients are encouraged by the mere sight of his presence. . . . They trust him and rely on him. . . . People often tell me, "You even walk like Professor Sawada!" Although such words are more or less sarcastic, I am utterly proud to hear them! (Lin 1983, pp. 22, 29)

Later in his autobiography, Dr. Lin told a story illustrating the mutuality of student-teacher affection:

> My research was progressing daily. But when I was about to start writing my dissertation, I ran into a big obstacle: the fee for printing the dissertation. . . . The figure [of the printing expense] was unthinkable to me. . . .
> One day I walked into Professor Sawada's office and said, "The

11. Hart's study is based on the Greek Resistance in the same period.

dissertation—I don't want to print it. The degree—I don't want it anymore!"

Professor Sawada . . . paused for a while and then said to me very calmly and kindly: "Well, let's use the funds of our lab to print it. You can pay it back when you have the money in the future."

To allow someone to use lab funds to print a dissertation was something that never happened before or after this. Professor Sawada's unusual support made me shed many grateful tears in private. (Lin 1983, pp. 57–58)

Dr. F expressed similar feelings in a straightforward manner: "At that time, we were very respectful to our professors. We always followed our professors' intentions" (Life-F). In interviews and memoirs, similar experiences were recounted by many other medical students and young doctors.[12] Later, in the immediate postwar years, these strong, interethnic professional ties served as an important mechanism to ease the transition of the Faculty of Medicine when Japan's Taipei Imperial University became China's National Taiwan University. The close interaction between young Taiwanese doctors and research associates and their Japanese mentors prepared them for taking over many responsibilities at the Faculty of Medicine once the Japanese left (Guoli Taiwan Daxue Yixueyuan Fushe Yiyuan, 1995).

The trust Taiwanese doctors placed in their mentors laid the basis for their internalization of a modernist professional culture. Through close teacher-student relationships, these Taiwanese doctors learned to favor the culture of the Japanese medical profession, such as in their preferences for medical subfields (Life-W; Wu 1978), principles of medical education (Life-C; Lin 1983), and even interest in tropical medicine (Du 1940). More important, they perceived in their Japanese mentors a zeal for rational, universal truth that obscured the borders between ethnic categories. For example, in the centennial anniversary publications of National Taiwan University Hospital (formerly Taipei Hospital), Dr. Chen quoted his diary on December 16, 1946, the day when his Japanese mentor departed for Japan: "Seeing Professor Kurosawa board the truck and leave us, I thought to myself: 'Mountains and oceans are being placed between us, but the physical distance will never weaken this teacher-student relationship that we've shared.

12. Several of my informants told me that they believed their medical training under the Japanese system had many advantages over the contemporary system (Life-C; Life-W; Life-CH). All ten of my informants said that they had, and continue to have, very good relationships with their Japanese mentors and classmates. Dr. Du Congming, the only Taiwanese who attained professorship at the Imperial Taiwan University, also made similar comments in his memoir (1989).

Rather, I will always remember my teacher's favors'" (Guoli Taiwan Daxue Yixueyuan Fushe Yiyuan 1995, p. 78). Dr. Chen's deep appreciation for Professor Kurosawa came from his "frequent interactions with the professor and . . . [his perception of Professor Kurosawa] as a role model for a true scholar" (ibid.). According to Dr. Chen, his Taiwanese colleagues shared the same respect for the Japanese professor and consequently arranged for Professor Kurosawa to revisit Taiwan in 1966.

The postwar reflections of Japanese doctors concerning their experiences in colonial Taiwan support the perceptions of Taiwanese doctors. For example, Dr. Mori Oto wrote, for a Japanese audience, in 1969:

> I donated my collection of medical books [passed down from my father Mori Ohgai] to the National Taiwan University [before I returned to Japan] at the end of the war. . . . I had come to this island to devote myself, until my death, to the research of its medical issues and to the development of this university. I hoped that the university's graduates and students, as well as its future students who would come here in my absence, could make use [of these books]. *Were these students Japanese, Taiwanese, or Chinese? Nationality was not my concern.* (Mori 1993, p. 354; my emphasis)

Similarly, Dr. Oda Toshio, former dean of the Faculty of Medicine at Taipei Imperial, expressed his belief that "the rulers of the land may change, but the knowledge accumulated in this land should remain unchanged as the land itself" (Oda 1964, p. 130). Both Mori and Oda expressed a commitment to the advancement of medicine across political and ethnic boundaries. Such attitudes convinced their young Taiwanese disciples of the irrelevance of ethnicity to professional life and, more broadly, to the pursuit of that which "truly mattered."

Overcoming Inequality

A second principal pattern in the life of Taiwanese doctors under Japanese rule reinforced a modernist orientation. Along the path into the medical community, Taiwanese medical students encountered and overcame countless incidents of unequal treatment based on ethnic identity. The experience of overcoming inequality left a deep impression on their perceptions of ethnic discrimination. More specifically, they developed a strong belief in the power of knowledge as the solution to this and other social problems, and displayed something close to an enlightenment mentality.

A few examples will help explain how these doctors conceptualized the power of knowledge. According to anecdotes volunteered by my informants illustrating their outstanding performances at various stages in their education, these doctors consistently emphasized school achievement as an important motif in their days under Japanese rule.[13] When asked about their acceptance to medical school, they invariably noted the academic excellence demonstrated by such an accomplishment. A quote from my interview with Dr. F illustrates the extent of their emphasis on personal academic excellence:

> LO: When you decided to go to medical school, how did your parents react? Did they encourage you?
>
> DR. F: My parents' opinion? Well, the point is, the entrance exam was very difficult.
>
> LO: How did your Japanese teachers react? Did they encourage you? Or did they *not* encourage Taiwanese students to go to medical school?
>
> DR. F: Well, the point is . . . you know, at that time, the Medical School only admitted about 60 people, 30 Japanese, 30 Taiwanese. And each year, there were about five to six hundred Taiwanese students who took the entrance exam. (Life-F)

After unsuccessfully trying to elicit Dr. F's comments on his parents' and teachers' attitudes toward his career choice, I realized that Dr. F thought my questions were irrelevant; in order to pass the difficult entrance exam, outstanding academic performance was far more important than the encouragement of his parents or teachers. His seemingly irrelevant answers to my questions turned out to resonate with the more explicit comments of other doctors about their own academic excellence. For example, when asked if family background played a role in affecting one's chance to enter medical school, Dr. L answered assertively: "No! No! From what I know, the chances of entering into medical schools depended on your performance at school, and on your own self-confidence" (Life-L).

Many of the doctors looked at the accumulation of knowledge as a path to ethnic equality that worked for both the colonizers and the colonized. Most of them believed that not only did they earn due respect from the Japanese with their outstanding performances, but their Japanese professors

13. For instance, a doctor who attended a Japanese-dominant primary school recalled that his and other Taiwanese classmates' admission was based on their excellent school performances (Lin, unpublished manuscript). Dr. L and his wife, who went to Taiwanese-dominant and Japanese-dominant primary schools respectively, both commented on how, being "outstanding students," they were treated very kindly (Life-L). Dr. Lu felt that his entrance into the Faculty of Medicine at Taipei Imperial was "predestined" by his excellent school performance (Shozawa 1998). Another doctor commented that Taiwanese students generally did much better than their Japanese classmates (Shozawa 1996).

and colleagues tended to develop a liberal, egalitarian attitude, when properly educated. In their interpretation, academic achievement led to ethnic equality for both the colonizers and the colonized. Or to put it more plainly, they trusted that well-educated people would respect each other, regardless of ethnicity. It was a mechanism that worked for them from primary school to job site.

Taipei Higher School[14] serves as a good example to illustrate this unusual interpretation of the relationship between knowledge and equality. Dr. Zhang remembered his professors at Taipei Higher School and Taipei Imperial University as excellent teachers as well as anticolonial liberals who truly respected their Taiwanese students (Shozawa 1995a).[15] Dr. Chen also recalled that social relationships at the Taipei Higher School were comparatively equal and that the teachers were, in contrast to the ones at his middle school, better scholars (Shozawa 1996). Dr. W contrasted the severe ethnic discrimination at his middle school with the equal, liberal, and academic atmosphere at Taipei Higher School. "After entering the Higher School, there was a lot of freedom! It was very different [from my middle school], very free! The teachers were wholeheartedly devoted to conveying knowledge to you. . . . The teachers you had close contact with were very caring" (Life-W; see also Life-C; Shozawa 1996).

The universities in Japan were another domain in which knowledge and equality seemed to progress hand in hand. Although many Taiwanese students at these universities noticed even before the war that they were treated more kindly and fairly than in Taiwan,[16] during the war the situation

14. Taipei Higher School (Taihoku Kōtōgakkō) was the only *kōtōgakkō* in Taiwan. According to the Japanese school system used before the end of World War II, middle-level education consisted of five years of *chūgakkō* (middle school) and three years of *kōtōgakkō*. The *kōtōgakkō* entrance exam was said to be very difficult to pass, but *kōtōgakkō* graduates were strong candidates for imperial universities.

15. Zhang remembered that many of his Japanese teachers at Taipei Higher School were critical of the discriminatory attitudes of other Japanese toward Taiwanese. Dr. Guo Weizu was also quoted by his biographer as remembering similar incidents (Cao 1996).

16. Taiwanese students in Japan were exposed to Japanese reform movements as well as to government supervision. Their experiences in Japan led many of them to participate in liberal reform activities after their return, especially in the 1920s. See Kaminuma Hachirō (1978) for an analysis of Taiwanese students in Japan. Without addressing this complex issue in detail here, it should be noted that these students encountered fewer instances of discrimination in Japan than in Taiwan. Many Taiwanese students commented that, in their encounters, the Japanese in the colony appeared much more conscious of the ethnic hierarchy than their counterparts in Japan. For example, see the section on "Experiences of Studying in Japan" in *Wei Huoyao xiansheng fangwen jilu* (Wei 1990).

offered a particularly sharp contrast to the repressive atmosphere that prevailed in the rest of the empire. In a published oral interview, Dr. Chen gave a detailed description of his impression of the academic and liberal environment at Nagasaki Medical University (Nagasaki Ika Daigaku). Dr. Chen noted to his interviewer, Professor Shozawa, that one Taiwanese doctor even reached the position of assistant professor at Nagasaki Medical University: "[This Taiwanese doctor] was able to attain the position of assistant professor. . . . Professor Takagi Jungorō was very fond of him. . . . The anatomy professor, [Dr. Takagi], was very nice to him, even though he was Taiwanese" (Chen, quoted in Shozawa 1996, p. 153).

Dr. Chen later added that the Japanese anatomy professor, Dr. Takagi (a different Takagi than the one who had directed the Taipei Medical School a few decades before), was very kind to Taiwanese students as long as they were hard-working and serious, because Takagi himself was a very serious scholar (Shozawa 1996, p. 153). Dr. Chen's comments, as well as the words of others about their experiences at Taipei Higher School, implied a belief that true scholars would respect each other regardless of their ethnicity. According to these doctors, a Taiwanese could gain respect from Japanese by excelling academically, and a Japanese, if a true intellectual, would also know how to respect Taiwanese.

Dr. Chen also spoke of an interaction that occurred between his Japanese professor and himself during the *kōminka* period. Dr. Chen had just received a letter from his father containing urgent instructions:

> My father wrote me a letter from Taiwan. I had already graduated at the time. . . . This must have been after the outbreak of the Great East Asian War. "Now you have no choice but to change your name. Change it to a Japanese-style name," wrote my father in his letter. I was with Professor Kageura that day, so I mentioned it to the professor. "How does he want you to change it?" asked my professor. "By adopting a Japanese-style name." "Don't you do such a silly thing! Chin Kanshō [the Japanese reading of Dr. Chen's name] is a first-class name for a great Japanese man," said my professor, "Don't talk nonsense. You've been called Chin Kanshō since your birth. Why would you change it to a Japanese-style name?" (Chen, quoted in Shozawa 1996, p. 154)

The Japanese professor's words explicitly contradicted the government policy of forced assimilation. Such a liberal attitude was peculiar during the war, but Dr. Chen recalled that liberal thoughts prevailed at Nagasaki Medical University. Perhaps influenced by this liberal atmosphere, most Taiwanese students at Nagasaki Medical University kept their Taiwanese names during the *kōminka* period (Shozawa 1996). Against the backdrop of wartime authoritarian rule, Japanese professors at Nagasaki Medical University were a distinct group that truly valued both knowledge and equality.

Taiwanese doctors continued to see knowledge and equality as mutually supportive at their work sites. Dr. Chen recalled that, after he started his own clinic in Taiwan, his degree from Nagasaki allowed him to attract many local Japanese patients, even though most Taiwanese doctors who had received their degrees in Taiwan saw Taiwanese patients almost exclusively (Shozawa 1996). Dr. L, who received his degree in Taiwan, also thought that a good degree exempted one from unequal treatment: "I didn't quite feel that there was [ethnic discrimination at work]. After all, the director in our Department of Pediatrics did attain such a high position. Well, maybe it [discrimination] did exist somehow? But he [the director] was a graduate from Tokyo Imperial University, very outstanding and therefore very well respected" (Life-L). Dr. H also remembered that his physician father enjoyed very good relations with the Japanese "because he was well educated" (Life-H).

Overall, as a group, the experiences of Taiwanese doctors convinced them that inequality would diminish with education, cultivating in them a strong belief in the legitimate power of knowledge. Knowledge would make, according to their thinking, the colonized respectable and the colonizers respectful. Instead of seeing their personal success as a rare privilege in the colonial society, they tended to consider it as an indication that their society was somewhat rational. Even when they recognized that colonial society was not humane or rational, they tended to believe that it could become so with education—education to change the attitudes of the colonizers and to improve the opportunities for the colonized. Inadvertently, these doctors became convinced of the value of personal solutions to structural problems of ethnic inequality. Dr. Zhang summed up this general attitude to ethnic relationships rather succinctly: "We should not be asking: Did they discriminate against us? Rather, we should be asking: Did we let them discriminate against us?" (Life-C).[17]

17. It is an interesting question to ask who the "we" refers to in Dr. Zhang's statement. Dr. Zhang was somewhat ambivalent in his elaboration of this issue during the interview. When probed, he explained that if the Taiwanese people of his time had worked harder and achieved more, they would have earned more respect from the Japanese. As he went on to illustrate his point, he used the example of the Taiwanese students at a few elite institutes at the time (e.g., Taipei Higher School and the Faculty of Medicine at Taipei Imperial University). As we will see later in the section on Anzu, Dr. Zhang further indicated that doctors were the representatives of the Taiwanese elite. At the same time, when probed, he acknowledged and criticized the

The Role of Community Leaders

Having internalized the culture of modernity and identified themselves as its carriers in Taiwan, many doctors saw fit to play the role of community leaders. Dr. F's words nicely summarize this common attitude concerning the role of doctors:

> DR. F: Doctors were the representatives of a society. . . . Therefore, it was not uncommon for doctors to concern themselves with politics. What else was there to do in the local community, after all? Seeing patients all day long?
>
> LO: So what precisely would they do?
>
> DR. F: They might run for elections for positions in medical organizations or local councils. That was very common then. (Life-F)

Although not always explicitly acknowledged in these interviews, most of the local medical organizations and councils were state-controlled agencies that implemented *kōminka* policies. What doctors referred to as service for the community could also mean participation in local branches of the state. Dr. Huang Wentao's story illustrates this ambivalence. Under its assimilation policy, the Japanese authority appointed him as a city council member during the war. He accepted the position, but issued very harsh critiques of the authority in his first appearance at the city council, and resigned the position afterwards (*Yiwang* 2, no. 2 [Feb. 1979] pp. 75–76). Other doctors tolerated the limitations on the power of the Taiwanese members in these organizations, arguing that such self-restraint was the basis for their continued participation (Life-F; Du 1989). Still others felt that the limitation of their power eventually marginalized their participation, regardless of the original intention. Some commented that both the medical associations and local councils were essentially organizations that implemented state policies, in which they gradually lost their voices.

These diverse attitudes notwithstanding, the postwar behavior of these doctors helps clarify their common interest in local politics. In contrast to their mixed attitudes toward Japanese-controlled political organizations, during the first few years after the departure of the Japanese many doctors actively occupied the center stage in local politics. Earlier studies show that

---

structural discrimination in the colony, implicitly suggesting that only a small number of Taiwanese could become doctors and have the capacity to refuse to "let them discriminate against us." The same pattern is observed in other doctors' narratives, too. They were aware of the structural inequalities of the colony but tended to focus on their positive experiences. They felt that their abilities and education earned them a great deal of respect from the Japanese, who were also capable and well educated.

doctors made up 35.45 percent of city and county council members and 28.57 percent of province council members between 1945 and 1951 in Taiwan (Li 1989, pp. 101–3).[18] Dr. F suggested that these were the same doctors who were temporarily silenced during the war, taking the liberty to express their opinions under Chinese rule. Along similar lines, Dr. H mentioned that his physician father became actively involved in local politics after the war. The interests of these doctors in local politics indicate their self-expectation as community leaders and a level of trust in the possibility for cumulative reforms within the system, at least until their postwar encounters with the Chinese convinced them that such trust was misplaced.[19]

THE FRAGMENTED CONSCIOUSNESS

I have analyzed how Taiwanese doctors developed modernist narratives. From their Japanese mentors they learned that modernization enhanced human welfare, no matter how it was introduced. From their experiences at school and at work they concluded that the accumulation of knowledge was the ultimate remedy to inequalities and discrimination. Their modernist narratives, however, contained rather than dissolved internal ethnic tensions. Their Taiwanese ethnicity at times became a subversive theme, which destabilized and frustrated the modernist thrust. For instance, at one moment in Dr. W's interview, he paused and deviated from his happy reflections on Taipei Higher School:

> To reveal to you my somewhat selfish thoughts, . . . after all, I thought making more money would probably make life more stable for me. After that, if my capacities allowed. . . . Many doctors, after they became relatively well-to-do, also began to engage in community service. [pause] I had the same hope at that time, that I would make some money, until I was about fifty, and then turn to politics and make some efforts to improve the fate of Taiwanese. That was my hope when I first decided to

18. It is surmised that the percentage might have been higher had the 1947 massacre not happened. In the incident, known commonly as the "2–28 Event" in Taiwan, a large number of Taiwanese elite were killed, and many others were sent into exile.

19. These doctors' postwar experiences are a complicated topic which merits a thorough study on its own. Many written documents, as well as my interviews, shed light on how these doctors and other Taiwanese elites became utterly disillusioned with systemic reforms in the first decade after the Chinese took over Taiwan. For some general discussions of postwar Taiwanese identity, see Cheng 1989; Kerr [1965] 1976; Lai 1991; Lo 1994; and Mendel 1970.

become a doctor. However, [in low voice] in my forties and fifties, seeing the kind of political environment in Taiwan, I no longer wanted to care. (Life-W)[20]

No matter how frequently they described themselves as modernized and Japanized (and they often equated the two), they could not really ignore their colonial existence. Occupying such an ambiguous position, Taiwanese doctors of this period manifested what I term a "fragmented consciousness." Generally speaking, in local colonial encounters, they admired and internalized aspects of "Japaneseness," but when facing colonialism and militarism as a whole, they considered themselves resentful opponents. Such a fragmented consciousness was manifest in the various ways in which these doctors rationalized, suppressed, and therefore manipulated certain categories of their life experience.

One important aspect of this fragmented consciousness was revealed in the artificial distinction these doctors asserted between their personal life and structural conditions. Dr. Zhang put it most explicitly: "I personally never felt that I was at all inferior to the Japanese. . . . My discontents concerning the Japanese did not pertain to my personal experiences, but rather, to the overall position of all Taiwanese students at the time. I made a lot of Japanese friends—on precondition that they held no discriminatory attitudes" (Life-C). His friend, Dr. W, made a similar observation: "Of course the Japanese that I had contact with were very nice to us. But after all, Japanese rule of Taiwan was a colonial one. There existed serious discrimination, not toward us, but toward the general masses" (Life-W). While critical of the social structure of the Japanese Empire, they believed that they could befriend and identify with "good" Japanese individuals.

The distinction between the structural and the personal enabled these doctors to sustain friendships during difficult times, such as at the end of the war.[21] At the same time, however, their actual experiences did not always

20. Like most of my informants, Dr. W was in his late teens and early twenties during the wartime period. When he reached the age of fifty, it was of course the postwar period, and the rulers of Taiwan had changed from Japanese to Chinese. He did not specify what types of community service he had in mind when he was young.

21. Dr. W told me that he and his friends were all ecstatic about the end of colonial rule while sad about the departure of their "good friends" who were being sent back to Japan (Life-W). For similar examples, see Mori 1993; Du 1989. The friendship among these doctors continued to develop well into the postwar period. The alumni of Taipei Medical School and its successor, the Faculty of Medicine at Taipei Imperial University, travel regularly between Japan and Taiwan to have their reunions. Students

support such an optimistic reading of their colonial existence. Occasionally, when they realized that their "friends" were a recognizable part of the unfriendly structure, their narratives conveyed a sense of betrayal. As Dr. Zhang indicated:

> After the end of the war, . . . we saw a photo album. . . . While looking at the photos, [someone said], "This is the Taiwan Sōtokufu Shokuminchi Seisaku Kengi Iinkai [The Colonial Policy Council of the Governor-General of Taiwan]. Ah! Professor Kawaishi is also in [the picture]!" That was very sad for me! The Taiwan Sōtokufu Shokuminchi Seisaku Kengi Iinkai was . . . the group that proposed that the distinctions between Japanese and Taiwanese should be "made much more explicit." Within such a group was my much-respected surgical professor, Kawaishi. Ahhh! At that time, I felt sad and lonely; it was very sad and lonely for me. (Shozawa 1995a, p. 179)

Another aspect of this fragmented consciousness is evidenced by these doctors' alternative interpretation of state ideology. Taiwanese medical doctors and students subtly readjusted state discourse on the "health of the empire." While working for a medical community that now mainly served the military state, they described their medical duties as being for the "people," not the "empire." This readjustment of the discourse on the "health of the empire" recentered the rhetoric on people rather than the state or the military, allowing doctors to view their participation in the wartime medical system in a more positive light. These doctors were able to maintain that the war was irrational and the dispatching of Taiwanese doctors unfair, while continuing to participate in the medical missions that assisted the military state. Dr. Han Shiquan, an activist in the 1920s, provides a good example. While highly resentful of the Japanese military, he nevertheless instructed his daughter that she should "perform her duty" on a team of war nurses— a duty that unfortunately cost her her life during an air raid (Han 1966, pp. 57–58).

Other examples can be marshaled to illustrate how Taiwanese doctors neutralized and depoliticized their wartime medical research or duty in their own accounts. Doctors often suppressed or bracketed certain experiences in constructing their narratives. For example, as Dr. F described his research

---

from the same school express a strong sense of community across ethnic lines. For some information on these alumni activities, see the alumni periodical of the Taipei Medical School, *Nanmei kaishi*. See also the *Centennial of National Taiwan University Hospital* (Guoli Taiwan Daxue Yixueyuan Fushe Yiyuan 1995) and a 1978 special publication at the fortieth anniversary of the founding of the Faculty of Medicine at Taipei Imperial University, *Tōneikai yonjūnen*.

during the war, he said, "For the military, blood transfusion was a very important issue. I did some research on blood transfusion." He continued to explain the details of his research, but without mentioning its military context. Instead, he focused on the value of such research to general patients: "I realized that this new method was safer and more convenient. Furthermore, I found out that it could be used for glucose injection. It was especially useful for treating very ill or weak patients" (Life-F). As he bracketed the military context of his research, Dr. F similarly chose *not* to mention in the interview his activities at one of the philanthropic hospitals in China—the hospitals that were designed to assist the Japanese expansionist ambitions there. Other sources recorded that Dr. F worked in one such hospital for some time, but Dr. F himself never mentioned this during his interview.[22]

Dr. Du's and Dr. Oda's contrasting accounts of the tenth convention of the Far Eastern Association of Tropical Medicine (FEATM) show again how a Taiwanese doctor might downplay the political and military nature of his medical activities during the war. Dr. Du Congming, the only Taiwanese medical professor at Taipei Imperial University in the colonial period, together with his Japanese colleague, Dr. Oda Toshio, attended this international convention on tropical medicine held in 1938 in Indochina. According to Dr. Oda's account of the conference, due to Japan's large-scale military actions in China, "There was something subtle in the way other nationals looked at [us] Japanese" (Oda 1974, p. 120). Dr. Oda further noted that the war eventually put an end to the conventions of the FEATM, making the meetings in 1938 the final ones. Dr. Du's memoir, on the other hand, completely omits the influence of the military atmosphere. His account emphasized the scholarly nature of the association. He described the convention as "serious and solemn," provided the title of his scholarly presentation, and mentioned, as an aside, the natural beauties of Indochina (Du 1989, pp. 106–7). Although he outlined a brief history of the FEATM, Du failed to mention that the war brought it to an end after its 1938 meetings.

Dr. Liang Yuming's account of his and his physician father's lives in Manchuria again serves as an example of how Taiwanese doctors attempted to neutralize and depoliticize wartime medicine in their narratives. In an oral interview conducted by a Taiwanese research team in 1993, Dr. Liang Yuming shared his memories of his father's medical career in pre-1945 Manchuria and his own impression of Manchuria Medical University

---

22. I learned of Dr. F's activities at the philanthropic hospital from another informant and from a medical journal. In order to protect the anonymous status of Dr. F, I omit specific citations of my sources here.

(Manshū Ika Daigaku). His father, Dr. Liang Zai, graduated from Taipei Medical School and worked for a hospital that belonged to the South Manchuria Railroad Company before he established a private clinic in Manchuria. Dr. Liang Yuming spent most of his childhood in Manchuria, received his secondary education in Japan, and entered Manchuria Medical University in 1942 (Liang and Liang 1994). Dr. Liang's firsthand account of wartime Manchuria made no mention of the Japanese political or military authorities as a factor in his or his father's medical careers, although scholars have long been sensitive to the suspiciously close relationship between the military and the medical community in Manchuria (e.g., Nakao 1993).[23] Instead, Dr. Liang focused on how Taiwanese and Japanese received equal treatment in Manchuria, and how his father served Taiwanese, Chinese, and Japanese patients alike and financially supported several Taiwanese friends in their studies at Manchuria Medical University (Liang and Liang 1994). As for his own experience at Manchuria Medical University, he gave a rather cursory description, providing only an outline of the curriculum (Liang and Liang 1994).

These contrasting accounts serve to problematize Taiwanese doctors' silence on the political nature of wartime medicine. The point is not to pronounce certain accounts as more accurate than others, but to consider the contradictions in these doctors' lives that might have compelled them to bracket certain memories. Behind the silence on certain topics in their narratives, I suspect, lies the discomfort of possessing a fragmented consciousness. In these previous examples, the doctors seem to have identified with and thrived under the Japanese system, but they desired to separate themselves from the war being waged by Japan. Their fragmented consciousness might have caused them to avoid recognizing their own involvement, however indirect, in the war.

These bracketed categories of experience rendered their narratives essen-

---

23. The Kwantung Army in Manchuria is especially notorious for having conducted inhumane, painful medical experiments on Chinese captives during the war. After the establishment of Ishii Unit in 1936 (renamed the Epidemic Prevention and Water Purification Department of the Kwantung Army in 1940 and more commonly known as the Manchukuo Unit 731), "many faculty members of the military medical school were sent to Manchukuo and became involved in experimenting on humans to develop biological weapons" (Tanaka 1996, p. 136). Recent studies point out that the Faculty of Medicine at Kyoto Imperial University in particular provided much support for the Kwantung Army's medical experiments (Nakao 1994; Tanaka 1996, especially pp. 136–37). Given its location, I suspect Manchuria Medical University might also have been heavily involved in what Nakao calls "the organized crimes of medical practitioners."

tially unstable, especially when confronted with the reality of the war. One doctor remembered the embarrassment he experienced when his professor, upon his request, recommended him for a job in mainland China. He said, "I was very interested in [the job], . . . but I thought that since I shared the same racial origin with the Chinese, it would be very awkward to be sent to China as a Japanese representative" (Zhou 1984, p. 58). For Dr. Wu Pingcheng, who was sent to Southeast Asia as a military doctor, the war did not leave any space for a coherent interpretation of the situation. His daily life in the military constantly reminded him that his fate was tied to the Japanese Army while his loyalty was not. In his wartime diary, published after the war, he recorded the unfair procedures in the selection of Taiwanese military doctors.[24] The war did not convince him of its value. In direct contradiction to the Japanese glorification of death on the warfront (referred to not as "death" but as *mugon no gaisen,* or a "speechless triumphant return"), Dr. Wu wrote, "I told myself that I would definitely come back [to Taiwan]. I should definitely not sacrifice my life for this meaningless, so-called sacred war. It wasn't worth it! I swore I would come back" (Wu 1989, p. 14). In the same diary, however, he recalled that he and other Taiwanese military doctors worried about the possible failure of the Japanese Army. They also enjoyed the respect and privilege they received as Japanese military officers. Dr. Wu admired his Japanese comrades who were prepared to devote their lives to the Japanese Army, even though he himself resolved to return to his hometown alive (Wu 1989).[25] Such contradictory sentiments coexisted uneasily with the universalizing narrative of modernity.

A Hybrid Identity

Contradictions, silence, and frustration, in short, symptoms of a fragmented consciousness, accompany the doctors' reflections on Taiwanese and Japanese ethnicity. In a certain sense, their confusion reflected generational experiences. As explained above, the Kōminka Era was a period when ethnic differences within the empire were forcefully absorbed into "protean Japaneseness." The "*kōminka* generation"—the group aged between fifteen and

24. Dr. Wu believed that the medical authority usually chose Taiwanese military doctors for political reasons. According to Dr. Wu, those who were suspected of "possessing dangerous thoughts" or who had unfavorable relationships with the police or the medical authorities were dispatched first. Other doctors also made similar observations (see Shozawa 1996; Life-L; Life-W; Life-F).

25. In contrast, the Japanese medical doctors and students described their experiences of the war in a seemingly more coherent way. They also recognized the connections between war and medicine more directly and willingly. For some examples of the Japanese perspective, see Tōneikai 1978, especially Parts 1 and 6.

twenty-five at the end of the war—had a confused identity. This generation was "born in colonial Taiwan at a time when the colony started enjoying the fruits of Japanese colonial rule" (Chou 1991, p. 224), and was therefore most thoroughly indoctrinated with *kōminka* ideology. They became a generation of Taiwanese who were raised to be Japanese.

As members of the "*kōminka* generation," the young medical students and doctors in my study went through professional experiences that had a specific bearing on their identity. Other scholars have also noted the impact of high social status of the medical profession in the Kōminka Movement:

> In general, both professions [teachers and doctors] were equally re-
> spectable, but physicians seemed to enjoy more social prestige because
> they received a higher level of education, came in smaller numbers, and
> not the least, had higher incomes than school teachers did. They were
> also, as revealed in various materials, the most Japanized. This point may
> explain why the numbers of physicians who adopted Japanese names
> were out of proportion to other professions at the outset of the name-
> changing program. (Chou 1991, p. 134)

Carrying this argument further, my analysis in this chapter shows that the experiences of Taiwanese doctors in overcoming inequality, their close rela- tionships with their Japanese mentors and colleagues, and, as a result, their internalization of a modernist professional culture together rendered their ethnic boundaries particularly blurred.[26]

I describe this blurred ethnic identity as a colonial hybridity, mixing not

26. Although my findings concur with Chou's in that doctors as a group were overrepresented in the Taiwanese population that had changed their names, neither Chou's nor my data deny the discrepancies between group-level tendency and indi- vidual doctors' choices. Lacking a social space and collective agency for the group, doctors did not have the chance to collectively reflect upon this issue or to formulate a position for the group.

Obviously, numerous doctors chose not to adopt Japanese names, and these indi- viduals might have had diverse reasons for their decisions. But their attitudes were by no means anti-Japanese; rather, they might have been expressing different degrees and forms of Japanization. For example, Dr. Chen, whose experiences at Nagasaki Medical University have been described, was convinced that he should keep his name, not because he held anything against Japanization but because his name, Chin Kanshō, was already "a first-class Japanese name." Like my two inform- ants who did not change their names throughout this period, Dr. Chen gladly accepted the Japanese reading of his name, which would have been Chen Hanshen in Chinese or Tan hanxieng in Taiwanese. Their attitudes were similar to that of Dr. Zhang, who did change his name to Hasegawa and claimed his Japanese identity, but felt it important to assert that he was Taiwan-born. In a sense, these doctors might have been pushing for a more inclusive notion of Japaneseness as they were becom- ing Japanized in different degrees.

only the categories of colonizer/colonized but also negotiating between the domains of ethnic and professional experiences. A hybrid identity, as argued in previous chapters, can be enriched by the experiences of transgressing the boundaries of original categories. Some doctors from the "*kōminka* generation" took pride in their hybrid identity. They drew on their multiple cultural traditions and attempted to "read Japan as heterogeneous." Probably best documented in a series of oral interviews with Dr. Zhang and his Japanese friend Dr. Izumi, the colonial hybrid turned the meaning of *kōminka* on its head:

> Dr. Zhang had a strong Taiwanese consciousness. But he also gradually identified with the Japanese. Dr. Izumi felt strong resentment toward *naichijin* [the Japanese-born Japanese] who abused their privilege, and he always considered Taiwanese no less Japanese [than *naichijin*]. . . . Dr. Zhang and Dr. Izumi defined "Japanese" differently than the way it is defined today. . . . They considered "Japanese" a multi-ethnic nation. (Shozawa 1995b, p. 234)

From the colonizer's perspective, Dr. Zhang signified the power of the assimilated over the assimilator; he became "Japanese" by redefining that identity.

But hybridity was only rarely experienced in such a creative and positive way. For most, a hybrid ethnic identity led to confusion and silence. For example, in my interview with Dr. H, he remembered the difficulty his physician father experienced in articulating an ethnic identity:

DR. H: My father definitely didn't think he was Chinese.

LO: So, did he think he was Japanese? Or simply Taiwanese?

DR. H: Well, under the authoritarian rule, he couldn't really say he was, . . . he had to say he was . . . well, he wouldn't say he was Japanese either, because he knew he wasn't. But he definitely wouldn't say he was Chinese. . . .

LO: So, do you know what he really thought to himself? Not what he said publicly, but perhaps what he said or thought privately?

DR. H: He definitely didn't think he was Chinese, I am certain about this. . . . At the end of the war, nobody was happy about the change of regime, because people didn't know what the Chinese regime was like. After the first Sino-Japanese War, Taiwan was given to Japan. The Taiwanese couldn't do anything about it. Now Japan wanted to give it back to China. And the Taiwanese couldn't do anything about that, either. . . .

LO: Did he ever say anything about Taiwanese independence?

DR. H: No! No! Back then I don't think my father had such

> thoughts. I think they felt a sense of powerlessness. Whoever
> wants to come and rule us is beyond our control. (Life-H)

Other doctors echoed this confusion regarding ethnicity, a confusion which
sometimes led to a sense of frustration about their inability to actively
define their own ethnic identities. Dr. L and his wife both recalled identifying with the Japanese before the end of the war, because they "were born as
Japanese, until the arrival of the Chinese, which abruptly changed our identity" (Life-L). But on the other hand, they "felt somewhat happy about the
end of colonial rule" (ibid.). Similarly, Dr. W felt he was very Japanized, but
"knew that [he] had Chinese blood" (Life-W).

When pressed to comment on what this meant for ethnic identity, these
respondents often became elusive. "We couldn't really talk about these
things openly then. It was during the war. . . . We wanted to avoid politics"
(Life-W). A doctor who spent the last few years before the end of the war at
a medical school in Japan simply said: "I didn't care about politics then. I
devoted myself completely to my studies" (Life-K). A Christian physician,
Dr. Guo, believed that his nationality could not be defined in this world. He
said at a church gathering in 1978:

> My ancestors were subjects of the Qing Dynasty. . . . But because China
> ceded Taiwan and Pescadores to Japan after the first Sino-Japanese War, I
> was Japanese at birth. At the end of World War II, I was forced to become
> Chinese by the [Chinese] Nationalist regime. Where should my national-
> ity really belong? The Bible says our nationality belongs in heaven. After
> serious consideration, I have come to believe that my true nationality
> belongs in heaven. (Cao 1996)

These unsuccessful efforts at defining the core of their ethnic identity gradually reveal "undefinability" to be the very core of their ethnic identity. But
their own silence frustrated them. Dr. W said pensively: "We Taiwanese . . .
were almost like slaves, after being ruled by all these different people. It's in
our mentality—we don't even know how to complain" (Life-W). "Upon
hearing that China was going to take over Taiwan," recalled Dr. K, "my sister and I were speechless. Then we could only say, the rulers were too self-
ish" (Life-K).[27]

---

27. Since many Taiwanese elite felt strongly that they were oppressed by the
Chinese who came with the KMT regime and even lost some family members during the "2–28 Event" in 1947, it is possible that their dislike for the Chinese intensified *after* the end of the war. How much, then, did these doctors' postwar experiences color their memories about their own ethnic identities before the war ended?
My findings suggest a generational difference. The *kōminka* generation seemed to

Eventually, doctors returned to their modernist narrative to anchor their identity. In interviews, they sometimes literally drew upon their professional experiences to answer a question about ethnicity. They asserted the universal value of medicine, which was supposed to transcend—or elide—the difficult issue of ethnicity. For example, Dr. F told me about his research during the war period, and, while showing me the journals in which his articles were published, he said, "I had always believed that my research on this topic would be very useful no matter what. . . . I am so glad I published these articles then. When I am dead, I can tell myself at least I have these" (Life-F). Expanding their quest for universal truth and good outside the realm of medicine, these doctors elaborated their life stories in terms of the advancement of knowledge. For example Dr. W described his life-long aspiration for knowledge: "My experiences at the Taipei Higher School influenced my personality greatly. Our classmates still get together regularly after all these years. We all have different kinds of careers, but we understand each other well. *The people who have been through higher schools are usually widely read and well learned* (Life-W; my emphasis).

Dr. Zhang used a postwar example to describe the same characteristics of Taiwanese educated elites of his generation:

> After the war, a number of us attended an informal get-together with some university students from Shanghai. We all had the same haircut

---

have internalized a strong Japanese identity before the war ended. They grew up speaking Japanese as one of their mother tongues (the other being their Taiwanese dialect), were trained in the Japanese educational institutes, developed close relationships with their Japanese mentors, and some even married Japanese (as documented by *both* prewar and postwar sources cited in this chapter). They tended to refer to the change of regime as a disruption in their life. Many doctors of the older generation, on the other hand, seemed to have a stronger Chinese identity. According to numerous written sources (e.g., Guoli Taiwan Daxue Yixueyuan Fushe Yiyuan 1995, pp. 84–86; Han 1964; Xu 1992, pp. 139–44), these doctors remembered feeling excited about the "return to our mother country" as the war ended and were happy to officially claim their Chinese ethnicity. They tended to refer to their postwar experiences with the Chinese as a disappointment or a betrayal.

Contemporary discussions of independence issues in Taiwan, I believe, provide outlets but not necessarily any dominant framework for these doctors to articulate their memories. As early as 1970, Mandel's study of Taiwanese nationalism documented widespread anti-Chinese sentiments among Taiwanese elites. In a 1992 interview, Dr. Cai recalled that an American official asked him about the "2–28 Event" after the event was over. He told the American he had no comments, but in reality he "dared to be angry but not to speak up" (*gannu buganyan;* see Xu 1992, pp. 139–44). The writings in *Anzu,* as we will see below, documented strong pro-Japanese sentiments in the years between 1943 and 1945. In short, the contemporary independence discourse in Taiwan mobilized rather than constructed these memories.

and wore school uniforms. The students from the mainland, in contrast, were more stylish—wearing suits and nice haircuts. Then our discussion began. The mainland students all had the same thoughts, basically repeating the opinions printed in the *Times, Life,* and so on. We Taiwanese students, on the other hand, came out with very diverse opinions. A very typical pattern. I think the same contrast exists between us and today's medical students. (Life-C)

In contrast with their silence about ethnicity, the theme of science and knowledge was stable and pronounced in the *kōminka* doctors' identity narratives. Their identity narratives hinge on the theme of modernity, precariously maintaining its coherence by avoiding the issue of ethnicity. As my interview analysis indicates, these doctors often refused the category of ethnicity when they talked about themselves, and they did so by supplanting it with the category of science and knowledge. In this sense, their hybrid identity developed along dual axes: they blurred ethnic boundaries in developing a fragmented consciousness, and they switched social categories (from ethnicity to profession) in "narrativizing" their identities.[28]

The Anzu Group

The story about a "submerged network" further illustrates the manner in which *kōminka* doctors attempted to articulate and define their hybrid identity at a group level. An informant for this study, Dr. Zhang, organized a study group called Anzu (Apricot) in 1943, when he was a student at Taipei Higher School. The group started with three core members and gradually attracted more students. By the time the group members decided to stop meeting in 1947, Anzu had more than thirty regular members. After the war, this group provided the core for a new Taipei student association. Anzu group members gathered together regularly, sometimes more than once a week. They also compiled their own magazines to circulate among group members about once every month. They read widely, including books on literature, philosophy, and theology. The liberal environment at Taipei Higher School and Taipei Imperial University facilitated their pursuit of knowledge; their magazines and meetings were left alone by school teachers and administrators despite the militaristic atmosphere of the empire.

Zhang and many of his friends in Anzu were aware of their elitist status

---

28. In one previously cited example, Dr. Guo used religion more than the profession to anchor his identity. Such individual differences are not to be denied. What I am establishing here is that the emphasis on modernity and the profession appears as a common pattern in the discussion of identities among this group.

as students at Taipei Higher School and expected to enter the most prestigious profession of their time, medicine. In the first issue of their group magazine, also called *Anzu*, the eighteen-year-old Zhang wrote an article entitled "Taiwan ikai ron," or "On the Medical Community in Taiwan." Dr. Zhang recalled writing the article:

> At that time, all students in Taiwan aimed for a medical career. Because of our social environment, becoming a doctor was a quick way to earn money and respectable social status. . . . So if a student entered medical school, his entire hometown would feel honored. Then, rich people would want to marry their daughters to him with abundant dowries. Eventually he would rise to the position of the local elite. Such was the ordinary life path of a doctor. My eighteen-year-old self proposed in the article that "we should stop studying for medical school if all we want is to follow this conventional path." "Before we become doctors, we should first become real humans. ". . . In my opinion, it was true that [at that time] medicine was the only road to success open to capable Taiwanese youth, but we could not forget that becoming a human was the premise for becoming a doctor. . . . In the end, we [the group] decided that we should become more diligent learners. (Shozawa 1995, pp. 169–70)

As part of Anzu's group narrative, Zhang's "Taiwan ikai ron" echoed the main themes in the narratives of doctors' identities discussed above. The spirit of modernity was emphasized in the article and regarded as the core of doctors' identity. Repeatedly, Zhang stressed the value of science and the spirit of humanism in his description of a "real doctor." For example, he proposed that doctors should "maintain their passions for science." "The young generation should develop a keen awareness of their passion for truth and for selfless service" (p. 15). In closing, Zhang repeated that, before a young Taiwanese man of his generation became a doctor, he should prepare himself by "experiencing the widest range of things, cultivating a most profound moral character, . . . and learning to be a true, altruistic doctor" (p. 16). Similarly, Zhang's article echoed the self-expectation of other doctors to be community leaders. "With Gotō Shimpei's scientific colonialism, it was obvious that Taiwan was destined to a path of development through science. It follows, then, that those who became familiar with the science of medicine should play powerful roles in the development of Taiwan, and that doctors should become leaders in both cities and the countryside" (p. 9).

Like many other doctors at the time, Zhang and his friends invoked Dr. Takagi's famous saying from the early years of the colonial period, "Before we become doctors, we should first become real humans." But perhaps beyond Dr. Takagi's prescription, Zhang and his friends also resorted to the pursuit of knowledge as an implicit way of self-empowerment in colonial Taiwan. Initially, Dr. Zhang organized the group to protect Taiwanese students, all of whom had experiences of being beaten up by Japanese classmates before entering Taipei Higher School. But after they became organized, according to Dr. Zhang, they intimidated their Japanese classmates without having to resort to violence. "Since we didn't have the chance to use our fists," recalled Dr. Zhang, "we thought to ourselves: Why don't we read some books?" (Life-C). Implicit in this statement was the desire to gain strength by studying in a society not too friendly to Taiwanese. His friend Dr. W also talked about how the pursuit of knowledge enriched their lives. He recalled that through the group he was exposed to classical music and started writing poems and short stories. Dr. W denied the political implication of their activities. But he believed they were making an effort to improve Taiwanese society:

> We wanted to contribute to the construction of a new and modern Taiwan. This task had to be taken up by us young people. . . . Although we all wanted to go to medical school, we also wanted to contribute to cultural developments. In fact, because all the good students went to medical school, few people were addressing cultural issues. So we thought: maybe we can help develop and liberalize the cultural sphere in Taiwan. . . . We were about twenty years old then—a romantic age [laughter]. We didn't care about politics, though. We were interested in cultural issues. (Life-W)

Anzu's *implicit* Taiwanese consciousness motivated many inconsistent words and deeds, echoing patterns of hybridity that we observed earlier in individual doctors' identities. For example, Zhang's "Taiwan ikai ron" addressed readers as "my fellow Taiwanese students" but was signed with his Japanese name, Hasegawa. The same ambiguity about their ethnicity became obvious again when Zhang tried to position himself between Taiwan and Japan's Greater East Asia. Zhang described Taiwan as his "home" and the Japanese Empire as his "country": "We should abandon the narrow idea of becoming a practitioner in our hometown, go beyond the boundaries [of our hometown] and reach to different points in the Greater East Asia. . . . If [our forerunners'] goal was to serve a town, let's target the whole country (*kokka*; see "Taiwan ikai ron," p. 16). With similar ambiguities regarding the relationship between Taiwan and Japan's Greater East Asia, the editor for a later issue of *Anzu* wrote in its preface:

> In Anzu, the blood of Greater East Asia and the will of the nation [*minzoko*] are bursting.
> Let's love truth more.

What advances our culture and saves it from corruption?
It is the mind that loves truth, the mind that respects truth.
It's the heart that loves Taiwan, the heart that loves our home.

(*Anzu* no. 3)

In both accounts, there are evident tensions between the desire to claim the Japanese Empire as their country and their nation, and to cherish Taiwan as their homeland.

Could it be that they were merely complying with wartime propaganda so that the military police would leave them alone? Dr. Zhang did not think so: "At that time, I didn't feel that changing my name would be a shame at all. We didn't change our names for the material incentives provided by the government. We didn't need material goods. Rather, we thought we were Japanese. Taiwan-born Japanese. I don't think there was anything to be ashamed of that we wanted to be part of the Japanese nation" (Life-C). His friend Dr. W remembered the group as less certain about their Japanese identity, but he also said that they loved Japanese culture and viewed it as a valuable resource for Taiwan. Dr. W recalled that the group's resolution to develop Taiwanese culture was actualized through the study of Japanese literary texts. It was not a problem for them, because "culture is not the property of a particular country. We wanted to learn, to research, and to absorb culture. But studying Japanese culture did not mean becoming Japanese" (Life-W). In general, they tried to draw from their experiences as Japanized Taiwanese. After all, it was an all-Taiwanese group with the explicit goal of upgrading Taiwanese culture, yet their magazine articles were almost exclusively written in Japanese. The case of Anzu shows that the tensions of a hybrid identity not only existed at an individual level, but in fact began to coalesce into a group narrative which creatively sought new identities in a time when old categories became unstable.[29]

---

29. They also played with different gender norms. Dr. Zhang said his older sister began to invite some of her friends into the group. Subsequently the female membership of the group began to increase. Dr. Zhang praised these female members as intellectual and mature. "Unlike the girls today," commented Dr. Zhang, "who are more concerned with beautiful clothes and good dancing places, these young women in our study group were very serious and diligent" (Life-C). While advocating the value of female intellect, the group nevertheless played with the implication of feminine characteristics:

> We developed very good friendships among the group members. Friendship, not so-called relationships. Well, everyone else said our group was a "rosy" club. I thought that was great, though. The military police would think the group was for love affairs. . . . At that time, study groups were closely observed by the Japanese military police. So we tried to encourage more females to join us. Then the military police would think, "Oh, it's just a social club." (Life-C)

The identity of "Japanized Taiwanese," though it did not motivate antisystemic political movements under Japanese rule, eventually bequeathed an important heritage to postwar Taiwanese nationalism in the medical profession, as discussed early in chapter 1.

IN THE ABSENCE OF THE COLOR CODE

As we have seen in this chapter, *kōminka*-generation doctors were domesticated by the surrounding relational configuration which was characterized by the colonial state's domination and regulation of the organizational, material, and cultural dimensions of their ethnic and professional communities. Two major patterns in their professional experiences (i.e., developing interethnic professional ties and overcoming ethnic inequality) resulted in the internalization of a modernist professional culture and further obscured the ethnic boundaries in their lives. Bracketing the political and structural context in the colony, they struggled to construct a coherent identity narrative that was mainly informed by professional experiences and culture. In this process, many of them developed a hybrid identity as medical modernists. As a group of colonial subjects who preferred to speak about their identity in terms of modernity rather than colonization, the experiences of these doctors illustrate an important aspect of ethnic relations within Japanese colonialism.

Ethnic Relations within the Japanese Colonial Empire

From the perspective of the colonizers, ethnic relations within Japanese colonialism served as a basis upon which Japan could distinguish itself from European colonizers. At the same time, it was a basic source of tension for the racial policies of the empire. Scholars have partially explained Japan's official ethnic ideology by depicting it as a "two-tier narrative." Historically, the duality might have originated from the efforts of Japanese colonial officials and scholars to learn from two divergent models:

> A paternalistic, racially separatist approach to colonial rule, which made racial distinctions within an empire, such as manifested by a number of modern European overseas empires, could lead, as in the case of British colonial doctrine in Africa, to concepts of indirect rule and imperial trusteeship, which themselves opened the way to the possibility of autonomy and independence of colonial territories. Yet a "continental" perspective, which insisted on the homogeneity of races and interests within an empire and which tightened rather than loosened the bonds between peoples of the homeland and the colonies, could also have served to diffuse throughout the empire the political rights and civil liberties

which existed in the mother country. The irony and tragedy of the Japanese case was that the colonial empire ultimately came to include the worst and most contradictory racial assumptions of both patterns. (Peattie 1984, p. 15; see also Jansen 1984)

These inconsistencies grew sharper as Japan attempted to position itself as the "anticolonial colonizer" in East Asia. On the one hand, Japanese colonial officials were replicating a social Darwinist idea of racial hierarchy evident in Western imperialism and, on the other hand, they were self-consciously articulating a moral rhetoric of "Japan's fraternal relationships with its neighbors" (Jansen 1984, p. 76). Weiner's (1997) recent publication, elaborating on Shimazu's (1989) concept of a "two-tier narrative of race," offers a succinct explanation of how these contradictory racial ideas worked to organize ethnic relations within the empire:

> The Japanese were thus identified as sharing the same "racial" origins as Chinese and Koreans. Nonetheless, this European-derived narrative of "race" did not preclude the existence of a further definition which identified "race" with nation, and which distinguished imperial Japan, in equally deterministic terms, from its Asian neighbors. . . . The subdivision of human species . . . imposed a set of obligations on Japan as Tōyō no Meishu (the Leader of Asia). These include not only raising colonial people to a level commensurate with their "natural" abilities, but preserving the essential and superior qualities of the Japanese within a carefully delineated hierarchy of "race." (pp. 13–14)

This "two-tier narrative" was at the core of the official conceptualization of ethnic relations in the empire. Japan, imagining itself as the "anticolonial colonizer," celebrated a pan-Asian brotherhood by accentuating the racial and cultural affinities between itself and other Asian countries and, at the same time, secured its leadership position by asserting its superior achievements in modernization. This ambiguous ethnic ideology, which rendered imaginable the *kōminka* ideology, fostered the view that the colonized were "not quite Japanese but capable of becoming Japanese."

However, it is unclear how, if at all, colonial subjects participated in the articulation of these ambiguous ethnic relations. Although abundant research has been done on explicitly anticolonial activities in the colonies,[30] little has been written that captures the more ambivalent reactions among colonized populations. Christy (1997) represents a rare exception; he asks why Okinawans came to accept the colonial formulation of Okinawan

30. For example, see Yanaihara 1929; Cai et al. 1983; Wakabayashi 1983; Zhou 1989.

identity as essentially a backward version of the Japanese. Stressing historical factors in the construction of ethnic identity, Christy found his answer in a combination of factors: the Okinawan experience of economic hardship, their sense of "sibling rivalry" with other colonies, especially Taiwan, and the limited availability of other frameworks for imagining their ethnicity. Suggesting the possibility that the Okinawans might have imagined their community as both Okinawan and Japanese, Christy concludes with an understanding of the agency of the colonized in redefining ethnic categorization:

> [The] attempt of many Okinawans to lay claim to both identities [i.e., Japanese and Okinawan] was, at least in part, an attempt to read Japan as heterogeneous. This opens the possibility that a homogeneous ideology such as *kōminka* could be transformed, at the margins, into a promise of plurality. In his defense of Okinawan dialects in 1940, Yanagi Sōetsu argued just this point. . . . [But] the heterogeneous promise of *kōminka* was the discomforting promise that those on the margins of the empire could also sacrifice themselves for the survival of the monolithic State. (p. 165)

Christy's work outlines some important historical conditions which merit consideration in the study of ethnic experiences in Japan's former colonies and occupied areas. Proceeding from his conclusion, this chapter further suggests the patterns of identity formation among the colonial subjects. Put differently, building upon Christy's answer to the "why" question (i.e., why did some members of the colonized community accept Japan's two-tier racial ideology?), I tackled the "how" question (i.e., how did they construct their ethnic identities under such conditions?). In this sense, this chapter offers a close examination of the processes, patterns, and difficulties of the articulation of the "heterogeneous promise of *kōminka*."

As shown in the example of *kōminka*-generation Taiwanese doctors, some colonial subjects' identity articulations registered important and previously overlooked imagination, and evidenced agency of the colonized, but were at the same time constantly interrupted and influenced by the politics and culture of colonialism. Consistent with Christy's study of the Okinawans, the Taiwanese case also provided occasional accounts of the attempt to "read Japan as heterogeneous" (e.g., some writings in *Anzu*). At the same time, however, I provide a more detailed assessment of the accessibility and effectiveness of such a multicultural ideal. Operating within their available cultural frameworks, the *kōminka*-generation doctors attempted to embrace both the Taiwanese and Japanese identities, which resulted in patterns of identity formation that, for the most part, manifested an imagination of reading modernity as nonethnic rather than reading Japan as heterogeneous. The heterogeneous promise of *kōminka* became a frustrated ideal at certain phases in Japanese colonialism. The colonial subjects articulated the ambiguities within the empire of the "anticolonial colonizers," leading to the rejection of the category of ethnicity rather than the consolidation of any particular ethnic identity.

Kōminka-generation doctors often refused the category of ethnicity in their identity narrative and, in contrast, embraced medicine as a universally positive science. They articulated their identity through the language learned in the cultural repertoire of the medical profession and constructed the role of "medical modernist" as the central theme of their identity narratives. To be sure, their ethnicity did not vanish; being Taiwanese still significantly affected their identity narratives. But it is through their "medical modernist" narrative that the impact of the omitted category of ethnicity can be traced. The bracketed categories, silence, and contradictions in their medical modernist narrative were all suggestive of their fragmented, unhappy consciousness regarding the Taiwanese-Japanese relationship. In this sense, *kōminka*-generation doctors developed a hybrid identity along two specific dimensions: they located themselves across ethnic boundaries and, furthermore, supplanted the category of ethnicity with that of the profession.

As we have learned from recent studies of ethnicity and nationalism, there is a need to give much closer attention than before to the contributions and experiences of social groups (Smith 1992, p. 2). Recognizing the group-specific nature of the identity formation process discussed here helps us to gain deeper understanding of the influences of the professional identity on the ethnic one. It was at the institutional site of the medical profession that these doctors negotiated a specific understanding of modernity that could, in their interpretation, be unhinged from the colonial project that delivered modernity to the colony in the first place. Major categories of their professional experiences served as paths through which they internalized a modernist worldview, with muted ties to colonialism. While the story of the "national physicians" illustrated well the influences of the ethnic community on professional group formation, the experiences of the "medical modernists" illuminate the roles of the profession in the transformation of ethnic identity. In studies of ethnic and colonial formation, the profession and cosmopolitan medicine in particular often become an important site for the advocacy of the bright side of modernity—a point to which I return in next chapter.

The Location of Culture

That the profession provided a cultural repertoire for the doctors to "read modernity as nonethnic" raises further questions about the location of culture in the process of ethnic (re-)formation. More specifically, while scholars often allocate culture to the "inside" and structure to the "outside" of ethnic groups, the Taiwanese case invites us to consider culture as both an "external" and "internal" factor in ethnic formation. In their studies of the role of economic forces in ethnic formation, Barth (1969) and his (critical) followers have long maintained that the "cultural stuff" enclosed by ethnic boundaries is less important than the boundary itself. Later, recognizing that economic interests alone do not determine ethnic boundaries, the constructionist approach broadens its analytical framework to include other, noneconomic dimensions in the formation and transformation of ethnic boundaries. Scholars have examined how ethnicity intersects not only with class, but also political institutions (Horowitz 1985; Espiritu 1992) and gender (Espiritu 1997; Frankenburg 1993; Kondo 1990). Still, the scholarly "division of labor" remains. While the construction of ethnic boundaries is recognized as "very much a saga of structure and *external* forces shaping ethnic options," the construction of culture is often regarded as "more a tale of human agency and *internal* group processes of cultural preservation, renewal, and innovation" (Nagel 1994, p. 161; my emphasis). Similarly, in his effort to disentangle the differential effects of content (what group members share) and circumstance (the situations they encounter) on ethnic processes, Cornell (1996) locates culture within the ethnic boundary and sees immigrant policies, economic structures, and so on as external. Anthony Smith, modifying his earlier thesis on the primacy of ethnic traditions, also suggests a need for closer attention to the interactions between culture and politics, yet he too assumes that culture is internal. Although he (accurately) recognizes the "ambivalence over alien cultures" and the tendency for a community to "compete with its neighbors by borrowing techniques and ideas," he still assumes that it "clings to its received traditions and life-styles and seeks to purify its culture of alien elements" (1996, p. 458). In short, when scholars argue for the importance of culture, they still seem to take it as given that culture *is* the stuff enclosed by ethnic boundaries.

This assumption about the location of culture, however, needs to be challenged by the structural, external view of culture discussed in chapter 1. The intersection of ethnicity and other social categories involves, among other things, the mixing of different cultural repertoires, among which the ethnic culture is not necessarily inherently more important than others. As detailed in this chapter, the *kōminka* doctors were embedded in both their ethnic tradition and professional culture, which were located *both* inside and outside of their ethnic boundaries. Thus, to question how their "internal" ethnic culture mediated the effects of structure or how it was (or was not) preserved only addresses part of their lived experiences. An equally relevant question concerns how they accessed their professional culture, used it, and contextualized this newly acquired cultural repertoire with their Taiwanese traditions.

In considering the locations of cultures in ethnic formation, I therefore suggest replacing the inside/outside framework with a notion of "multiple cultural toolboxes." Borrowing Swidler's (1986) famous conceptualization of culture as a toolkit of symbols, stories, values, and worldviews, I view ethnic cultural tradition as but one of numerous powerful and stable toolboxes that nevertheless does not need to assume the greatest importance. Colonization (or ethnic mixing in general) may bring about new cultural toolboxes grounded in recently introduced institutional practices. These various cultural repertoires have different degrees of accessibility and importance to different social groups. Social groups can—and must—creatively select ideas from accessible toolboxes to organize action and construct identity.

6 Borders of Medicine
The Dōjinkai Projects in China

INTRODUCTION

Medical missions, as depicted in preceding chapters, were construed as a foundational practice of Japan's "scientific colonialism" and later the "East Asian Co-Prosperity Sphere." While Japan's colonial medical practices were originally developed in Taiwan, its first colony, which renders it a particularly important case, a proper understanding of the role of medicine in the Japanese Empire requires recognition of the breadth and the variation of its application. To this end, the medical system in the Japanese informal empire in China provides a good comparative case.[1]

The Japanese informal empire in China differed greatly from its colonial presence on Taiwan. China was never a formal colony of Japan, and China's role as a former cultural mentor for Japan was commonly acknowledged, if differently interpreted, by Japanese intellectuals, government officials, and military men in the rising Japanese Empire.[2] Furthermore, in contrast to its

---

1. As Peter Duus points out, since the late Qing period, Western imperialist powers had built an "informal empire" in China with the structure of unequal treaties. The concept of the "informal empire" describes a form of collective imperialism in which various powers attempted to gain access to economic privileges in China while avoiding direct conflict with one another. "The rules of collective informal empire were reformulated in the doctrine of the Open Door. The treaty powers realized that maintaining a balance-of-power equilibrium in China was less costly than risking conflict through competition, and they reaffirmed the basic rules of the game under the same free-trade ideology that had justified the establishment of the treaty in the first place" (Duus 1989, p. xix).

2. Akira Iriye's (1980) edited volume provides a good analysis of the different modes of interaction between the Japanese and the Chinese during this period. In his introduction to the volume, Iriye summarizes some of the diverse opinions among the Japanese regarding the "China problem":

secure position as the singular colonizer in Taiwan, in China Japan faced strong competition from European and American powers. Due to a number of factors, Japan also provoked much stronger hostility among the population in China than it ever did in Taiwan.[3] As a result of these differences, Taiwan and China dramatize the opposing legacies of Japanese colonialism. The official discourse of Japan as an "anticolonial colonizer" developed into two contrasting narratives in these two drastically different contexts. Whereas Japanese colonial officials characterized their colonial projects in Taiwan as an attempt to share Japan's achievements in modernization with their less advanced Asian "brothers," many viewed their actions in China as a way to repay past cultural debts to a once superior civilization.[4]

Cosmopolitan medicine, an important tool of imperialism in both places, assumed different trajectories in Taiwan and China. Initially, many of Japan's medical plans in China appeared similar to efforts in Taiwan, but the different contexts eventually led to different paths of development. Japan's medical plans in China essentially took a very different direction due to factors such as Japan's competition with other hegemonic powers, its escalated

---

Naitō Konan, the historian, was concerned with the problem of culture and power. . . . Naito asked how the Chinese could seek to maintain their cultural integrity in the midst of foreign influences. The answer was to stress Japan's unique mission in China as the inheritor of Chinese culture and center of a new Asian civilization that was to be generated through Sino-Japanese cooperation. . . . For Ishibashi Tanzan, the journalist, on the other hand, Japanese behavior in China was important as an indicator of Japan's own development. Okamoto's essay stresses Ishibashi's call for a peaceful and reformist Japan that eschewed imperialism for peace and coprosperity. . . . The opposite of such views was the position of General Ugaki Kazushige. . . . Ugaki was the archetypical imperialist with no interest or concern for China per se; China was important merely as an object of Japanese needs. (p. 6)

3. Peter Duus (1989), for example, discusses how the rising Chinese nationalism in the 1920s presented a key factor in shaping Japan's imperialist plans towards China.

4. "From the outset, many Japanese argued that Japan's relationship with China was qualitatively different from that of the Western powers. After all, as men as diverse as Okakura Tenshin and Yamagata Aritomo often pointed out, the two peoples shared a 'common culture and common race' (*dōbun dōshu*), and it was natural for Japanese to think that they had a special sympathy for China or a depth of understanding that Westerners did not. The Chinese and the Japanese, moreover, shared a recent historical experience in common. Both had been the objects of Western gunboat diplomacy, and in the Bakumatsu period some Japanese even proposed that Japan make common cause with China in resisting the Western encroachment. But in the 1890s, when the failure of China to modernize and its defeat in the Sino-Japanese War precluded any notion of common alliance or common cause, there emerged the notion—embodied in the 'Ohkuma doctrine,' or the idea of 'the yellow man's burden'—that the Japanese, in repayment of their cultural debt to China, should take an active role in pulling China up the steep path toward 'civilization'" (Duus 1989, p. xxvi).

militarism, and the rising anti-Japanese sentiment among the Chinese population. The end result was that the Japanese medical personnel in China delivered service but not science. Japanese hospitals in China treated significant numbers of patients in the first half of the twentieth century, but they never cultivated any significant body of native practitioners in the profession, as they did in Taiwan. Rather than a project under scientific colonialism which focused on gradual, "natural," and thorough transformation of the colony, Japan's medical activities in China were used as a quick fix for the immediate obstacles in the empire's aggressive plans there.

Thus, in contrast to the outcomes of unintended ambiguities and tensions that we witnessed in the Taiwanese case, the intersections and interactions of Japan's professional and colonial projects in China were largely determined by the parameters of the imperial state's cultural and political agenda. One central ambiguity that characterized the intersection of colonialism and professionalism in wartime Taiwan, the tension between ethnicity and modernity, took on very different meanings in the Chinese case. When dispatching doctors and health personnel to China, Japanese colonizers often wished to transgress national borders and construct their medical activities as a borderless, philanthropic act, to help legitimize their presence. Behind this evangelistic gesture, because of their attempt to defeat other imperial powers already present in China, Japan was most concerned about the issue of national boundaries, and watched closely which nation sent doctors where. Instead of an identity dilemma that confronted a group of native professionals, this ambiguity was now articulated as a central contradiction in the colonizers' desire to simultaneously universalize and nationalize professional expertise.

THE JAPANESE "MEDICAL EMPIRE" IN CHINA: THE CASE OF "DŌJINKAI"

Dōjinkai and Colonial Medicine in China: A Brief History

In the history of Japan's medical activities in China, Dōjinkai, which can be roughly translated as "the Universal Benevolence Organization," played a crucial role.[5] Founded in 1902 and established as an incorporated foundation

---

5. The governor-general in Taiwan also sponsored a hospital system, the *hakuai byōin*, in southern China (see chapter 4). But Dōjinkai was involved in a larger scope of medical activities, including establishing medical schools, translating medical textbooks, sending Japanese students to China, and so on. Similar activities also took place in Manchuria. Several Japanese organizations, together with the South Manchuria Railway Company (*mantetsu*), sponsored a fairly well-developed medical system in Manchuria. See Jie Shen's (1996) *"Manshūkoku" shakai jigyōshi.*

in 1903, Dōjinkai grew quickly in its membership base and soon developed strong ties to the government. At first, Dōjinkai relied on individual contributions for its financial sources, but it soon attracted attention and support from the Japanese state. "In 1907, an imperial award of five thousand yen lent the Dōjinkai considerable luster, and in 1914 the association was again honored when the Taishō Emperor agreed to assume the title of Dōjinkai president. . . . When the China Cultural Affairs Bureau was formed in 1923, the Dōjinkai became one of the recipients of the Boxer funds" (Lee 1989, p. 298). From 1923 to 1936, the association received a total of roughly 5.59 million yen from the Japanese government's China Cultural Affairs Bureau (Huang 1982, p. 73).

In 1923, "close to forty thousand doctors, industrialists, and government officials were members" (Lee 1989, p. 298). An issue of the organization's magazine, *Dōjin*, that was published in the same year grants us a glimpse of the composition of the organization as it approached maturity. Included among the thirty names listed as core leaders of the foundation (i.e., its president, chairman, managers, counselors, and the board of directors) were five medical doctors, one pharmaceutical doctor, three viscounts, and three barons. The numerous aristocratic titles indicated the imperial state's involvement with this foundation. For example, the president of Dōjinkai was a royal prince. Gotō Shimpei, now possessing the title of viscount, was also listed as a counselor.

The founders of the Dōjinkai, like those of another cultural exchange institute, the Tōa Dōbunkai, believed in the principles of nonintervention and cultural exchange (Huang 1982; Lee 1989).[6] The association's formal goal was to "spread medical and pharmaceutical knowledge and skills to China and other Asian countries to protect the public health and aid the sick among these populations as well as in Japan" ("Dōjinkai kisoku gaiyō,"

---

6. See Reynolds 1989 for a detailed discussion of the role and history of Tōa Dōbunkai. Focusing on the case of the Tōa Dōbun Shoin, Reynolds provides a detailed account of the history and ideological persuasion behind Japan's cultural exchange projects in China in the late nineteenth century and the first half of the twentieth century. His analysis shows the complex politics of such cultural exchange projects, concluding that even with the best intentions, Japanese in China inevitably became the tools of Japanese imperialism.

Similarly, Sophia Lee's study of Japan's Foreign Ministry's Cultural Agenda for China also argues that "cultural diplomacy is undeniably fraught with tension between the desire to seek knowledge and express creativity without constraints and the need to conform to domestic and international orthodoxies" (Lee 1989, p. 272). My study of the Dōjinkai hospitals in China in this chapter explores this very tension and seeks to understand its various meanings.

Gaimushō Gaikōshiryōkan; see also Lee 1989). Consistent with this statement, Dōjinkai was actively involved in overseas medical activities even though it was based in Tokyo. In its 1923 issue, *Dōjin* describes the process by which, upon its establishment, the organization sent off a total of 329 doctors and pharmacists to China, Korea, and Southeast Asia. After 1906, the focus of the foundation changed from dispatching medical personnel to establishing medical institutes in Manchuria and Korea, where several hospitals were subsequently opened. With the establishment of the South Manchuria Railroad Company (SMRC) and the annexation of Korea, the Dōjin Hospitals in these areas were handed over to the SMRC and the governor-general in Korea. Meanwhile, starting in 1914, Dōjinkai began to work diligently in China, establishing Dōjin Hospitals in Beijing, Hankou, Qingdao, and Jinan.[7]

The Dōjinkai also attempted to participate in medical education in China, although they were not as active in this aspect. A Dōjin medical and pharmaceutical school with the specific purpose of training overseas students from China was founded in Tokyo in 1906, but financial difficulties forced the school to close in 1911 (Huang 1982, p. 99). In 1923, Dōjinkai began to draw a plan for building a medical school in Shanghai, which never materialized.[8] The Dōjin Hospital in Jinan also showed signs of cooperation with a local Japanese-sponsored university ("Kimitsu no. 302," Gaimushō Gaikōshiryōkan; "Kimitsu no. 88," Gaimushō Gaikōshiryōkan). A short-lived Qingdao Medical School was established under the supervision of the Dōjinkai Qingdao Hospital from 1924 to 1930 (Huang 1982, p. 101).

With such an extensive involvement in colonial medicine, the Dōjinkai attempted to position itself as the center of the Japanese medical empire in China. In 1923, Dōjinkai discussed its role among the major Japanese hospitals in China. These hospitals included the Beijing and Hankou Dōjin Hospitals, the Guangdong, Xiamen, and Fuzhou Hakuai Hospitals (sponsored by the governor-general of Taiwan), the Qingdao and Jinan Hospitals,[9] the Fengtian Hospital (run by the Manchuria branch of the Japanese Red

7. Since these are four well-known Chinese cities, it will probably be much easier for readers to recognize them by their original Chinese names than their Japanese pronunciations. For this reason, I will refer to these locations by their Chinese names. The Japanese pronunciations are: Pekin (Beijing), Kankō (Hankou), Chintao (Qingdao), and Sainan (Jinan).

8. Japan's Foreign Ministry did establish a Shanghai Science Institute in 1928, but this school accommodated Japanese students almost exclusively (see Lee 1989, pp. 288–92).

9. Jinan and Qingdao Hospitals were run by other Japanese authorities at this time; they were both handed over to Dōjinkai in 1925.

Cross), as well as various hospitals run by the South Manchuria Railroad Company. Based on this survey published in *Dōjin*, Dōjinkai argued that it was the most active Japanese organization in the medical activities in China. Thus, it was suggested that Dōjinkai should take up the responsibility of integrating various Japanese-sponsored medical institutes in order to foster a coherent and effective plan for enhancing Sino-Japanese amity ("Taishi iryōjigyō no tōitsu an: Dōjinkai wa yoroshiku korega chūshin tare," Gaimushō Gaikōshiryōkan). Historical materials do indicate that Dōjinkai played an increasingly important role in the history of Japan's colonial medicine in China, as will become clear in the following discussion of the Dōjin Hospitals.

Each of the four Dōjin Hospitals in China had a Japanese director and was staffed by both Japanese and Chinese doctors. But Japanese doctors outnumbered their Chinese colleagues by about three to one (Lee 1989, p. 299). These hospitals provided good medical service to a significant number of Chinese patients. One scholar notes that "because of its reasonable, graduated rates for Chinese patients, the [Beijing] hospital attracted a large Chinese clientele. It also provided free cholera immunization to Chinese residents in Peking [Beijing]. According to one source, in 1917 all the hospitals in Peking treated a total of 81,604 persons. During that year, the Peking Dōjin Hospital treated a total of 20,871 patients" (Lee 1989, p. 299).

Table 6 lists the numbers of patients treated at the four Dōjin Hospitals in China during 1930 and 1931. Patients were categorized as Chinese, Japanese, and foreign (though no definition of "foreign" was provided). The decline of Chinese patients in 1931 was due to new developments in Sino-Japanese relations, most notably the Manchuria Incident in 1931 which dramatically heightened anti-Japanese sentiments in China. In fact, throughout the operation of Dōjin Hospitals, the number of patients fluctuated according to the relative intensity of anti-Japanese feelings in China. But "each time, after a slump induced by a Sino-Japanese incident, the number of Chinese patients would gradually increase and sometimes even surpass the pre-incident level" (Lee 1989, p. 299).

After the outbreak of the second Sino-Japanese War in 1937, all four Dōjin Hospitals were forced to close down temporarily. When the hospitals reopened, they underwent major reorganization and served a very different purpose—cooperation with the Japanese military. On September 24, 1937, in a telegram labeled "secret," the Japanese Minister of Foreign Affairs instructed the Chairman of Dōjinkai to cooperate with the Japanese military and dispatch medical teams to war-stricken areas. The purpose, wrote the Minister of Foreign Affairs, was to "take care of Japanese and Chinese

Table 6. Numbers of Patients at the Dōjin Hospitals in China

	Beijing		Hankou		Qingdao		Jinan	
	1930	1931	1930	1931	1930	1931	1930	1931
Chinese patients	12,206	4,672	12,364	3,393	12,622	6,936	13,007	8,011
Japanese patients	3,415	2,587	7,018	4,927	19,335	23,868	9,355	6,591
Foreign patients	122	41	257	212	1,080	1,047	103	89

SOURCE: Adapted from "Dōjinkai kaiin keieihi chōsho," Gaimushō Gaikōshiryōkan

patients and to facilitate the pacification teams of the Military" ("8420–1," Gaimushō Gaikōshiryōkan).

From the government's perspective, it was quite clear that colonial medicine was to service propaganda and co-optation in China. A document stamped with the label "top secret" and circulated in the Ministry of Foreign Affairs (dated October 21, 1937) provides a useful summary of Japan's plans for medical activities in China. Focusing on the dispatch of immunization teams to northern China, the document stated that poor health conditions and insufficient immunization efforts in northern China should be improved to facilitate future activities and trips by Japanese in these areas. Equally important for Japan, sending immunization teams to China would be an extremely valuable piece of propaganda. To these ends, the document outlines a list of proposed activities, including:

1.   Conducting surveys and research regarding immunization.
2.   Investigating the conditions of local immunization facilities and planning for the establishment of new ones.
3.   Providing assistance to Chinese immunization agents.
4.   Treating Chinese patients.
5.   Submitting reports on their activities, surveys, research, and suggestions. ("Taishi bōeki kyūgo-han haken ni kansuru jigyō-an," Gaimushō Gaikōshiryōkan)

In short, immunization teams were supposed to improve local health conditions, gain medical knowledge about these areas, and co-opt local Chinese in preparation for the eventual takeover planned for by the Japanese.

Following this government instruction, Dōjinkai sent two kinds of med-

Table 7. Number of Patients Treated by the Clinic Teams

	Clinic Teams Sent by Hankou Hospital	Clinic Teams Sent by Qingdao Hospital	Clinic Teams Sent by Jinan Hospital
Total number of patients treated (10/18/37–3/31/38)	56,899	53,637	83,994

SOURCE: Adapted from "Shina haken Dōjinkai shinryō-han seryō kanja-hyō," Gaimushō Gaikōshiryōkan

ical groups, clinic (*shinryō*) and immunization (*bōeki*) teams, to provide medical treatment and immunization services to Chinese residents in cities and villages in many areas in northern and central China. These touring medical teams covered a great area and reached many remote corners beyond the influence of the original Dōjin Hospitals. But Dōjinkai medical missions were also transformed into a tool of the Japanese military in this process (Huang 1982, p. 97).

The words of some of the participating doctors provide a concrete sense of what their role was on these medical teams. In 1938, some of these doctors returned from China and held a public meeting in Japan, which consisted of a series of short reports for an audience of educators, practitioners, and other groups in the field of medicine. These speeches, reprinted by Dōjinkai, indicated the nature and the extent of their activities. Consistent with the secret telegram from the Minister of Foreign Affairs, the vice-chairman of Dōjinkai emphasized the pacifying nature of these medical teams, stating that Dōjinkai understood that it was important "to take care of the refugees in Japanese-occupied areas ... and elsewhere" ("Hokushi chūshi ni okeru Dōjinkai no shinryō bōeki jigyō ni tsuite," Gaimushō Gaikōshiryōkan). Within a year, from the start of the war to the time the report was delivered, Dōjinkai sent about 250 people on the clinic teams, at a cost of about 2 million yen (ibid.). Similarly, immunization efforts were made in these areas, according to the instructions of the Japanese government. "With the new affiliation with the military and an understanding that war-stricken areas tended to be vulnerable to attacks of epidemic diseases," Dōjinkai was commanded by the Ministry of Foreign Affairs to send various immunization teams to northern and central China. Three hundred people were sent on these teams (ibid.). From October 18, 1937, to March 31, 1938, the Hankou, Qingdao, and Jinan Dōjin Hospitals sent nine clinic teams, which made a total of nineteen visits to various cities and towns in China (see table 7).

Competition among Multiple Hegemonies

Much like Gotō Shimpei's original formulation of the thesis of "scientific colonialism," Japan's colonial medicine in China was meant as a way to disseminate the gospel of modernity and science and to spread Japan's cultural and political influences. However, engaged in hegemonic competition with various other imperialist powers in China, the Japanese practitioners of "scientific colonialism" self-consciously constructed a contradictory narrative that both erased and emphasized the "nationality" of modernity and science. Although the Japanese often described their medical activities in China as a borderless service that transcended national boundaries, just as in Taiwan, they emphasized these medical activities as a specifically *Japanese* enterprise, to be distinguished from American and British hospitals.

Dr. Shimose Kentarō, in a memo about his visit to Shanghai, candidly questioned the existence of the "spirit of universal benevolence" among Japanese doctors in China. He admitted that, unlike Western missionaries, Japanese doctors did not go to China because of the spirit of universal benevolence:

> In today's Japan, or even in the near future, there will not exist people who are genuinely interested in China and at the same time take the monetary issue lightly. In other words, we will not see people who are like the missionaries that sacrifice themselves and are willing to die in Asia after long years of hard work.
>
> It is probably asking too much to expect [Japanese] people to be philanthropic, interested in China, and dedicated to Chinese people's well-being. ("Zakkan," Gaimushō Gaikōshiryōkan)

Dr. Shimose then proposed a solution to this problem, asking Japanese educators in the field of medicine to cultivate these desired attitudes in themselves and their students:

> It is highly desirable that the deans, presidents, and professors at imperial and private universities and medical schools take the initiative to understand the spirit of universal benevolence. It is also urgent that they display an interest in foreign countries, especially China.
>
> However, lip service about being interested in China is to be avoided. Rather, one idea is to give the powerful figures in medicine some opportunities to learn and understand:
>
> The spirit of universal benevolence; an interest in foreign countries; and Humanitarianism.

>   Another possibility would be to invite a few carefully selected
> presidents and professors to visit our colonies and China so that they
> can develop their own ideas about the medical practices [of Japanese
> hospitals there].
>   Maybe some of them will get interested in today's China and will
> want to participate in the development [of medicine in that country].
> Alternatively, perhaps I can pinpoint the right people and approach
> them about the possibilities of taking the positions in China. (ibid.)

Why was it so important for Japanese doctors to become interested in
China? The answer lies in the instrumentality of medicine in a hegemonic
competition. Japanese colonial medicine in China, represented by Dōjinkai's
activities, was part of a larger hegemonic competition among imperial powers. In 1923, the *Dōjin* editorial board wrote a preface entitled "A War without Weapons" ("Buki naki ikusa"). This "war" was the "trade and industry
battle" among "world powers," competing for access to the raw materials in
China as well as the trust of Chinese people ("Buki naki ikusa," Gaimushō
Gaikōshiryōkan). The preface cautioned the Japanese that they seemed to
trail behind the Americans in this competition. Using language acquisition
in China as an indicator, it stated that "more and more young people spoke
English in China now, and they would even ask the Japanese they encountered whether they could converse in English" (ibid.).

The role of medicine in this "war" was discussed explicitly in the first
article in this issue of *Dōjin*. Entitled "The Handshake of Two Nations"
("Ryōkokumin no akushu"), this article argued that Japan needed to win
this "war" because the cooperation between Japan and China was crucial for
regional peace. "The spiritual handshake between these two nations was key
to the foundation and maintenance of peace in East Asia" ("Ryōkokumin no
akushu," Gaimushō Gaikōshiryōkan). To ensure a close relationship between
China and Japan, a so-called Sino-Japanese friendship, the most effective
strategy was the delivery of medical services to Chinese people. Noting that
the Americans had been doing exactly the same thing (e.g., establishing
educational and medical facilities in China), the article nevertheless concluded on an optimistic note, arguing that shared racial and cultural origins
(*dōbun dōshu*) would ensure Japan's ultimate success in this "war without
weapons."

Notwithstanding the differences between the optimism in the *Dōjin*
magazine and the pragmatism in Dr. Shimose's memo, these two pieces both
made explicit the importance of the *nationality* of cosmopolitan medicine.
For Japan, to be the leading deliverer of medicine was considered more
important than the actual delivery of medical services to China. On a spec-

trum from well-intended cultural diplomacy to outright hegemonic war, the Dōjin Hospitals moved from one extreme to the other with the rise of Japan's militarism. Nevertheless, one thing that remained unchanged throughout was that, viewing medical evangelism as a self-imposed mission, the Japanese insisted on being *the primary agent* in the project of modernizing China.

Once dispatched, the Japanese in China became even more conscious of and enthusiastic about their instrumentality for the hegemonic competition with other imperial forces. For example, in a document sent by the Japanese Consulate in Jinan to the Japanese Ministry of Foreign Affairs in 1930, the consulate enthusiastically argued that Jinan Dōjin Hospital needed government financial aid by stressing the hospital's contribution to important "cultural affairs." From the examples provided in the document, it becomes clear that "cultural affairs" here referred to outreach efforts to local Chinese residents. The Japanese Consulate praised the Jinan Hospital for increasing the percentage of Chinese nationals among its patients over the years (55 percent in the previous year). The consulate argued that, although the hospital suffered a recent loss of Chinese patients due to the rise of Sino-Japanese tensions in Jinan, the Ministry of Foreign Affairs should continue its financial support of the hospital to sustain its outreach efforts. It was further emphasized that the Jinan Dōjin Hospital faced stiff competition from a local university hospital sponsored by a number of Western churches ("Kimitsu no. 302," Gaimushō Gaikōshiryōkan).

Two years later, the same issue was brought up again in another correspondence between the Ministry of Foreign Affairs and the Japanese Consulate in Jinan. The Jinan Hospital suffered an even greater loss of Chinese patients as the local Sino-Japanese tensions intensified. The consulate insisted on the need to maintain the same level of activities at the hospital because it was not simply a business but a "cultural battle," with the church-sponsored university hospital still the chief enemy ("Kimitsu no. 88," Gaimushō Gaikōshiryōkan). From this example, it appears that the Dōjin Hospitals and the Japanese Consulate in Jinan were thoroughly convinced of the importance of competing with other American- or European-sponsored hospitals; they were enthusiastic players in Japan's cultural war in China.[10]

10. That the Dōjin Hospitals in China were engaged in a cultural battle was also acknowledged by the larger Japanese populations in China, who were not affiliated with the state or the hospitals. For example, in a telegram sent from the [Japanese] Resident Group of Jinan to Yoshizawa Minister of Foreign Affairs in 1932, the local Japanese used the argument of cultural battles to support their argument against the downsizing plans proposed by the Dōjinkai headquarters in Tokyo:

The same tendency among the Japanese medical practitioners in China became even more pronounced once the war began. For example, when Dr. Seo worked on the Dōjinkai immunization team in Shanghai, he stressed the need to reflect upon the reputation of Japanese medicine when practicing medicine in such an "international city" ("Korera no shinryō narabini Shanhai ni okeru Shinajin no shippei ni tsuite," Gaimushō Gaikōshiryōkan). Because he was working in Shanghai, the doctor became aware of the competition from "the clinics sponsored by different countries in the Leased Territory" (ibid.).

A doctor who helped organize the Dōjinkai medical teams, Dr. Masuda Taneji, made similar points when he delivered a lecture in Japan on October 10, 1938, in which he surveyed the conditions of health facilities in China on the eve of the second Sino-Japanese War. Contextualizing Japan's medical activities in China in the history of metropolitan medicine in that country, Professor Masuda argued that Japan should take up the responsibility of helping Chinese doctors modernize their field ("Jihen chokuzen ni okeru hokushi chūshi no eisei shisetsu ni tsuite," Gaimushō Gaikōshiryōkan). But when he further evaluated Japan's achievements in this regard, it became clear that Professor Masuda's focus was not on the advancement of cosmopolitan medicine in China per se; instead, his main concern was that Japanese doctors maintain more influence on China than Western doctors, in particular, American, doctors. For example, he compared the numbers of Japanese-run and American-run hospitals in China. He also traced the educational backgrounds of the leading figures in major medical schools in China and, much to his dismay, found that most had received their training in the United States. Thus, Dr. Masuda described the American influence as a threat that demanded serious consideration on the part of Japanese medical personnel. In general, the medical service of the Dōjinkai touring clinics appeared to be used not only as a pacification tool during the war but also as the continuation of prewar hegemonic competition between Japan and other imperialist powers who also wished to "bring modernity to China."

Jinan Hospital has provided a large population in Shandong Province with medical services and has alleviated the negative feelings of local [Chinese] residents after the Jinan Incident as well as various other incidents. The Hospital has also contributed greatly to the public health in remote areas, and the importance of its presence is felt more keenly than ever. But at this very moment, Dōjinkai ignores its mission, makes poor use of its national subsidies, and asks the Dōjinkai Jinan Hospital to downsize unreasonably in their attempt to use the money for other purposes. . . .

Jinan Hospital has received the privilege of being a part of the cultural enterprise in China. Therefore, it is regrettable that the trustworthiness and the reputation of the Hospital no longer measures up to that of the past. ("Shōwa 7, Yoshizawa gaimu daijin," Gaimushō Gaikōshiryōkan; my emphasis)

SUPPORT FROM THE JAPANESE
MEDICAL COMMUNITY

As Young (1998) argued eloquently for the Manchurian case, Japanese imperialism involved the total mobilization of society rather than simply a few "bad judgments" by some government and military leaders. Similarly, without extensive support from the medical community in Japan, Dōjinkai alone would not have been able to conduct these activities. Some traces of such "crimes of medical doctors" are to be found in historical documents. An article appeared on May 18, 1938, in the weekly journal *Iji eisei shinbun*, in which a Professor Taniguchi commented on his proposal to the Ministry of War and the Ministry of Foreign Affairs. His comments provide an example of the active support of doctors for colonial medicine. Professor Taniguchi, formerly in charge of the immunization teams in central China, returned to Japan with a plan to establish an immunization research institute in central China. Allegedly, he suggested that "just as the immunization institute in northern China had been staffed mainly with the researchers at Tokyo Research Center on Epidemics (Tokyo Densenbyō Kenkyūjo), the new center in central China can rely on the support of Osaka and Hokkaidō Imperial Universities" ("Bōeki kenkyū shoin wa denkenkei ga dokusen—Taniguchi kyōju Nankin de kataru," Gaimushō Gaikōshiryōkan). Similarly, Dr. Miyagawa, vice-chair of Dōjinkai, formally spoke to the deans and presidents of medical schools and universities at the Japanese Medical Association, asking them to actively support Dōjinkai's activities in China ("Minshū o i de senbu—Senkentai sudeni shuppatsusu," Gaimushō Gaikō-shiryōkan). Overseas Japanese medical colleges were also recruited to facilitate similar activities. Both the Manchuria Medical University (Manshū Igaku Daigaku) and Seoul Imperial University (Keijō Teikoku Daigaku) were in charge of organizing clinic teams in Manchuria in the aftermath of the Manchuria Incident ("Kōfutsū 236" [August 3, 1934]; "Kōfutsū 544" [May 8, 1933], Gaimushō Gaikōshiryōkan).

Another example of the extensive cooperation between the medical community and the Japanese military is documented in Yuki Tanaka's study. Tanaka carefully examines the role of the Japanese medical community in the notorious Unit 731 in Manchuria. Unit 731, known for its brutal experiments on Chinese POWs, was initiated by Ishii Shirō, a prominent physician and graduate of Kyoto University. Ishii traveled to Europe in 1928 to investigate the situation concerning biological weapons and, after his return, became firmly convinced of the need for Japan to develop biological weapons. Tanaka recounts this forgotten history:

In 1932 Ishii set up the Epidemic Prevention Laboratory within the military medical school in Tokyo with the full support of the military. At the same time, Ishii set up in Manchukuo a small and secret subgroup, the Tōgō Unit, in the village of Bei-inho, 100 kilometers southeast of Harbin. Remote Manchukuo was chosen primarily because researchers wanted to conduct medical experiments on human beings, which were difficult to carry out in Japan. Experiments on humans using Chinese prisoners began as soon as the Tōgō Unit was established. Thus, research on defensive methods against biological weapons was conducted mainly in Tokyo, and research on offensive use and actual production of such weapons was carried out in Manchukuo. . . . In 1925 the Geneva Convention prohibited the use of chemical and bacteriological weapons. Ishii obviously knew that his plans contravened the convention. . . . The Ishii group sought out all bacteria and viruses that could prove useful as weapons and for which vaccines could be developed so as to protect the Japanese forces using them. (1996, p. 136)

Ishii was not working alone. Like the leaders of Dōjinkai, Dr. Ishii actively sought the support and help of his colleagues. He quickly established branch units in many locations in and beyond China. As a graduate of Kyoto University, Ishii was able to use his connections there in his recruitment efforts:

Ishii started recruiting young elite medical specialists from various Japanese universities a few years before the establishment of Unit 731 in 1936. Professors in the medical school of Kyoto University in particular assisted Ishii with this recruitment. Branch units were set up in Beijing, Nanjing, Guandong, and Singapore; these units conducted experiments on weapons developed by Unit 731 and made plans for waging biological warfare within those regions. At this time Colonel Ishii had 3,000 staff in Unit 731 and as many as 20,000 staff under his command if all members from the branch units were totaled. (Tanaka 1996, pp. 136–37)

Many doctors trained by Ishii became heavily involved in the detailed planning of specific biological warfare operations. A number of them became prisoners of the Allies and admitted under interrogation the role of Japanese medical schools in the functioning of Unit 731.

The support of the medical community for both Dōjinkai and Unit 731 was indicative of close state-medicine interaction and cooperation during this period. Recruitment instead of coercion was the main mechanism for the involvement of Japanese doctors in colonial medicine. This observation leads to an important question: Why were doctors interested in such activities that contradicted their professional ethics either explicitly (e.g., Unit 731) or implicitly (e.g., Dōjin Hospitals)? In the next section, I turn to this troubling issue by examining how these contradictions were rationalized or glossed over in individual and public discourses.

DOUBLING: "WARRIORS IN WHITE"

In a sense, the question of doctors' involvement in imperialism is about the ambiguous relationship between nationalism and modernity. Doctors were asked to serve both the goal of the empire and the ethics of medicine. In contrast to wartime Taiwanese doctors who struggled with comparable ambiguities as part of their quest for a coherent identity, the challenge for the Dōjinkai and the Japanese public media was more involved with the production of a consumable narrative for the public. How could they reconcile the proclaimed goal of improving the public health conditions in China on the one hand, with their actual involvement in a war that was destroying countless lives and facilities on the other? How, in other words, was the theme of universal benevolence appropriated and manipulated in a project centered on the national interests of Japan? Though much of the answer to these questions was buried or destroyed with the passing of the war itself, a few remaining documents lend themselves to the formulation of some informative speculations.

At the individual level, doctors involved in these activities developed a strategy of "doubling" to reconcile their roles as humanist life-savers and accomplices of the war (Tanaka 1996). The doctors of Unit 731 "were able to create a logic of sorts that justified their actions. Once this logic was created, . . . Maruta [the label for Chinese prisoners] were no longer human beings but a means to the end of gaining knowledge. That knowledge was supposed to help save the lives of Japanese people. In sum, there was the conviction that valuable lives saved outweighed any concern that worthless lives might be lost. . . . This, of course, means that the willingness to dispose of certain lives did, in fact, coexist with the desire to save the lives of others" (Tanaka 1996, p. 162). Tanaka compares this coexistence of conflicting desires to what Robert Jay Lifton observed in the Nazi doctors. For both groups, the strategy of "doubling" led the doctors to see their brutal acts as consistent with the high moral cause of serving "more valuable" lives and authorities. They justified the specific agenda of their nation by equating it with a higher, broader moral cause, such as that articulated in Japan's slogan about the Greater East Asia Co-Prosperity Sphere.

Expanding Lifton's and Tanaka's analyses to the collective level reveals that the Japanese public discourses about Dōjinkai's medical activities were also constructed with a "doubling" strategy. Unlike the experiments conducted by Unit 731, which qualified as outright criminal acts and were kept from public knowledge, Dōjinkai's medical missions were highly publicized in Japan through news reports and public speeches. Yet, like the Unit 731 doctors, the Dōjinkai and the Japanese public media developed a strategy of "doubling" that constructed and connected the two roles of the Dōjinkai medical missions: imperial soldiers and benevolent philanthropists.

Dōjinkai Doctors in Japan: An Imperial Troop

To the extent that the Japanese state depicted their war against China as a moral obligation—a "sacred war"—to deliver the Chinese people to the prosperity and civilization of the Japanese Empire, the role of Dōjinkai doctors in the war was recognized positively in the media. For example, as a formal gesture of submission to the imperial state, members of medical teams paid a worshiping visit to the Meiji Shrine—the first public structure dedicated to the memory of the Meiji Emperor, and a symbolic center of the empire. Equally suggestive of their connection to the war, when they formally embarked on the trip from Tokyo station, most team members were wearing a military-style uniform. Similarly, in a newspaper article published on April 23, 1938, the immunization teams were described as "immunization armies," and their trips to China were called "military advancement" ("Bōeki butai no shingun," Gaimushō Gaikōshiryōkan). The article acknowledged that the immunization teams were sponsored by the Cultural Affairs Bureau (Bunka Jigyōbu) in the Ministry of Foreign Affairs, and described these activities as one example of the "mobilization of the sciences *towards the battlefield*" (*senjō e no kagaku dōin*; my emphasis; ibid.). From these texts, it is clear that the Japanese public media explicitly and positively acknowledged the Dōjinkai doctors' connection to the war.

Dōjinkai Doctors in China: The Spirit of Universal Benevolence

Even if Japan's invasion of China was euphemized as a "sacred war," its connection to the Dōjinkai medical missions still needed to be toned down once the Dōjinkai doctors were dispatched beyond the periphery of the empire. Once in China, the construction of their public images subdued the imperialist theme and instead emphasized the spirit of universal benevolence.

Some pictures taken in China appeared in Japanese newspapers in 1938 and, along with narrative descriptions of the scenario in these pictures, they preserved traces of the discursive manipulation of the public images of the Dōjinkai doctors. In contrast with their military uniforms at the departing moment in Tokyo, members of medical teams wore white lab coats when working in China. The narrative descriptions of such pictures referred to the medical missions as "compassionate treatment provided for the Chinese people," and emanated a touch of the medical evangelism suggested by the pictures ("Shina minshū ni jōnoshinryō," Gaimushō Gaikōshiryōkan). Likewise, in their self-presentation before the Chinese people, Dōjinkai doctors depicted themselves as agents of modern civilization. It was claimed that the purpose of these overseas medical missions was to enhance human welfare indiscriminately across national boundaries. For example, a flier prepared by the medical tour teams sponsored by the Jinan Dōjin Hospital described Japanese doctors as "pure humanists." Dōjinkai doctors wrote the text of the flier in Chinese, and although they made a few grammatical mistakes, their general points were quite clear:

> Everyone! Here comes a good chance!
> Why is the good chance here?
> Be patient! Let me explain it clearly for you and you will understand.
> Starting from May 12, . . . we will open a temporary Jinan hospital clinic (currently scheduled for five days). Two Japanese doctors that will be here are both excellent healers.
> Jinan hospital is the biggest hospital in Jinan County; it's the Dōjin Jinan Hospital run by the Japanese.
> The purpose of this hospital is for Japan to spread modern medicine and pharmacology in China and East Asia, in order to improve the general health conditions in these areas.
> So, for the purpose stated above, we especially come here this time to introduce the most advanced Japanese medical knowledge to you all. The medical fees and drug prices are especially discounted, and examination fees are waived. So please, everyone with an illness, come and receive treatment from our clinic.
> The five of us on this tour welcome you all.
> *Dōjinkai Jinan Hospital Touring Clinic*
> ("Dōjinkai Jinan iin junkai shinryō hōkoku,"
> Gaimushō Gaikōshiryōkan; my emphasis)

The doctors' "mobilization of the sciences toward the battlefield," as described in the Japanese newspaper, was presented as a medical evangelism once they arrived in China.

Similarly, a poster about immunization shots at Dōjin Hospitals emphasized service to the people in China (as opposed to the interests of the empire). The text reads:

> Smallpox vaccination
> Provided at no charge
> Good citizens
> Hurry to the Dōjin Hospital.
> ("8420–1," Gaimushō Gaikōshiryōkan)

In contrast to their imperialist ideology, which gave rise to the dehumanizing label of Maruta for the Chinese prisoners in Unit 731 only a couple of years earlier, Chinese people were addressed here as "good citizens" (*ryōmin*). Dōjinkai doctors were portrayed as a group of well-intentioned providers of modern science.

Furthermore, Dōjinkai doctors linked their self-assigned mission of medical evangelism to the tradition of Chinese culture. Explaining why Dōjinkai picked this name, the vice president of the organization said it was because "the ancient saint taught us the virtue of *isshi dōjin,* or universal benevolence." The "ancient saint" referred to Confucius, and the term *isshi dōjin* was originally a Chinese saying ("Hokushi chūshi ni okeru Dōjinkai no shinryō bōeki jigyō ni tsuite," Gaimushō Gaikōshiryōkan). In a newspaper article published in Japan during 1937, which reported that Dōjinkai sent medical teams to provide medical assistance to Chinese residents in areas afflicted by the battles, this teaching of the "ancient saint" was again quoted as the guiding principle for Dōjinkai doctors. The title of the article reads, "While these were Chinese residents, the Dōjinkai medical teams provided treatment with the spirit of *universal benevolence*" ("Shina no minshū nara, isshi dōjin ni, Dōjinkai kara kyūgohan," Gaimushō Gaikōshiryōkan; emphasis in original). Some pictures published on May 8, 1938, in another Japanese newspaper, *Tokyo asahi shimbun,* presented images of Japanese doctors busy providing treatment to Chinese patients. Another picture showed a group of Japanese medical personnel treating Chinese patients under a tablet inscribed with Dr. Sun Yat-sen's famous saying "The World Belongs to All" (*Tian xia wei gong*). The tablet, centrally located in this picture, was described as an appropriate caption for the picture ("Shina minshū ni jōnoshinryō," Gaimushō Gaikōshiryōkan).[11]

11. Japan's claim to the role of authentic inheritor of the Chinese tradition can be traced to the early days of the Colonial Empire. In a speech delivered in the early 1900s, Gotō explicitly invoked China's legendary past in his reflection of Japan's colonial medicine in Taiwan. He compared the colonizers' health policies to the concerns for people's welfare shown by great ancient emperors in China, such as Yao, Shun, and Qin Shihuang. He argued that the efforts of Japanese colonial officials in public health showed their true appreciation for the value of human life, "just as Qin Shihuang had once sent his agent Xu Fu to look for the legendary longevity medicine" ("Gotō minsei chōkan enzetsu hikki," Kokkai Toshokan). (The fact that Emperor Qin Shihuang's quest for longevity medicine was not only futile but also completely self-serving, naturally, was not part of Gotō's analogy.) The Japanese government, argued Gotō, "had truly learned to recognize the importance of medicine in the last 30 years" (ibid.). In contrast, the contemporary Chinese government had deviated from its own great heritage, for it "greatly overlooked the role of the medical science and, by the same token, overlooked the importance of life" (ibid.). In this sense, Gotō portrayed Japan as the true inheritor of ancient Chinese wisdom.

In contrast, Japanese accused the contemporary Chinese government of having deviated from and forsaken its own great tradition. Time and again, the Japanese accused Chinese armies of using biological weapons on their own people. In a 1938 Dōjinkai speech in Tokyo, the vice-chair of Dōjinkai, Dr. Miyagawa, commented specifically on this issue. While the Japanese immunization teams were reported to have labored diligently to bring the epidemics under control, the Chinese armies were accused of spreading the bacteria of cholera in areas that had fallen under Japanese occupation. According to Miyagawa's report, cholera epidemics broke out in places like Jiujiang, Shijiaban, and Tianjin, due to "the evil deeds" of the Chinese army or plainclothesmen ("Hokushi chūshi ni okeru Dōjinkai no shinryō bōeki jigyō ni tsuite," Gaimushō Gaikōshiryōkan). Dr. Miyagawa thus concluded his report by saying that "based on our first-hand experience this time, there is no doubt that the Chinese are using biological weapons. There is abundant evidence for these inhumane acts. We must learn the lesson and treat the threat of biological weapons very seriously in our future immunization work" (ibid.).

Around the same time, a Japanese newspaper, *Tokyo asahi shimbun*, published an article with a similar claim. The article concludes with an attack on Chinese authorities, condemning their brutality in using biological weapons on their own people for the sake of weakening the Japanese military forces.[12] Other Japanese newspapers, such *Yomiuri shimbun* and *Kokumin shinbun*, also published similar accounts ("Hiretsu na teki no saikin senjutsu" and "Bōgyaku jikokumin ni mukuyu," in Gaimushō Gaikōshiryōkan). All these reports attempted to present a picture which contrasted the kindness of the Japanese with the brutality of the Chinese. The message of these reports was clear: while ancient Chinese philosophers taught us the virtue of "universal benevolence," it was the Japanese who really took it to heart and developed it in practice.

12. The article reported that the Japanese army found powerful evidence to confirm their suspicion that the Chinese army was using biological weapons in the war. According to the article, the Japanese army learned from the Chinese refugees and captives that cholera was going around in the city of Jiujiang right before the arrival of the Japanese army. It further claimed that after the Japanese troops entered Jiujiang, some Japanese soldiers who drank from local wells were also stricken by cholera. Most importantly, the Japanese found a couple of ampoules in a well in the city that "looked completely different from the ones that were made in Japan and therefore must be things left by the enemies. Since there is no reason why ampoules should be lying around in the bottom of a well, we can judge from solid ground that it was a strategic act of the enemy army upon their retreat" ("Teki no saikinsen bakuro—Wagagun tsuini kakushō o nigiru," Gaimushō Gaikōshiryōkan).

The Dōjinkai doctors were often described with labels that were rather contradictory: "*Compassionate* treatment provided to the Chinese people—the *warriors in white* from Dōjinkai" ("Shina minshū ni jōnoshinryō," Gaimushō Gaikōshiryōkan; my emphasis). Another news article described Dōjinkai's medical activities in China as "a fight against the bandits' counterattack" ("Hizoku no gyakushū to tatakau, ijutsu no senbuhan, mezamashii Dōjinkai no katsuyaku," Gaimushō Gaikōshiryōkan). While these reports acknowledged that Dōjinkai doctors were part of the war, it was the war against the brutality of the Chinese government, which used biological weapons on its own people, not an imperialist act committed by an aggressive Japanese government.

In short, Japanese public media attempted to connect these two faces of the Dōjinkai doctors—as simultaneously belligerent warriors and benevolent philanthropists. Like the doctors in Nazi Germany and Unit 731, the Japanese newspapers adopted a strategy of collective doubling. To justify the means by the end, the Japanese media excused and even praised Dōjinkai doctors' involvement in the war on the grounds of fabricated noble purposes of the war, and the fictional description of Japan as the true heir to the ancient wisdom of Chinese saints.[13] The unification of these two roles—the soldiers of the "sacred war" and the agents of "universal benevolence"—represented the operation of the "doubling" strategy at a collective level. But unlike the doctors in Nazi Germany and Unit 731, the Dōjinkai doctors

13. Alternatively, and unlike the cases of the Nazi or Unit 731 doctors, the media sometimes did just the opposite, isolating Dōjinkai's medical activities in China from their imperialist purposes and focusing on their immediate actions, which appeared to be merely innocent, virtuous, medical activities. These two (somewhat contradictory) strategies worked together in constructing a positive meaning for the two faces of Dōjinkai doctors.

In one example, medicine was deliberately construed as an apolitical and purely professional service. An internal document produced by the Hankou Dōjin Hospital recorded that Chiang Kai-shek stopped by the hospital to visit a Chinese general who was receiving treatment there. Although the specific date of the document was not preserved, judging from the context it was probably prepared in the late 1920s. The author, apparently one of the medical personnel at the hospital, noted that Chiang, an important leader in the Chinese Army (who was to become a major opponent of the Japanese Army in the future), visited the hospital for purely medical reasons. Indeed, it was recorded that Chiang's conversation with the Japanese doctor who prepared this document concentrated solely on the medical record of the patient whom he was visiting, the history of the Hankou Dōjin Hospital, and other medical issues. In conclusion, the author reemphasized the nonpolitical aspect of medicine: "Although we don't know how General Chiang's attitude will change in the future, the natural feelings developed from human interactions can be said to transcend national boundaries anytime anywhere" ("Hankou chihō no jikyoku jōhō," Gaimushō Gaikōshiryōkan).

needed to persuade not only themselves but also their Chinese patients. As the next section illustrates, this goal demanded careful and conscious efforts and calculations on the part of the Japanese medical doctors and authorities.

A CAREFULLY DESIGNED ACT

In this section, I focus on Dōjinkai's internal reflections about how to proceed with its medical activities. Dōjinkai doctors carefully considered the rhetoric and techniques necessary to manipulate the relationship between science and the nation. At times, doctors wanted to emphasize that they represented Japan; at other times, they needed to argue that science and medicine had no nationality.

The self-reflections of the Dōjinkai doctors who participated in these medical missions often indicate that they were most concerned about how much their medical services changed Chinese people's attitudes toward Japanese and alleviated anti-Japanese feelings. In some cases, effective medical service was what it took to sway local residents' opinions. For example, in a 1938 Dōjinkai speech, Dr. Sotoda gave a self-evaluation of their work and concluded that they "served to give [the Chinese patients] a new impression of us Japanese as well as to induce their trust in Japanese medicine to a certain extent" ("Shijiazhuang, Zhengding, oyobi Jinan ni okeru shinryō taiken," Gaimushō Gaikōshiryōkan). To illustrate his point, Dr. Sotoda recounted a story that he considered very significant for "Sino-Japanese friendship and cooperation." According to the doctor, a Chinese gentleman visited their medical team shortly after their arrival in Jinan. With tears, this Chinese gentleman told them that a Chinese friend of his was treated at Jinan Dōjin Hospital in the past. As the war broke out, the Dōjin Hospital closed down, and his friend was transferred to a local Chinese hospital and unfortunately passed away. Before he died, according to the Chinese narrator of the story, the patient kept calling the names of his Japanese doctors at the Dōjin Hospital, earnestly desiring their help to save his life. Although the patient eventually passed away, he was said to have been very touched with the warm treatment he received at the Japanese hospital and felt that he got to know Japan better. Although this Chinese patient was originally an American-educated, anti-Japanese government official, as a result of his medical experience he developed pro-Japanese attitudes. Dr. Sotoda used this story as a real example that characterized their mission, concluding that "they ought to work hard to fulfill their wishes for Sino-Japanese friendship and cooperation in this manner" ("Shijiazhuang, Zhengding, oyobi Jinan ni okeru shinryō taiken," Gaimushō Gaikōshiryōkan). The key to successful co-optation, in this story, was for Chinese patients to recognize the benefits of cosmopolitan medicine brought to them by *Japanese* doctors. In these incidences, doctors indeed regarded the "nationality" of their medicine as a crucial component of their work in China.

Other "success stories" supported and substantiated this point. Many examples were contained in a collection of Dōjinkai doctors' self-reflections compiled by the Jinan Dōjinkai medical team. During their five-day visit to Qufu in Shandong Province, the medical team cured a very ill three-year-old boy. On the fifth day, the boy's father brought several other patients to the temporary clinic and "got down on his knees to thank the doctors and to ask them in tears to prolong their stay" ("Dōjinkai Jinan iin junkai shinryō hōkoku," Gaimushō Gaikōshiryōkan). Again, the doctor who recorded the story concluded that effective medical service helped make the Japanese welcome in a Chinese village.

Alternatively, medical teams also recognized the need to garner support from local Chinese *before* they had a chance to deliver their medical service, in which case they emphasized the "borderless-ness" instead of the "Japaneseness" of their medicine. The medical team visiting Qufu (the same one that cured the three-year-old) discussed this aspect of their co-optive efforts. Qufu, the hometown of Confucius, was said to be a place permeated with traditionalist culture. By the time the medical team arrived, there was not a single cosmopolitan physician in residence, nor were railroads approved to come near town. Despite the potentially adverse environment, the medical mission was said to be relatively successful, due largely to the help of a Mr. Gong. Mr. Gong graduated from a vocational college in Japan some thirty years before and therefore "understood things Japanese." He welcomed the visit of the medical team and helped them select the location of their temporary clinic and distribute their fliers. Mr. Gong's help was seen as crucial for the medical team to successfully attract local patients. If not for Mr. Gong, the medical team "could have ended up like the German missionary doctors that visited here about ten years ago," who apparently failed to see even one patient during their visit ("Dōjinkai Jinan iin junkai shinryō hōkoku," Gaimushō Gaikōshiryōkan). The Japanese medical team did better—they managed to attract 164 patients in their five-day visit. Although this number was not particularly impressive in comparison to some of the other medical teams' statistics, it was not bad for this town.

Interestingly, Mr. Gong advocated in favor of the activities of the Japanese by emphasizing that there was nothing particularly Japanese in what they were doing. In explaining his motivation for helping the medical team, Mr. Gong stated, "I am not pro-Japanese in particular. However, I would like to assist—across national boundaries—in the things that should be done" ("Dōjinkai Jinan iin junkai shinryō hōkoku," Gaimushō Gaikō-shiryōkan). The narrator of the story, a Japanese doctor on the medical team, elaborated on this theme of "borderless medicine" and added his own thoughts. "I, too, didn't start out with thinking too much about the issues of pro-Japanese versus anti-Japanese attitudes, or the distinctions between Japanese and Chinese. Rather, I think of myself as nothing more than an ordinary doctor. I believe in the value of performing a doctor's duties simply as a doctor" (ibid.). By constructing their activities as a borderless, life-saving mission, the medical teams sought to enlist the help of sympathetic Chinese political and social elites and to eschew awkward political implications. Thus, the Japanese doctors' success depended on their ability to convincingly present an image of "borderless medicine" *and then* emphasize the nationality they represented.[14]

In short, depending on the context they faced, the medical teams needed to be able to swiftly mobilize two narratives: one that emphasized their nationality and the other that erased it. Taken together, these stories illustrate one interesting central ambiguity in the relationship between medicine and nationality that was articulated by this imperialist project. Dōjinkai doctors' "success stories" testified to their capacity for exploiting and manipulating this ambiguity.

In addition to these "success stories," the medical teams also reflected upon their failures and improvement plans. In one of the Dōjinkai reports delivered in Japan in 1938, Dr. Okazaki explored the cultural reasons for the failure of their medical team, which he listed as language barriers, local superstitions, and Chinese people's lack of medical knowledge. Reflecting upon his experiences in Nanjing, Doctor Okazaki reported that the "Japanese-style Chinese" of their team members hindered communication, and local Chinese people's inadequate medical knowledge deepened their mistrust of the medical team. Local customs constituted another barrier. For example, according to Dr. Okazaki, because Chinese people believed in reincarnation, they protested against the incineration of the victims who had

---

14. There were other stories about local Chinese elite helping the medical teams. For example, a medical team dispatched to a small county called Qihe, also by the Jinan Dōjin Hospital, reported a relative success with their three-day visit there. They were greeted warmly by the Chinese officials, including the head of the county. The medical team concluded that "the unexpected success in Qihe was largely due to the understanding and supportive attitudes of the local officials and residents" ("Dōjinkai Jinan iin junkai shinryō hōkoku," Gaimushō Gaikōshiryōkan).

died from epidemics, which slowed down the team's immunization efforts ("Nanjing ni okeru shinryō taiken narabi shinajin no tokushu shippei ni tsuite," Gaimushō Gaikōshiryōkan).

Other accounts discussed political and economic reasons for the failure of medical teams. In the pamphlet compiled by the Jinan Dōjinkai medical team, many participating doctors offered careful reflections upon their activities after the completion of each round of the medical tours. After the first medical tour in 1937, the medical team commented on the factors that influenced the result of their mission. In addition to the selection of locations and the presentation of fliers (e.g., the fliers with pictures worked better than those with drawings), the attitudes of the local authorities were a decisive factor. "Since we are working in the inner lands where the cultural level is low, perhaps most local people do not care that much about the political climate. In this context, the leaders in the local authority have a great say in deciding the situations. Thus, we must look at our medical tours from a radically different perspective than how we normally think about medical practice in *naichi* [at home]" ("Dōjinkai Jinan iin junkai shinryō hōkoku," Gaimushō Gaikōshiryōkan).

The author continued to provide examples of how "local authorities" affected the activities of the medical team. For instance, when the Japanese Consulate in Jinan contacted the head of the Shandong Province about the medical teams, they received an outright rejection. Likewise, some representatives of local authority blatantly refused to meet with members of the medical team. In other instances, the Chinese authorities explained to the local residents that the medical teams were really drug dealers in disguise (ibid.). Economic factors were another consideration. In poor areas, even after the teams reduced medical fees, they still could not attract enough patients. The medical team's strategy for addressing this issue (i.e., offering medical coupons to low-income residents) did not work. The medical team reportedly relied on local authorities to distribute these coupons to the poor, yet the Chinese officials ended up distributing them among themselves, their friends, and their families ("Dōjinkai Jinan iin junkai shinryō hōkoku," Gaimushō Gaikōshiryōkan).

Later that year, after one medical team completed its second tour, the participating doctors reconsidered their strategies carefully. The team listed eight items to be considered in the future:

1. It would be more efficient to start [our work] in places closer to Jinan—where residents might have been familiar with our hospital—and then gradually expand to more remote places.

2. It is necessary to re-visit three or four times the places where our medical team had visited before.
3. Our fliers need to be more accessible to local people, preferably with illustrations.
4. We need to work harder to widely distribute our fliers inside and around the towns we are visiting.
5. Our activities will not yield much result in the villages unless they are free of charge.
6. For the location of our temporary clinic, it's better to use hotels rather than official buildings.
7. The distribution of fliers and other types of advertisement should be done at least once every ten days.
8. The touring clinic should plan a 7–10 day visit [at each location]. Otherwise, doctors [of the touring clinics] will not be able to provide sufficient treatment [to the local residents]. Remote villages which are beyond the reach of our advertisement efforts will require 10–20 day stays. ("Dōjinkai Jinan iin junkai shinryō hōkoku," Gaimushō Gaikōshiryōkan)

Generally speaking, the main concerns remained location, propaganda, and economic considerations. Local Chinese authorities also continued to be a challenge, but this time, the medical team seemed to decide to distance themselves, choosing local hotels over official buildings to house their temporary clinic.

In sum, the medical teams considered a wide range of factors in their self-analyses. They discussed technical issues (i.e., flier preparation and distribution), cultural barriers (i.e., language problems and local customs), economic factors (i.e., medical fees), as well as political considerations (i.e., Chinese officials' attitudes). If the "success stories" illustrated the importance of the discursive manipulation of the relationship between medicine and the nation, these "failure stories" further revealed an array of material conditions that demanded meticulous consideration if the discursive manipulation of these doctors was to be effective.

GOVERNMENTALITY AND NATIONALITY: MODERN MEDICINE IN IMPERIALISM

This chapter has provided a survey of the Dōjin Hospitals and medical teams in China. My analysis demonstrates that Dōjinkai's initial plans included many projects that were similar to the ones that had been carried out in Taiwan (e.g., dispatching doctors, building hospitals, training native medical practitioners), but for various reasons, Japan's colonial medicine did not take root in China. The Dōjinkai was more successful in providing medical treatment than in delivering training. In its involvement in Japan's wartime mobilization, Dōjinkai's medical projects exposed one central ambiguity in the relationship between nationality and modernity. In contrast to the wartime Taiwanese doctors who struggled with comparable ambiguities as part of their quest for a coherent identity, the Japanese doctors on the Dōjinkai medical teams coldly dissected this ambiguity and manipulated it masterfully.

In a sense, this ambiguous relationship between nationality and modernity was a function of the peculiar relationship between China and Japan. My analysis concurs with Duus's argument that, in their attempt to monopolize control over China in the context of the informal empire, the Japanese had to insist on their mastery of modern sciences as well as a shared past with the Chinese.[15] But the story of the Dōjin Hospitals further accentuates a third claim made by the Japanese, that is, that they were the contemporary, authentic inheritors of the great Chinese tradition of "universal benevolence." In other words, the formula of Japanese colonialism did not exactly prescribe a linear progression from an Asian tradition to Western modernity; rather, it challenged this great divide with an attempt to appropriate China's past for contemporary use. Japanese colonial discourses intended to position the empire as the embodiment of "Asian modernity," switching between presenting itself as the agent of a universalistic modernity and the "big brother" with particularistic ties. It is partially because of this peculiar position that the connection between medicine and nationality became so ambiguous and perpetually slippery in the Japanese medical projects in China.

These ambiguous relationships also reflect the complex roles of colonial medicine in Japanese imperialism. While medicine in Taiwan was developed as an integral part of Japan's scientific colonialism, which focused on gradual, "natural," and thorough transformation of the colony, it served a rather different function in China. Japanese medical activities in China improved

15. The Japanese colonizers often positioned themselves as the Asian pioneers in exploring Western civilization. "Although there are numerous countries in East Asia, the only nation that managed to appropriate Western civilization to enhance the welfare of its people is Japan" ("Gotō minsei chōkan yenzetsu hikki," Kokkai Toshokan). Gotō, among others, took great pride in the speed at which Japan was catching up with Western countries. "It's only been 30 years since we initiated the Meiji Restoration, and yet our nation, as it stands now, is highly competitive. Our achievements in medicine are no less outstanding than other countries', except perhaps for the one nation Germany" (ibid.).

health conditions in areas under Japan's occupation and influence and to some extent served as useful propaganda for Japanese imperialism. But these endeavors left little impact on the institutional practice and professional culture of medicine and failed to cultivate any significant body of native agents for the empire. Though designed as a tool of colonialism in both cases, in Taiwan colonial medicine developed along a course which gradually embedded it in local communities, whereas in China similar professional enterprises evolved as an extension of the imperial state.

At a more general level, this discussion completes the attempt in this book to examine the intersection of professionalization with imperialism. As pointed out in earlier chapters, because the groundwork for the sociology of professions was laid by Western European and North American scholars, the social embeddedness of professions in imperialism has gone largely unexamined. This book attempts to provide better historical and theoretical understandings of the different patterns in the relationships between the profession and race / ethnicity. In this vein, while the discussions in chapters 3, 4, and 5 focused on the mutual embeddedness of ethnicity and the profession, the analysis of Dōjinkai's medical activities in China engages recent scholarly efforts to reexamine the ties between the modern expansionist state and professional expertise.

Recently, a burgeoning literature has offered a critical reevaluation of the assumption of professional autonomy, most eminently formulated by Freidson.[16] For example, Terry Johnson (1995) fundamentally questions the assumption of professions' autonomy of expertise within Europe. Adopting a Foucaldian concept of "governmentality,"[17] Johnson sees the professionalization of expertise as part and parcel of the process of governing. The crys-

16. In his rather sophisticated model, Freidson (1994) considers the question of whether a profession can be truly autonomous when it must submit to the protective custody of the state. His answer: professions submit to the state when it comes to social and economic aspects, but they control the technological aspect of their work. For Freidson, the autonomy of technique is what defines a profession as well as its relationship with the state.

17. Johnson offers a concise recapitulation of Foucault's concept of governmentality:

> Governmentality is a novel capacity for governing that gradually emerged in Europe from the sixteenth century onwards in association with the invention, operationalization, and institutionalization of specific knowledge, disciplines, tactics, and technologies. The period from the sixteenth until the eighteenth century was . . . notable for the appearance throughout Europe of a series of treatises on government: on the government of the soul and the self; on the government of children within the family; on the government of the state (Foucault 1979: 5–9). This rethinking of the various forms of governance was associated both with the early formation of the great territorial, ad-

tallization of expertise and the growth of professional associations in nine-teenth-century Europe, argues Johnson, were directly linked to the rise of the modern state and its new techniques of ruling, which included "the clas-sification and surveillance of populations, the normalization of the subject-citizen, and the discipline of the aberrant subject. The establishment of the jurisdictions of professions like medicine, psychiatry, law, and accountancy, were all . . . products of government programmes and policies" (Johnson 1995, p. 11). From this perspective, the autonomy of expertise is only granted to the professions insofar as it works as a convenient and useful technique of state rule. The interests of the state, ironically and perhaps counter-intuitively, are best served by granting technical autonomy to pro-fessions rather than withholding it from them. Johnson thus makes a sweeping critique of the professions literature: "We cannot understand what is happening to the professions today if we frame our questions around the issues of autonomy and intervention. . . . *Freidson's view that the distinctive feature of a profession, autonomy in controlling its own technical work, is always contingent*" (1995, p. 21; my emphasis).

While Johnson's critique of the professional autonomy assumption is welcome, much empirical work remains to be done to understand the dif-ferent patterns of interaction between the state and professions in varying contexts, especially outside of Europe and North America. Some researchers have begun to move in this direction by studying this issue in colonial soci-eties, which represent one context where the central role of the state in shaping professional activities and developmental trajectories cannot be ignored. For example, Manderson's (1996) study of health policies in colo-nial Malaya explores the linkage between health conditions, ideological legitimization, and social order. As Johnson found in his analysis of profes-sional expertise in Europe, Manderson finds that colonial medicine enabled British colonial officials to improve the material conditions in the colony, to solidify the ideological legitimacy of the colonial rule, and more important, to create—and impose—order on this new space. Colonial health programs

---

ministrative states and colonial empires, and with the disruptions of spiritual rule asso-ciated with the reformation and the counter-reformation." (Johnson 1995, p. 8)

This process signals a radical break with the Machiavellian assumption that the power of the prince was best deployed in securing sovereignty. Rather the new assumption holds that

Governing was no more than the "right disposition of things" leading to the "common welfare and salvation for all." This novel discourse which began to conceive of popular obedience to the law as the sole source of legitimate rule . . . also made it possible to identify . . . the means of governing, those tactics and knowledges developed in order to regulate territories and population." (ibid., p. 8)

were aimed specifically at influencing individuals and their social environments in order to transform them into clean and useful entities for the colonizers. In justifying these health and social welfare programs and expenditures to the government in London, the Colonial Office situated these activities in terms of the legitimacy of the polity, and thereby revealed their political calculation about colonial medicine. More broadly speaking, colonial medicine was also a tool for "knowing" about the unknown territories: "The obsession of colonial officials to categorize was reflected in their efforts to establish order where there was, if not chaos, *terrain vague;* the imposition of order onto colonial space was part of the exercise to know, claim, and control" (Manderson 1996, p. 235).[18]

In many ways, the Dōjin Hospitals can be considered another interesting case that illustrates the complicated and inadequately studied dynamics between medicine and the state in a colonial context.[19] More important, this case raises a new question about the issue of nationality with regard to discussions of professions and governmentality. Like Manderson's British doc-

---

18. Manderson explains how medical knowledge about the colony facilitates the establishment of social order: "At the micro level this occurred, I suggest, with the incorporation of nature into culture through inscription, categorization, cataloguing, and labeling, a task that drove laboratory scientists employed at the Institution of Medical Research, for example, into their efforts to 'know' about tropical diseases. At the macro level, it was the role of the state to replace anarchy with government, shape plantations and farms from primeval jungle, and, through educational, judicial, and medical systems, establish institutional and ideological order" (1996, p. 236).

19. There are, of course, some studies on the relationship between the state and the professions that do not proceed from a "governmentality" approach. For example, Elliott Krause's (1991) earlier work is situated in the former Eastern bloc. He notes that "until recently, . . . we have not often brought the state back in' to the analysis of professions," and he picks up this task by studying Eastern Europe, where "it is impossible to ignore the central role of the state in professional group activity" (p. 3). In this vein, Krause proposes a few other analytic dimensions: the state itself (including state structure, power, efficiency, and legitimacy); the strength of an intelligentsia tradition in the nation; and relatedly, the social role of the university in professional training. Krause's systematic analysis of the situation in Eastern Europe yields a useful and more context-sensitive schema for understanding relations between the state and professions. This framework allows us to explore questions such as how the state, in most authoritarian regimes, seeks to manufacture the loyalty of professional groups and how professional groups may or may not seek to counteract state control.

Along similar lines, Hoffman (1997) critically reconsidered Freidson's theorization of professional autonomy. Having carefully examined the case of Czech medicine under state socialism and revealed how the medical profession constantly struggled with the state, she proposes that to take technical (or "clinical," to use her word) autonomy as a given is only appropriate for analyzing professions in more pluralist societies.

tors in Malaya, the Dōjinkai doctors served and represented an imperial state that claimed to be the disseminating agent of modernity. But they were perhaps unique in that these diligent students of comparative colonialism faced competition from their masters and had to deal with the fact that they were not the only, or even the most powerful, representatives of modernity. Whereas the studies of Foucault, Johnson, and Manderson all suggest that the profession serves the function of naturalizing and legitimizing state control in the name of modernity, these studies commonly assume the presence of a singular state. The history of Japan's colonial medicine in China reminds us that, on the stage of global competition, a state that extends its influence in a foreign land seeks to naturalize and legitimize not so much the state writ large, but the *nationality* of that particular state. As a profession is mobilized by the state to engage in such international competition and, accordingly, to provide service in a foreign country, it is compelled to carefully package the piece of modernity that it promises to deliver. In such contexts, the profession is charged with the task of articulating the connections between the service it offers and the nation it represents. In this increasingly globalized era, we need to be mindful of the ties between professions and the state, and, more important, of the connections between professions and the nation. Indeed, the ties between professions and the nation make up a central part of a community's endeavor to "claim" modernity; this understanding fundamentally challenges any universalistic implications of modernity.

7 Professional Identities, Colonial Ambiguities, and Agents of Modernity

After the Japanese defeat at the end of World War II, Taiwanese doctors continued to face changing structural forces and articulate new identities. This chapter, however, brings temporary closure to their ongoing story, and considers the three moments of their colonial experience. In the following pages, I review the changing identities and structural positions of Taiwanese physicians and speculate on the theoretical implications of the history of this group.

Informed by the analytical framework developed in chapter 1, I traced how Taiwanese doctors were collectively situated in their surrounding "relational configuration" by highlighting the intersections of the material, cultural, and organizational dimensions of the Taiwanese medical and ethnic communities. This broadly conceived relational configuration was further situated against the background of the colonial state and the Taiwanese civil society. With this analytical framework, I charted the structural transformation of this relational configuration and reconstructed the narrative articulations of doctors' collective identity during three time periods. In the 1920s (see chapter 3), as doctors began to enjoy a certain degree of organizational autonomy, they became relatively insulated from state regulation in both their professional practice and political attitudes. Their professional culture further inspired significant critiques of the extensive, institutionalized ethnic inequalities in the colony. At the same time, this professional culture also promoted a critical attitude toward many traditional cultural practices in their ethnic community, and their market position distanced them from their Taiwanese co-ethnics. A relatively liberal civil society mobilized the progressive aspects of the profession and encouraged its participation in anticolonial movements. In this context, doctors developed an identity narrative as "national physicians," which defined the central role of the profession in terms of its service to the nation.

Chapter 4 addresses the changes in the doctors' identity narrative and their surrounding relational configuration during the years between the Manchuria Incident in 1931 and the outbreak of the second Sino-Japanese War in 1937. In this period, the tightened grip of the state threatened to destroy the nascent Taiwanese civil society that had developed during the previous decade. This fiercely regulatory state also encroached upon the relative autonomy of the profession, dictating its goals and directions. These intensified state-profession ties cultivated an expanding professional market, which in turn further integrated the Taiwanese medical community into the imperial medical system. The expanding professional market, along with other new economic trends in the colony, consolidated the class differences between doctors and their co-ethnics. The cultural connections between their professional and ethnic communities were further attenuated. In short, the medical community developed stronger ties with the colonial state in place of many of its old connections with the Taiwanese ethnic community. Under these circumstances, the profession gradually lost the legacy that identified its members as "national physicians"; it failed to register a collective identity narrative during this time.

During the Kōminka Era (1937–1945), Taiwanese doctors were placed in a relational configuration of total state control; the organizational, material, and cultural dimensions of their ethnicity and profession were subject to intensive state regulation. Meanwhile, the profession's elevated market position and its weakened cultural connections to the ethnic community remained little changed. Bracketing these structural conditions in the wartime colony, and through the cultural repertoire of their profession, Taiwanese doctors developed an identity narrative as "medical modernists." In this narrative, doctors defined themselves as "modern" and read modernity as non-ethnic, signaling one of the most profound moments of confusion over ethnic relations in an empire constructed by the "anticolonial colonizers." The experiences of the "medical modernists" provide a telling case that illustrates the role of the profession as an important institutional site for the transformation of ethnic relations and identities.

With the more complex historical details and meanings of this process bracketed temporarily, we can identify four general changes in the profession's relational configuration: the ethnicity-profession ties declined; the state-profession connections intensified; the state-ethnicity ties grew; and state domination over civil society prevailed (see charts 5–7). These four structural changes explain the shifting "positionality" of these ethnic professionals. To recast the analysis in more specific terms, professional autonomy appears as the key factor that encourages the social mobiliza-

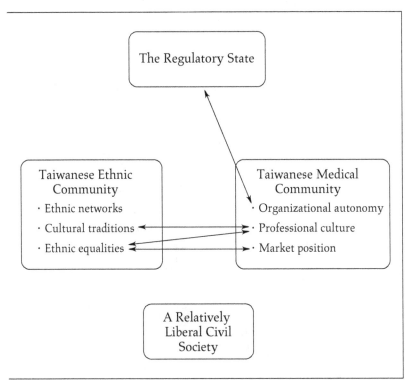

Chart 5. Doctors' In-between Position—National Physicians, 1920–1931

tion of the profession, whereas market position is the main factor that pulls it back. Professional culture as a source of imagination can be drawn upon either to establish or deny the connection between professional and ethnic communities. The larger context of the state/society relationship is important in shaping the expression of the ambiguous political potential of the profession; the profession participated actively in a liberal civil society and withdrew rapidly from such participation as state regulation increased.

While changing structural conditions may explain doctors' mobilization, demobilization, and assimilation, they do not dictate the specificity of doctors' collective identities. Doctors developed the narratives of national physicians or medical modernists as they lived through particular historical junctures and drew upon these experiences to imagine and articulate their identities. The formation of these identity narratives was not determined by

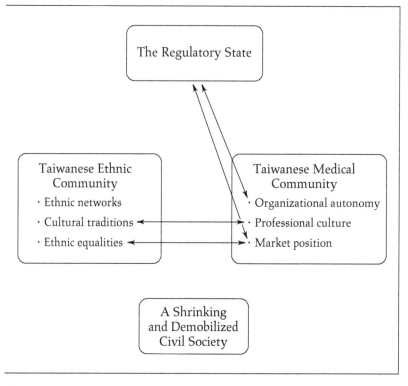

Chart 6. Doctors' In-between Position—Years of Public Demobilization, 1931–1936

any general logic within the relational configuration. Structural conditions do not necessarily generate particular identities.

A RACIALIZED HISTORICAL SOCIOLOGY OF PROFESSIONS

The study of Taiwanese doctors expands our sociological imagination about the social roles of professions. The theorization of these doctors' positionalities, which took shape in the intersected histories of professionalization and colonization, makes essential the need for a historical sociology of professions that can adequately account for their structural locations and identity narratives. In part, the analysis in the preceding pages has established a perspective from which the profession is conceptualized as a category in constant interaction not only with the market and the

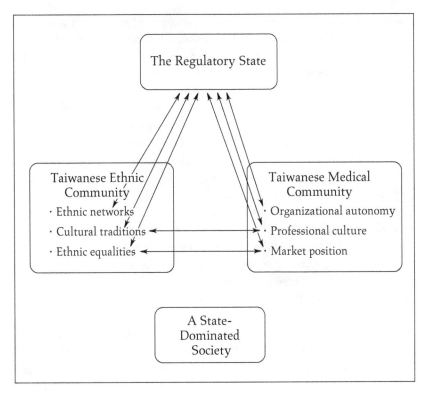

Chart 7. Doctors' In-between Position—Medical Modernists, 1937–1945

state, as we traditionally see it, but also with other social categories, such as race, ethnicity, or gender. In this sense, my study endorses and expands Abbott's idea that professionalization occurs "in a context that helps determine its course" (1988, p. 23). While Abbott argues for the importance of interprofessional relationships in shaping the course of professionalization, I have broadened his focus on group-level relationships to include the interactions between professions, ethnicity, and, by analogy, race and gender.

But what does it mean to argue that the profession is structured by ethnicity, race, or gender? On the surface, the answer can be easily found in the numerous and familiar accounts of unfair job opportunities and wage differences. At a deeper level, the inequalities in opportunities and rewards manifest a "deep structure" that takes shape through the process of the social formation of the profession. This "deep structure," alternatively described as an "institutional thought structure,"[1] provides the framework through which the profession produces collective narratives about what it is, how it operates, what it attempts to accomplish, or, in a nutshell, how the profession defines its identity. What I wish to emphasize is that, due to the interactive processes through which the "deep structure" of the profession is formed and transformed, the collective identity of the profession is gendered and racialized, yet is often unrecognized as such. So race, ethnicity, and gender are not informal mechanisms of exclusion (Freidson 1986), but internalized components of a profession's identity. In this vein, we face not only the issue of how to increase the number of Taiwanese doctors, black lawyers, or gay managers at a given place and time, but also the more fundamental question of how the "deep structure" of the profession was formed and may be changed. Herein lies a genuine need to understand the formation and operation of the "default" race, ethnicity, and gender of a profession and to recognize its importance not just for minority professionals but for the entire profession (and sociologists of professions). In other words, sociologists will have to more consciously racialize and gender agents of professionalization.

From the relational perspective adopted and advanced in this book, discussions of the identity formation of the profession necessarily raise questions about its relationship with the identity narratives produced through other social institutions. The minority professionals whose ethnicity, race, or gender differs from the dominant ones in their profession are compelled to reconcile, integrate, and make choices about these competing sources of identity. For these "in-between" professionals, the profession becomes an insti-

---

1. The concept of institutional thought structure was born at the interface between the sociology of knowledge and institutionalism. "An institutionalized thought structure is a highly speculative concept, an entity that cannot be proved to exist, cannot be described in its totality, and cannot, of course, be measured. But it is important, not least because the actors in the field frequently evoke it, directly or indirectly. It is a set of basic assumptions or norms that are taken to be axiomatic; that is, it is assumed that they exist, that they are shared by the majority in the field, and their presence is evoked whenever an action is questioned (literally, as in a press interview, or metaphorically, as when they are infringed)" (Czarniawska-Joerges 1997, p. 67).
Other scholars have used a similar concept, institutional logic, to discuss this topic. "Each of the most important institutional orders of contemporary Western societies has a central logic—a set of material practices and symbolic constructions—which constitutes its organizing principles and which is available to organizations and individuals to elaborate. . . . These institutional logics are symbolically grounded, organizationally structured, politically defended, and technically and materially constrained, and hence have specific historical limits" (Friedland and Alford 1993, pp. 248–49).

tutional site of identity contestation which shapes their ethnic (or racial and gender) consciousness. The identity of Taiwanese doctors formed in interaction with their profession's "default" identity as servants of Japanese colonialism. Though this is a specific historical case with limited generalizability, it contributes to the establishment of the in-betweenness of minority professionals as a universally important question for the sociology of professions. I have, in other words, used a particular case to raise a general question.

My focus in this book rests on the collective level, leaving the issue of individual choices and struggles for other discussion forums. Informed by studies that have recognized and confronted the default ethnicity, race, or gender in the profession as structural problems (e.g., Kanter 1977; Woods 1993), I wish to advance the argument for the need to formulate, facilitate, and better understand *collective* struggles against these problems.[2] Although the structural problems that ensue from a profession's "default" ethnicity, race, or gender identity are most often experienced as profoundly and painfully personal issues, and should be understood as such, it is crucial that these problems are also studied in the context of *collective* identity struggles. A structural problem calls for a collective solution. Thus, the organizations and submerged networks formed by groups of minority professionals can become important sites for collective and creative articulations of mean-

2. It has been recognized by various sociologists of professions and scholars of race/ethnicity and gender that there exists a strong structure of assimilation in the professional world, even though they might differ on their explanations for the nature of this structure. Larson (1977) explains how evolving notions of professionalism have established a dichotomy between the professional and particular identities, firmly subscribing to the idea that "properly trained and socialized workers could (and should) transcend their particular differences when working together" (Woods 1993, p. 242). The image of a nonsexual, nonracial, and non-ethnic professional, however, is maintained not by truly resolving or respecting these differences in the professional world but by suppressing them. In her now classic book *Men and Women of the Corporation* (1977), Kanter pays special attention to how and why women tend to be marginalized in the corporation. Using a powerful concept "homosocial reproduction," Kanter explains how managers attempt to increase mutual trust in the workplace by homogenizing its personnel, resulting oftentimes in decisions to hire and promote their social peers who share their cultural backgrounds, assumptions, and communication styles. Similarly, focusing on the experiences of gay professionals in America, Woods (1993) explores what the image of the "asexual professional" involves and how it in effect naturalizes heterosexuality in the workplace. Illustrating a similar pattern, Sheppard's (1989) and Gutek's (1989) work also discusses how professional women are encouraged to "desexualize" their dress, speech, and demeanor. In a less theoretical language, Graham (1995) discusses how black managers develop different individual strategies to sidestep the issue of their "blackness" in corporate America. His discussion also ultimately exposes the inadequacy of individual solutions to a structural problem.

ingful new identities (of which the Taiwanese doctors discussed in this book offer a good example). These identity narratives integrate, often with difficulties and ambiguities, the "deep structure" of their profession with the experiences and voices that are marginalized by it. In short, I argue for the need to study the process through which the "deep structure" of the profession not only produces unequal opportunities but, more important, imposes a particular identity on those who do manage to obtain the opportunities normally unavailable to their group. Furthermore, I view it as an urgent issue, both academically and practically, that we produce more and better research about how these minority professionals struggle with multiple and often conflicting identity narratives at an organizational level.

This focus on the "default" professional identity and struggles against it partially answers Zald and McCarthy's (1994) call for greater scholarly effort to specify the conditions under which organizational intellectuals become politicized. The puzzle, as Zald and McCarthy put it, "is how institutionally employed intellectuals can criticize social arrangements" (p. 97). With the qualification that professional cultures are formed in specific professions at specific locations, Zald and McCarthy propose to view professional culture as the main source of professionals' critical thinking. For example, "In some societies medical doctors may be an elite cultural group deeply involved in politics and general cultural affairs (as in Latin America), while in other societies doctors may be technocrats relatively neutral to political life" (1994, p. 111). More specifically, Zald and McCarthy maintain that professions differ in their assumptions about the relation of means to ends, and therefore in their prescriptions for change. "Lawyers are trained to see the world differently from economists. And a lawyer and an economist equally committed to ameliorating poverty will be very different in the tactics they choose, the programs they see as having payoff, and the skills that they bring to any program" (ibid.).

The study of Taiwanese doctors advances Zald and McCarthy's conclusions. At one level, this book supports and substantiates Zald and McCarthy's observation that professionals are likely to subscribe to different "formulas" for social change. For example, while all intellectuals in Taiwan were exposed to the dominant narrative of modernism in the colonial period, the doctors' modernist ideology was specifically grounded in the institution of colonial medicine and produced distinct "social diagnoses." Furthermore, tracing the formation of these "social diagnoses" suggests that they are not only informed by professional culture but also mediated by professionals' collective identity narratives produced at specific times and places. In other words, professionals can draw upon their professional culture in numerous ways to formulate discourses on broader, nonprofessional issues. How they do it is shaped by their collective self-identities. The contrast between national physicians and medical modernists illustrates this point. In the 1920s, Taiwanese doctors devoted themselves to "curing" the social ills in their ethnic community through modernization efforts. But in wartime, though still immersed in a modernist professional culture, they embraced the universalistic promise of modernity and thereby suppressed the particularities of ethnicity. In both periods, the "formulas" for social change developed from the same professional culture, but they evolved along different lines of identity narratives and eventually emerged as contrasting perspectives. Thus, this book emphasizes that the formation of professional identities is crucial in shaping professional "formulas" for social change. How much the situation of (anti)colonial professionals can be generalized to other cases is a question that awaits further research, but this study highlights the general importance of collective identities in sociological studies of professionals.[3]

My emphasis on the collective identities of professionals reinstates professions into the heart of civil society. Max Weber and his Frankfurt successors noted that professionals can be important players in the public sphere but unfortunately tend to withdraw from it (Habermas 1989; Marcuse 1964; Weber 1968). By virtue of their organizational autonomy, professional associations constituted a major sector of Western European public spheres at their originating moments. However, professionals were gradually "split apart into minorities of specialists who put their reason to use nonpublicly" (Habermas 1989, p. 175), and became preoccupied with further enhancing their organizational autonomy and elevating their collective market position. Habermas (1984) described this process as part of the colonization of the lifeworld by the system. This perspective establishes

3. This perspective will also help us better understand earlier studies that document, without explicitly theorizing, the importance of professional identities. For example, in her study of doctors who provided abortion before and after *Roe v. Wade*, Joffe shows that although "the AMA resolution stated that abortion policy should be based on 'sound clinical judgment' and 'the best interest of the patient'" (1995, p. 46), this resolution did not forge one common attitude among doctors. Many doctors in their practice witnessed "the lengths to which women would go" to have abortions (Joffe 1995, chapter 3), but only the "doctors of conscience" politicized their role on this issue (ibid., see especially chapter 4). Although Joffe does not explicitly trace the group identity of these doctors, she identifies conscience as the main theme in their narratives and implies the emergence of a group identity among abortion-sympathetic physicians.

the assumption that professionals can, but often do not, play a significant role in the public sphere.

But this assumption does not hold true in the face of the recognition that within the professional sphere a social space exists that accommodates critical reflections upon competing sources of identity. In particular, the segments of the profession that embed their agents in multiple social networks and cultures can potentially become sites for the mobilization of collective actions or articulation of critical narratives. The size and dynamics of these "in-between" segments will vary according to specific historical context, but the tensions therein between competing sources of identity are likely to sustain an open discourse and thus preserve a "realm of the social." In this fuzzy, flexible space, the parameters of public discourses are more inclined to adapt to the changing concerns of different groups than to dictate their articulations.

This "realm of the social" lays the basis for the vitality of a civil society:

> The public sphere of civil society cannot be simply a realm in which representatives of state authority vie for attention with economists claiming to predict the economy like the weather on the basis of its reified laws. It must include an institutionally organized and substantial capacity for people to enter as citizens into public discourse about the nature and course of their life together. This capacity depends not just on formal institutions, but on civil society as a realm of sociability. (Calhoun 1992, p. 311)

To the extent that segments of the professional world can accommodate such a "realm of sociability" for cultivating the capacity to "enter public discourse," they constitute an important basis for civil society. Within this "realm of sociability," contention over professional identity raises challenges to dominant cultural schema and inspires the formulation of new ones.[4]

---

4. Scuilli (1986) argues that professions are important sites that accommodate voluntaristic actions and resist authoritarian social integration. He proposes an empirical hypothesis: "To the degree any enterprise establishes and maintains the collegial form of organization and thereby honors the integrity of procedural legality, that enterprise inherently restrains arbitrary power and simultaneously establishes a social basis for broader movements of non-authoritarian social integration" (Scuilli 1986, p. 761). My study supports Scuilli's argument for the potential of the professional sphere for non-authoritarian movements, but it suggests a different basis for understanding such potential. Scuilli's emphasis on the procedure and organizations of the professions, I argue, is questionable. Liberal procedure and autonomous organizations per se are not sufficient guarantees for meaningful pluralism, as evident in numerous discussions about the "liberal market" and deliberations on the political controversy surrounding multiculturalism (see Taylor et al. 1994).

With the articulation of this point, I have come full circle to the notion of "relational thinking" which I developed in the beginning of this book. As I explained in chapter 1, we should regard group identities as a changing group narrative in response to certain social situations that is often communicated through public statements, cultural symbols, communal rituals, and so on. Identity narratives, I have argued, are tangibly located at organizational sites, such as submerged networks, social movements, group organizations and so forth. Many of us, however, will find ourselves in the "in-between" categories, confronted with competing identity narratives, and perhaps motivated to organize new organizational bases to articulate a new collective narrative, thereby expanding new "realms of sociability."

JAPANESE COLONIALISM IN TAIWAN: STRUCTURES AND IDENTITIES

Despite varying emphases, most studies of Japanese colonialism are more concerned with the structural forces of colonialism than the individual and group experiences of this history. On the one hand, scholars informed by the modernization thesis focus on the infrastructures and cultural institutions that the Japanese built during their fifty-year rule in Taiwan. It is by now a familiar argument that "the Japanese, for all their faults, promoted economic developments on a considerable scale in Korea and Taiwan" (Gann 1996; see also Gold 1988). On the other hand, taking a postmodern perspective, some scholars turn the modernization thesis on its head and instead question the colonial nature of modernization. For example, drawing on Mitchell's study of British colonialism in Egypt, Cumings reads Japanese colonialism primarily as a history of Japan's internalization of Western modernity and part of the expansion of a Western-centered hegemonic web. "This web has a spider: first England/America, then America/England, then war and defeat, then unilateral America, then (about 1975 down to the present) trilateral America. Japan, South Korea, and Taiwan industrialized mostly within this web" (Cumings 1995, p. 51). The agents of modernity at different phases in history, identified as the "spiders" in this sprawling hegemonic web, are all guilty of absorbing nation after nation into the modern regime of disciplinary power:

> [They put their] citizens through a regimen of public education that seemed perfectly designed to develop the industrious political subject, with the vices of self-surveillance and repression that Mitchell analyzed for British Egypt. . . . And there we see the undeniable legacy (and the irony) of Japanese colonialism: they were colonizers and modernizers. . . .

> Threatened by the modern project in the form of Western imperialism,
> after 1868 the Japanese internalized it, made it their own, and imposed it
> on their neighbors: a highly disciplined, rational, almost Weberian type
> of colonialism, but one that was ultimately irrational because it could not
> last over time without creating its own competitors, and thus its own
> grave. (ibid., pp. 8–9)

Thus, despite their radically different interpretations of "modernity,"
both modernist and postmodernist scholars read Japanese colonialism in
Taiwan as mainly a history of the island's incorporation into the hegemonic
world order of "modernity." Defining the Japanese Empire as a link in a
chain of colonization/modernization, Cumings differs little from his mod-
ernization-minded colleagues in his emphasis on structure over agency.[5]

Among other things they have accomplished, the monumental three-
volume series on Japanese colonialism and imperialism by Duus, Myers, and
Peattie (Myers and Peattie 1984; Duus, Myers, and Peattie 1989, 1996)
takes us significantly beyond this framework. Thanks to this and other
recent scholarly endeavors (e.g., Young 1998; Morris-Suzuki 1998), we have
traveled far in the fruitful direction pointed out by Peattie in his introduction to the first volume of their series:

> For the Japanese in their colonies were not a faceless elite of uniformed
> oppressors, no more than they were all marble exemplars of progress and
> civilization, but were earnest administrators and calculating speculators,
> wealthy landlords and tenant farmers, teachers and ruffians, housewives
> and prostitutes, doctors and adventurers, who collectively embodied
> Japanese visions and prejudices, plans and passions, knowledge and igno-
> rance, altruism and greed. *When contemporary scholarship begins to*
> *populate the Japanese colonial landscape with living, active individuals,*
> *Japanese colonialism will at last begin to take on a humanity, if not a*
> *humaneness, which it does not yet possess.* (1984, p. 52; my emphasis)

Studies of concrete group experiences are more useful than broad, abstract
colonial categories in developing understandings of Japanese colonialism.
Extending Peattie's argument further, we should recognize that the "Japanese
colonial landscape" is also populated by "living, active individuals" gener-

5. With his emphasis on the Japanese Empire as merely a link in the chain of colonization, Cumings sees little reason to treat Japanese colonialism as an anomaly.
He proposes that "with a conception of Foucauldian power and Foucauldian modernity, ... there is no fundamental distinction between second phase (i.e., late-
nineteenth-century) colonialism and the modern industrial project itself, and, thus
no basic distinction between Japanese colonialism, American hegemony, and South
Korean, North Korean, or Taiwanese modernization" (1995, p. 8).

ally referred to as the category of the colonized. The Taiwanese, Koreans, Chinese, Manchurians, and others who lived under different forms of Japanese imperialism also need to be recognized in their roles as peasants, teachers, doctors, merchants, peddlers, prostitutes, and so forth, rather than as a group of faceless colonial subjects, differing only along the continuum from resistance to collaboration. It is through careful analyses of the heterogeneous social and cultural experiences of both the "colonizers" and the "colonized" that we can better comprehend the processes and legacies of Japanese colonialism. This is not simply filling in the gaps; approaching colonial histories from the standpoints of groups among the colonized uncovers meanings of their experiences that are inaccessible in a colonizer-centered framework of thought.

This perspective applies particularly well to discussions of ethnic identities and relations within the empire. Through studies of heterogeneous group experiences rather than formalized colonial categories we can develop a nuanced understanding of this aspect of Japanese colonialism. The Japanese official colonial discourse emphasized the close racial and cultural ties between the colonizers and the colonized while insisting on their hierarchical distinctions. The ambiguity thus generated could not derive its meanings from the logic of the official discourse. "Unlike the European encounter with its racial Others, [the] absence or invisibility of otherness [in Japanese colonialism] posits a moment where a deferral between seeing and knowing, perceiving and conceiving is enacted, an instant where difference would be suspended and displaced if silence was kept" (Ching 1998, p. 65). Rather, the ambiguity in Japanese colonial relations only became meaningful as different groups struggled to make sense of it. In Oguma's words, "For the people who actually lived through such situations, [colonial relations] were not simply an either-or choice. . . . The colonized attempted to express their own standpoint, which was something inexpressible by the 'political vocabulary' of inclusion and exclusion" (1998, p. 13). While recent scholarship has begun to address various Japanese articulations of colonial identities (e.g., Young 1998), we also need more studies of how the colonized struggled with the ambiguous, or the inexpressible, so as to uncover their political and cultural imagination, which reproduced and redefined the parameters of colonial relations.

It would, of course, be unwise to assume that such ambiguities were unique to Japanese colonialism. Rather, empires are to be recognized as full of "overlapping, jostling, discordant 'imagined communities'" (Morris-Suzuki 1998, p. 161) and therefore produced many blurred categories of identity. As Stoler observes, those groups that were positioned between colonial and colonized were, in particular, confronted with a profound identity ambiguity, for they were subject to "a frequently shifting set of criteria that allowed them privilege at certain historical moments and pointedly excluded them at others" (1989, pp. 154–55). But these colonial ambiguities were perhaps more central to the experiences within the Japanese Empire because its official ideology emphasized "Asian brotherhood." Morris-Suzuki expounds the particular salience of this issue in the Japanese Empire:

> First, the nature of the Japanese state, and therefore the circumstances of its creation, produced a vision of citizenship in which the sense of individual autonomy and rights was relatively tenuous and the emphasis on duty (particularly on the duty to defend the nation) relatively strong. Second, . . . Japanese colonization . . . evoked no allusions to "empires on which the sun never sets," but instead provoked . . . a passion both for detailing the links that bound colonizer to colonized and for assiduously tending the frontiers that kept them apart. The intellectual legacy of this ambivalence survives to the present day. (1998, p. 162)

This book has traced this ambiguity in Japan's scientific colonialism and subsequently the *kōminka* ideology. As the ambiguous ethnic ideologies were incorporated into policies of scientific colonialism, which evolved around the central thesis of "natural" modernization, the Japanese administration was led by its own logic to cultivate native agents who, located in both the colonial system and local communities, could effectively bridge the two. By the same token, this specific colonial endeavor also created social positions in the colony that were inherently contradictory. Even in the last years of the colonial rule, when "natural" Japanization gave way to forced assimilation, similar structural contradictions persisted. The slogans of the Greater East Asia Co-Prosperity Sphere (GEAPS) accentuated common cultural and racial affinities, common economic interests, and the creation of a new East Asian culture in the region (Duus, Myers, and Peattie 1996); to use today's social science language, such ideological constructions appealed to the promise of a pan-ethnicity.[6] But the promise of a pan-ethnic empire was never consistently realized in colonial policies. For example, many *kōminka* policies reflected a combination of the demands for the colonial subjects'

6. Oguma points out that the official discourse recognized the multi-ethnic nature of the empire. For example, "the definition of Japan's citizens [*kokumin*] provided by official school textbooks in the 1930s included residents in—quite naturally for the time—Okinawa and Hokkaidō, but also [as might not have been expected] Korea, Taiwan, Sakhalin, etc." (Oguma 1998, p. 4). But, as Oguma's study explains in detail, the official discourse of this "pan-ethnicity" was itself changeable, inconsistent, and ambiguous.

total loyalty to the Emperor on the one hand and the deliberate delays in granting them full citizenship rights on the other (Oguma 1998, pp. 9–12).

Through the experiences of Taiwanese doctors we observe some of the most profound confusions and creativity of the colonial subjects who faced such ambiguous colonial relations. This is because Taiwan, among Japan's formal and informal colonies, came closest to being a "success case" for the imperialist objectives of "scientific colonialism" and, later, to molding a GEAPS ethnicity (Peattie 1984). At the same time, medicine was widely regarded by the colonizers and to some extent by groups among the colonized as the benchmark for this "success." Taiwanese doctors, in their role as "native agents" largely responsible for this "success," were confronted with deep-rooted structural tensions and struggled with many difficulties for coherence in their identity narratives. While the shifting structural configurations conditioned their anticolonial mobilization, demobilization, and assimilation, their collective efforts to forge a coherent identity defined the meanings of their actions. Their identity narratives expressed standpoints of the colonized which Oguma described to be inexpressible in the official framework of dichotomous choices.

From national physicians to medical modernists—from resistance to assimilation—their identity narratives both internalized and subverted the colonial ideology and manifested different modes of transcending the colonizer/colonized dichotomy. In their initial moment, these Taiwanese agents of "scientific colonialism" claimed "modernity" for their nation and envisioned themselves as nationalistic agents of "healing" writ large. Although this period is considered their anticolonial moment, these doctors empowered themselves vis-à-vis colonial rule by adopting certain institutional and cultural aspects of Japanese colonialism. Toward the end of the empire, in contrast, Taiwanese doctors attempted to lay claim to a universalistic modernity and to articulate a modernist identity that transcended ethnic boundaries. Although it would appear that doctors were highly assimilated during this period, their assimilation also resulted in their suppression of the category of ethnicity per se, which altered the original meaning of the official *kōminka* ideology. In both moments, doctors' identities deviated from the ideology of scientific colonialism (and later that of the GEAPS) as they defined themselves as agents for higher purposes than are defined by the Japanese Empire—that is, those of the Taiwanese nation or of "modernity." Their story illustrates how colonial subjects' interpretations of the ambiguous colonial relations in the Japanese Empire altered the meanings of the official colonial discourse and shaped their own identity.

To speak of resistance and assimilation from this perspective, then, cautions us against any analysis that rests on the assumption of the colonizers and the colonized as stable categories that represent coherent interests. Although there were numerous groups that embodied such categories and interests, as documented in past studies and reviewed earlier in this book, a better understanding of the in-between groups is required for advancing our knowledge of this colonial history. The in-between groups often shared, to varying degrees and in different forms, the beliefs in the racial and cultural affinities and the promise of an East Asian modernity within the empire. But their critiques challenged the colonial fiction that this reading of East Asia's past and future should dictate (as did Japanese colonial officials) specific policies, actions, and interactions. Their resistance centered not so much on the promise of colonial modernity as on their limited agency in the delivery of this promise.

When these in-between groups downplayed the agency issue in their identification with the universalistic appeal of modernity, their assimilation could not be a coherent process either. To take the univeralism of modernity at its face value, these social groups often had to separate the fruits of modernity from the violence of imperialism, when in reality the two developed in tandem in their societies. While victims of Western imperialisms were burdened with a Du Boisian "double consciousness" as they attempted to embrace both tradition and modernity, one can argue that the in-between groups in the Japanese Empire sometimes manifested a "fragmentary consciousness" as they sought single-mindedly to anchor their identity in modernity. Black intellectuals have had to struggle with the recognition of their identities' being shaped by modernity but not fully part of it, of having both an African and an American self, of the violence that "America" committed against "Africa" (Gilroy 1993). In contrast, Taiwanese doctors' whole-hearted embracing of modernity resulted in their unstable identity narratives, which were disrupted by suppressed and bracketed experiences.

Such tensions in the narratives of assimilated identities exposed the central hypocrisy in a colonialism whose official discourse celebrated the alleged similarities between the colonizers and the colonized. As I have argued elsewhere, while the categories of the civil and the uncivil encouraged and justified Western imperialisms, the same divide entails a fundamental irony in Japanese imperialism:

> The pursuit of civility in Japan started with a self-conscious effort to achieve that status in order to maintain national integrity and to interact equally with other nations. . . . The family/other divide operates as an important cultural motif in [Japan's] civility; Japan is much more con-

cerned with maintaining the integrity of "the family" than in proselytiz-
ing its virtue. . . . Whereas the evangelical imperialism of Western states
was rationalized as an attempt to spread the gospel of civility to uncivil
pagans, . . . [Japanese] imperialism faced the problem of having to both
inscribe the national family and include extra-national members. Given
these contradictory demands, it is likely that authoritarianism alone could
deny the contradiction and prevent ideological fragmentation. (Lo and
Bettinger 2001, pp. 269–70)

AGENTS OF MODERNITIES

This reading of Japanese colonialism raises a broader question: Does it matter *by whom* science is being delivered to a local community, so long as it is
delivered? While Japanese colonial officials were fundamentally flawed by
their arrogance in assuming that they were the only legitimate agents for
modernity in Asia, Taiwanese doctors were also centrally concerned with
their role as the local designated agents in the process of East Asian modernity. Through a lengthy engagement with this history, this book illustrates
the complex roles of "agents" of modernity, and contributes to our understanding of the ways different groups negotiate between universalistic narratives of science and the concrete sociopolitical relationships through which
science is being delivered, developed, and received. Modernity can never
exist outside of the culturally specific plans of its deliverers and the culturally specific evaluations of its receivers. To the extent that there is no
modernity that exists void of human agency, there is no modernity that is
not localized. Despite its universalistic appeals, the spread of modernity constitutes an inherently relational process.

This perspective facilitates our understanding of the history of modernity in two ways. First, it questions any normative assumptions about the
modernities developed in Western Europe and North America. This perspective joins recent scholarship that critiques the "acultural" theories of
modernity that have prevailed in Western social sciences. "It should be evident that the dominant theories of modernity over the last two centuries
have been of the acultural sort. . . . The changes have been explained partly
by culture-neutral social developments, such as Emile Durkheim's move
from mechanical to differentiated, organic forms of social cohesion or Alexis
de Tocqueville's assumption of creeping democracy (by which he meant a
push toward equality). In Max Weber's interpretation, rationalization was a
steady process, occurring within all cultures over time" (Taylor 1999, p.
155). The "acultural" theories are guilty of misclassifying "changes that

reflect the culture peculiar to the modern West as the product of unprob-
lematic discovery" (ibid., p. 160).

Instead, a cultural theory of modernity has to be able to recognize that
"outside of those cases where the original culture is quite destroyed, and the
people either die or are forcibly assimilated—and European colonialism has
a number of such cases to its discredit—a successful transition [into moder-
nity] involves a people finding resources in their traditional culture which,
modified and transposed, will enable them to take on the new practices"
(ibid., 162). Modernity, then, is not driven by any internal logic, but develops through site-specific encounters where a "different start[ing] point for
the transition . . . leads to [a] different outcome" (Gaonkar 1999, p. 15; see
also Gilroy 1993, Rofel 1999).

Second, to conceptualize modernity as site-specific encounters demands
a fuller recognition of the varying modes of participation of the marginalized in the modernity projects. In colonial contexts, the actions of the colonized are typically understood in terms of co-optation and anticolonial
resistance. For instance, scholars like Partha Chatterjee (1993) argue that
integration of any aspect of the colonial legacy with the native society
inevitably facilitates the colonial enterprise. Bhabha, on the other hand, sees
colonial hybrids as "intercultural brokers in the interstices between nation
and empire, producing counter-narratives from the nation's margins to the
'totalizing boundaries' of the nation" (Pieterse 1995, p. 56). Both positions,
however, ultimately suggest that we understand colonial subjects within a
framework in which the colonizers remain the primary reference point.
Although the colonial imposition of the modernity project is always violent
and intrusive, the experience of the marginalized should not be read *solely*
as a critique of this imposition. To do so would risk again treating their experiences as a commentary (albeit a critical one) of those at the center and thus
reinforcing their "otherness."

Rather, it is important to understand the creativity of the marginalized in
their experiences of the double consciousness, fragmented consciousness, and
the like. Their attempts to participate in the modernity project, although
often frustrated and ignored, generated new cultural legacies, new meanings
of modernity, and new possibilities for articulating the relations between traditions and modernities. As an unintended consequence (from the perspective of the center), these agents of modernity on the periphery redefine
aspects of modernity, as in the case of the Japanese "anticolonial colonizers,"
the Taiwanese "national physicians," and the kōminka "medical modernists."

The modernity project, then, is less a teleological unfolding of reason
than a series of site-specific encounters that can be described as a process of

hybridization.[7] Since not every loop in the chain of hybridization/modernization is alike, one central question concerns how to differentiate among different kinds of hybrid. Some propose that "it might be tempting to say that the institutions and practices converge, while the cultures find new forms of differentiation" (Taylor 1999, p. 164). Others argue that we should "construct a continuum of hybridities: on one end, an assimilationist hybridity that leans over towards the center, adopts the canon, and mimics the hegemony, and, at the other end, a destabilizing hybridity that blurs the canon . . . [and] subverts the center" (Pieterse 1995, pp. 56–57). These conceptual frameworks, however, can only be a first approximation. As modernity develops through unequal social, political, and economic relationships, those on the margin who attempt to make themselves modern (rather than being made modern) are compelled to enter this web of unequal relationships and, as they do so, must come to terms with issues of their self-positioning and ontology. In this process, as they struggle for a coherent "modern" identity of their own, they must develop cultural and political imaginations that allow them to meaningfully negotiate the institutional/cultural or resistance/assimilation divide. The attempt at integration, tension-ridden as it may be, cannot be reduced to the dichotomous frameworks imposed on them. These ontological narratives are indeed an integral part of the cultures of modernity.

To argue that the modernity project unfolds through a history of hybridization, I wish to broaden the hybridization perspective beyond the

7. The term *hybridity* as it has been used throughout history has multiple connotations. As Robert Young (1995) points out in his study of the genealogy of this term, the concept of hybridity is an integral part of the very colonial system that today's scholars seek to dismantle. According to Young, the usage of the term *hybridity* in the vocabulary of the Victorian extreme right presupposes the existence of "pure" and distinct racial categories and centers on the issue of the fertility of interracial "hybrids."

Recent scholarship in postcolonial studies, however, has radically transformed the meaning of hybridity. The central concern here is about the creativity and cultural imagination of the hybrid, which are located in between categories. These writers find no reasons to assume hybridity as a blending of two *distinct* cultures, races, or ethnicities. For example, Paul Gilroy's discussion of the modernity of the black Atlantic explicitly rejects any essentialist notion of ethnicity. For him, the two cultures that inform the "double consciousness" of intellectuals in the black Atlantic are diverse, messy, and incoherent in and of themselves (see Gilroy 1993). It is in this latter tradition that I position my engagement with the concept of ethnic hybridity. Hybridity, then, signifies the encounter, conflict, and/or blending of two ethnic or cultural categories which, while by no means pure and distinct in nature, tend to be understood and experienced as meaningful identity labels by members of these categories.

field of colonial and postcolonial studies. Hybridization is not a process that occurs exclusively in non-Western societies, as if "the West" were left "uncontaminated" and represented the "authentic" modernity. Rather, in the continual creation and recreation of "modern" institutions and cultures, in Western and non-Western societies alike, different groups deploy and define the framework of "modernity" in their specific contexts. As suggested by the relational perspective adopted and developed in this book, instead of remaining conceptually confined by fixed categories, we should seek to better understand the complexity of social experiences and use these understandings to refine our conceptual categories.

Perhaps the writing of this book is in itself one effort to make explicit this hybridity. I travel conceptually from American social science categories to Taiwanese colonial histories and come back to raise challenges to "Western" scholarship. As social scientists in North American academic settings, do we have to care about the story of Taiwanese doctors? One generation ago, perhaps we would have easily decided to hand this case over to our colleagues who are "area specialists," yet it is now no longer so easy to dismiss the relevance of the experiences on the periphery. We are, instead, challenged to consider how the social histories of the formerly excluded serve to denaturalize our familiar concepts, such as professions, modernity, and colonialism. In short, we are compelled to appreciate more fully the historicity of our own discipline and thereby prepare ourselves better for an open, humble, and full-fledged dialogue that is so long overdue.

APPENDIX
Sources and Data

I provide here a brief explanation for the historical materials that are cited frequently in this book. These materials consist of four major categories.

Taiwanese Activities and Discourses in the Public Sphere

(a) *KE—Taiwan Sōtokufu keisatsu enkaku shi* (A Developmental History of the Governor-General's Police in Taiwan), a detailed secret record kept by the Japanese police bureau in Taiwan on any activities that seemed "oppositional" in their eyes (translated into Chinese as *Taiwan shehui yundong shi*)

(b) *MP/SMP—Taiwan minpō*, the only major newspaper not affiliated with the state in colonial Taiwan, started in 1923 and renamed *Taiwan shinminpō* in 1930

(c) *Anzu*, an unpublished, literary journal circulated among a group of Taiwanese educated elite between 1943 and 1947, edited by a Taiwanese physician and founded when he was a student at Taipei Higher School

Professional Experiences within the Medical Arena

(a) *TIGZ—Taiwan igakkai zasshi* (Journal of the Medical Association of Formosa), the official journal of the medical association in Taiwan

(b) *Jiayi [Kagi] igakkai zasshi*, a journal published by a local medical association in the city of Jiayi

(c) *Tōnei kaishi*, a newsletter published by the Faculty of Medicine at the Taipei Imperial University and later by its alumni association

(d) *Nanmei kaishi,* a newsletter published by Taipei Medical School and later by its alumni association[1]

State Policies and Regulations

(a) *FH/KH—Taiwan Sōtokufu fuhō; Taiwan Sōtokufu kanpō* (Official Bulletin of the Governor-General of Taiwan)

(b) *MJST/JST—Taiwan Sōtokufu minsei jimu seiseki teiyō,* renamed in 1919 as *Taiwan Sōtokufu jimu seiseki teiyō* (Outlines and Summaries of the Administration of Civil Affairs), published yearly by the governor-general of Taiwan

(c) *Taiwan Sōtokufu rinji jōhōbu buhō* (Newsletters of the Governor-General's Temporary Information Department in Taiwan), a wartime government publication

(d) *Taiwan jihō* (Taiwan Times), a journal published under the direction and supervision of the governor-general of Taiwan

Life Stories

I was introduced to my first informant, Dr. Zhang (also one of the founders of *Anzu*), by a Japanese scholar, Professor Shozawa Jun. I located other doctors through Dr. Zhang, his friends, and other channels. Since it is extremely difficult to approach doctors of this generation in Taiwan without obtaining an appropriate introduction, I was unsuccessful in my attempt to interview the physicians whom I located from associational mailing lists. I interviewed ten physicians: eight in Taiwan and two in Japan, all in 1994. Each interview lasted from two to three hours on average. Two informants agreed to be interviewed again after our initial conversation. Except for Dr. Zhang, who allowed me to use his last name when quoting him, the informants asked to remain anonymous. They have each been assigned a letter. Quotations from these interviews are referenced in the text as Life-[letter]. I conducted these interviews in Taiwanese and Japanese and translated the transcriptions into English. Nine of my ten interviewees were male.

All ten of them were ethnic Taiwanese, that is, descendants of Han-Chinese immigrants who arrived in Taiwan a few generations ago. They all came from middle- to upper-middle-class families. It is worth mentioning

---

1. For (c) and (d), only an incomplete collection was preserved. But in the postwar period, the alumni of both institutes continued to publish either books or newsletters, which also provide glimpses of the professional life before the war.

that these doctors all displayed a critical attitude toward the Kuomintang (KMT), the ruling party in Taiwan for more than a half century, since 1945. (The first regime change in post-1945 Taiwan finally took place after the KMT defeat in the 2000 presidential election.) Some of them were more political than others and would volunteer their criticisms of the KMT, but when being probed, all of them were clear about their dislike of the KMT. There was no clear consensus among them, however, regarding what the best alternative should be to KMT rule. These doctors all preferred to speak in Taiwanese for our conversations, despite the fact that Mandarin Chinese is presently the official language in Taiwan. It was also not uncommon for some informants to switch to Japanese during our conversations. Their choices of language sensitized me to the multiplicity of their ethnic self-identifications from the beginning of the interview process.

Methodological Reflections

Like many studies of public mobilization under repressive regimes, this project faces the difficulty of nonsystematic data. In colonial Taiwan, the types of available data on public mobilization varied according to the drastic changes in the public sphere. The press was able to publish critiques of the colonial state and society in the 1920s, and I rely on newspapers as a steady record of doctors' public activities and discourses for this period. In the 1930s, the press was subject to increasing state censorship; instead, literary activities began to flourish in Taiwan. I rely on literary journals, as well as some studies of the first public election in 1935, in order to understand doctors' participation in the public sphere during these years. After the outbreak of the war in 1937, the colonial state controlled almost all the newspapers and journals in Taiwan: it imposed wartime propaganda on much of the media space, officially outlawed the publication of Chinese materials in 1937, and eventually forced all newspapers to merge into one government-controlled press in 1944. The same degree of state control was said to interfere with the second public election in 1939. Heavy state control, together with the bombing at the end of the war, destroyed most written records on the public life of Taiwanese during these years. I use oral interviews and published oral histories as my main sources for understanding doctors' experiences in this period.

The variation of data could affect my findings in a number of ways. First, published materials and oral interviews provided two very different environments in which the doctors reflected upon their public roles. Could the difference in the environment account for some of the differences I find in their discourses? Second, my informants were in their twenties during the war, and they could not provide detailed information on older generations' wartime experience. Third, since I was only able to interview a limited number of doctors, how much can I generalize their words for all Taiwanese doctors' wartime experiences?

In fact, the first problem turns out to strengthen, rather than weaken, my findings. While the press under the Japanese regime tended to adopt an implicit, moderate language in its reports on anticolonial activities or discourses, the newspaper articles from the 1920s still indicate Taiwanese doctors' active participation in anticolonial mobilization. The oral interviews conducted in present-day Taiwan allow the informants to freely discuss or even magnify their anti-Japanese sentiments, but instead the interviews document these Taiwanese doctors' positive evaluation of their Japanese heritage. In other words, if I could have used both newspaper articles and oral interviews as my sources for both the 1920s and the wartime, I might have found an even sharper contrast between these two groups of doctors.

Another likely suspicion is that the postwar interactions between the Chinese and the Taiwanese might have strengthened the latter's pro-Japanese sentiments and thereby inadvertently encouraged them to cast their recollection of the colonial period in a more positive light. Along the same line, one might wonder how, given the pro-independence atmosphere on the island in the 1990s, the timing of the interviews might have biased my informants' memories of the Kōminka Era. To answer this question, one needs to compare and contrast the writings and other materials left from the pre-1945 and the post-1945 periods. The strong pro-Japanese sentiments that emanated from the writings in *Anzu*, as discussed in the body of the book, would seem to suggest that these feelings were not postwar reconstructions. On the other hand, my field experiences led me to believe that these doctors were cautious but honest in sharing their political opinions. Instead of seeing the 1990s as a time when they could finally celebrate their Japanese heritage, these doctors seemed to still feel the need to be cautious about what they said under the KMT regime. They (except for Dr. Zhang) requested that their names be kept in strict confidence, occasionally asked me to turn off my tape recorder, and wanted to make sure that I was an ethnic Taiwanese myself before they would discuss certain issues. At the same time, after obtaining my promise of confidentiality, they tended to open up, to offer their honest opinions, and to display a strong enthusiasm about sharing the experiences of their youth.

Still, one may question whether these doctors' dislike of the KMT or their nostalgia for their youth might have romanticized their lives during wartime. Likewise, the small number of informants could also challenge the validity of my findings. To compensate for these problems, I triangulate the oral interviews with written sources, such as the prewar and postwar publications by the Faculty of Medicine at Taipei Imperial, publications by its alumni organizations, published memoirs, autobiographies, oral histories, some writings by Japanese doctors who resided in Taiwan during wartime, as well as the unpublished materials produced by the aforementioned group, Anzu. While these different types of data may be biased in different ways, they tend to converge on major patterns in the collective identity of *kōminka*-generation doctors—that is, on their focus on a modernist professional culture, their self-awareness as community leaders in Taiwan, and their general liking of the Japanese heritage. At some points, discrepancies do exist between different types of data and are noted as unsolved parts of the puzzle left to us by this turbulent and intriguing time period.

Finally, available data do not represent a complete picture of older physicians' wartime experiences. As a result, the discussion about doctors' wartime experience cannot sufficiently separate cohort effect from the impacts of historical process. It does not tell us if the wartime assimilation process transformed the previous anticolonial physicians in the same way it transformed the younger generation. Without a rigorous answer to this question, I should not generalize my findings about Taiwanese doctors' wartime experience beyond the generation of my informants. Indeed, the scarcity of the data on wartime Taiwan remains a challenge to the students of Taiwanese history. My findings about wartime Taiwan are a small contribution to this field.

Glossary

CHINESE GLOSSARY

aiyong [aiyū]	隘勇	Jiayi	嘉義
baojia	保甲	Jinan	濟南
Chen Qimai	陳其邁	Lai He	賴和
Chen Yisong	陳逸松	Lin Xiantang	林獻堂
Danshui	淡水	Liu Juchuan	劉鉅橡
Du Congming	杜聰明	Lu Xun	魯迅
Fengshan	鳳山	*Nanyin*	南音
Fengtian	奉天	Pingdong	屏東
Fujian	福建	Qihe	齊河
Fuzhou	福州	Qing	清
Guangdong	廣東	Qingdao	青島
Guo Xiucong	郭琇琮	Qufu	屈阜
Guoli Taiwan Daxue Yanjiu Tushu-guan 國立臺灣大學研究圖書館		renshu	仁術
		Shantou	汕頭
Guoli Zhongyang Tushuguan Taiwan Fenguan 國立中央圖書館臺灣分館		shifei juan	實費卷
		Shijiazhuang	石家莊
		Tainan	臺南
Han Shiquan	韓石泉	*Taiwan wenyi*	臺灣文藝
Hankou	漢口	*Taiwan xinwenxue*	臺灣新文學
Huang Wentao	黃文陶	Wu Xinrong	吳新榮
Jiang Weishui	蔣渭水	Xiamen	廈門

Xianfa budui	先發部隊		Zhanghua	彰化
Yang Kui	楊逵		Zheng Chenggong	鄭成功
Yongqing	永清		Zhengding	鄭定
Zhang Zuolin	張作霖			

JAPANESE GLOSSARY

bōeki	防疫		Keijō Teikoku Daigaku	
Chikamatsu Monzaemon			京城帝国大学	
近松門左衛門			Kodama Gentarō	児玉源太郎
chō	庁		kōgakkō	公学校
chōchō	庁長		*Kokka sōdōinhō*	国家総動員法
Den Kenjirō	田健治郎		kokugo katei	国語家庭
Densenbyō yobō kisoku			kōminka	皇民化
伝染病予防規則			Koxinga [Kokusenya]	国性爺
dōbun dōshu	同文同種		ku	区
Dōjinkai	同仁会		Kyōeiken Kōsei Burokku	
Ebara Soroku	江原素六		共栄厚生ブロック	
gaishō	街庄		*Kyōgaku-rei*	共学令
Gotō Shimpei	後藤新平		Manchukuo	満州国
gun	郡		Manshū Ika Daigaku	
gunkoku no fujin	軍国の婦人		満州医科大学	
hakuai byōin	博愛病院		Mantetsu	
Harima	播磨		満鉄 (南満州鉄道株式会社)	
hokō	保甲		Maruta	丸太
hontōjin	本島人		Masuda Taneji	増田胤次
Horiuchi Tsuguo	堀内次雄		minzoku ishi	民族医師
iken	医権		Miyakawa Yoneji	宮川米次
Inoue Kaoru	井上馨		mugon no gaisen	無言の凱旋
Ishibashi Tanzan	石橋湛山		Musha Incident	霧社事件
Ishii Shirō	石井四郎		Nagasaki Ika Daigaku	
Ishii Unit (Unit 731)	石井部隊		長崎医科大学	
isshi dōjin	一視同仁		naichijin	内地人
jukubanjin	熟蕃人		Naitō Konan	内藤湖南
Kawaishi (Kunio)	河石九二夫		Nettai Igaku Kenkyūjo	
			熱帯医学研究所	

Ohkuma (Shigenobu) 大隈重信

Okakura Tenshin 岡倉天心

Okazaki Giyō 岡崎祇容

ryōmin 良民

Sakuma Samata 佐久間左馬太

seibanjin 生蕃人

senjō e no kagaku dōin 戦場への科学動員

shi 市

shichō 支庁

shikai 市会

Shimonoseki Treaty 下関条約

Shimose Kentarō 下瀬謙太郎

Shinminkai 新民会

Shintōa Igakkai 新東亜医学会

shobō 書房

shū 州

shūkai 州会

Sotoda (Rinzō) 外田麟造

Tagawa Daikichirō 田川大吉郎

Taihoku 台北

Taihoku Bengoshi-kai 台北弁護士会

Taihoku Kōtōgakkō 台北高等学校

Taiwan ahen rei 台湾阿片令

Taiwan Bunka Kyōkai 台湾文化協会

Taiwan Chihōjichi Renmei 台湾地方自治連盟

Taiwan chūō eiseikai kisoku 台湾中央衛生会規則

Taiwan Hōkō Ishidan 台湾奉公医師団

Taiwan igyō kisoku 台湾医業規則

"Taiwan ikai ron" 台湾医界論

Taiwan Minshūtō 台湾民衆党

Taiwan Seinen 台湾青年

Taiwan Seinenkai 台湾青年会

Taiwan Sōtokufu Igakkō 台湾総督府医学校

Taiwan Sōtokufu Igaku Senmon Gakkō 台湾総督府医学専門学校

Taiwan Sōtokufu seiyakujo kansei 台湾総督府製薬所官制

Taiwan Sōtokufu Shokuminchi Seisaku Kengi Iinkai 台湾総督府植民地政策建議委員会

Taiwan Sōtokufu Taihoku Igaku Senmon Gakkō 台湾総督府台北医学専門学校

Takagi Tomoeda 高木友枝

Takao 高雄

Takasago (zoku) 高砂 (族)

Takekoshi (Yosaburō) 竹越 (与三郎)

Tōa Dōbunkai 東亜同文会

Tōgō Unit 東郷部隊

Tokyo Densenbyō Kenkyūjo 東京伝染病研究所

Tōyō Idō Kai 東洋医道会

Tōyō no meishu 東洋の盟主

Uchida Kakichi 内田嘉吉

Ugaki Kazushige 宇垣一成

wansei 湾生

Yamagata Aritomo 山県有朋

Yamaguchi Hidetaka 山口秀高

Yanagi Sōetsu 柳宗悦

Yokokawa Sadamu 横川定

Zheng Chengkong [Tei Seikō] 鄭成功

References

ENGLISH MATERIALS

Abbot, Andrew. 1993. "The Sociology of Work and Occupations." *Annual Review of Sociology* 19: 187–209.
———. 1992a. "What Do Cases Do? Some Notes on Activity in Sociological Analysis." Pp. 53–82 in *What Is a Case? Exploring the Foundations of Social Inquiry,* ed. Charles C. Ragin and Howard S. Becker. Cambridge: Cambridge University Press.
———. 1992b. "From Causes to Events: Notes on Narrative Positivism." *Sociological Methods and Research* 20: 428–55.
———. 1988. *The System of Professions: An Essay on the Division of Expert Labor.* Chicago: University of Chicago Press.
Anderson, Benedict. 1991. *Imagined Communities: Reflections on the Origin and Spread of Nationalism.* 2nd ed. London: Verso.
Arnold, David. 1993. *Colonizing the Body: State Medicine and Epidemic Disease in Nineteenth-Century India.* Berkeley: University of California Press.
Asad, Talal, ed. 1973. *Anthropology and the Colonial Encounter.* London: Ithaca Press.
Balibar, E., and E. Wallerstein. 1991. *Race, Nation, Class: Ambiguous Identities.* Trans. Chris Turner. New York: Verso.
Balzer, Harley D. 1996. "Introduction." Pp. 3–38 in *Russia's Missing Middle Class: The Professions in Russian History,* ed. Harley D. Balzer. Armonk, NY: M. E. Sharpe.
Barclay, George W. 1979. *Colonial Development and Population in Taiwan.* Princeton, NJ: Princeton University Press.
Barlow, Tani, ed. 1997. *Formations of Colonial Modernity in East Asia.* Durham, NC: Duke University Press.
Barth, Fredrik. 1969. "Introduction." Pp. 9–38 in *Ethnic Groups and Boundaries: The Social Organization of Culture Difference,* ed. Fredrik Barth. Boston: Little, Brown.
Beasley, W. G. 1990. *The Rise of Modern Japan.* London: Weidenfeld & Nicolson.
Berezin, Mabel. 1996. "Non-liberal Politics: A Social and Cultural Analysis." Lecture given at the Center for Studies of Social Transformation, University of Michigan.

Berlant, Jeffrey. 1975. *Profession and Monopoly: A Study of Medicine in the United States and Great Britain.* Berkeley: University of California Press.

Bhabha, Homi. 1994. *The Location of Culture.* New York: Routledge.

Bledstein, Burton. 1976. *The Culture of Professionalism.* New York: Norton.

Bourdieu, Pierre. 1977. *Outline of a Theory of Practice.* Trans. Richard Nice. Cambridge: Cambridge University Press.

Breuilly, John. 1982. *Nationalism and the State.* Manchester, England: Manchester University Press.

Brint, Steven G. 1994. *In an Age of Experts: The Changing Role of Professionals in Politics and Public Life.* Princeton: Princeton University Press.

Brooks, Clem, and Jeff Manza. 1997. "The Social and Ideological Bases of Middle-Class Political Realignment in the United States, 1972 to 1992." *American Sociological Review* 62 (2): 191–209.

Brubaker, Rogers. 1992. *Citizenship and Nationhood in France and Germany.* Cambridge, MA: Harvard University Press.

Burrage, Michael. 1990. "Introduction: The Professions in Sociology and History." Pp. 1–23 in *Professions in Theory and History,* ed. Michael Burrage and Rolf Torstendahl. London: Sage Publications.

Calhoun, Craig, ed. 1994. *Social Theory and the Politics of Identity.* Cambridge, MA: Blackwell.

———. 1993. "Nationalism and Ethnicity." *Annual Review of Sociology* 19: 211–39.

———, ed. 1992. *Habermas and the Public Sphere.* Cambridge, MA: MIT Press.

Chatterjee, Partha. 1993. *The Nation and Its Fragments: Colonial and Post-Colonial Histories.* Princeton, NJ: Princeton University Press.

———. 1990. "A Response to Taylor's 'Modes of Civil Society.'" *Public Culture* 3 (1): 119–32.

———. 1986. *Nationalist Thought and the Colonial World—A Derivative Discourse.* London: Zed Books.

Chen, Ching-chih. 1984. "Police and Community Control Systems in the Empire." Pp. 213–39 in *The Japanese Colonial Empire, 1895–1945,* ed. Ramon H. Myers and Mark R. Peattie. Princeton, NJ: Princeton University Press.

———. 1967. "The Police and the Hokō Systems in Taiwan under Japanese Administration (1985–1945)." Pp. 147–76 in *Papers on Japan,* 4, ed. Albert Craig. Cambridge, MA: Harvard University Press.

Chen, Edward I-te. 1984. "The Attempt to Integrate the Empire: Legal Perspectives." Pp. 240–74 in *The Japanese Colonial Empire, 1895–1945,* ed. Ramon H. Myers and Mark R. Peattie. Princeton, NJ: Princeton University Press.

Cheng, Tun-jen. 1989. "Democratizing the Quasi-Leninist Regime in Taiwan." *World Politics* 41: 471–99.

Ching, Leo. 1998. "Yellow Skin, White Masks." Pp. 65–86 in *Trajectories: Inter-Asia Cultural Studies,* ed. Kuan-Hsing Chen. London: Routledge.

Chou, Wan-yao. 1996. "The Kōminka Movement in Taiwan and Korea: Comparisons and Interpretations." Pp. 40–68 in *The Japanese Wartime Empire, 1931–1945,* ed. Peter Duus, Ramon H. Myers, and Mark R. Peattie. Princeton, NJ: Princeton University Press.

———. 1991. "The 'Kominka' Movement: Taiwan under Wartime Japan, 1937–1945." Ph.D. diss. Yale University.

Christy, Alan S. 1997. "The Making of Imperial Subjects in Okinawa." Pp. 141–70 in *Formation of Colonial Modernity in East Asia*, ed. Tanie Barlow. Durham, NC: Duke University Press.

Cohen, Jean. 1979. "Why More Political Theory." *Telos* 40: 70–94.

Cohen, Jean, and Andrew Arato. 1992. *Civil Society and Political Theory.* Cambridge, MA: MIT Press.

Cooper, Fred, and Ann Stoler. 1989. "Introduction: Tensions of Empire: Colonial Control and Visions of Rule." *American Ethnologist: The Journal of the American Ethnological Society* 16: 609–21.

Copper, John F. 1993. *Historical Dictionary of Taiwan.* Metuchen, NJ: Scarecrow Press.

Cornell, Stephen. 1996. "The Variable Ties That Bind: Content and Circumstance in Ethnic Processes." *Ethnic and Racial Studies* 19 (2): 265–90.

Corrigan, Philip, and Derek Sayer. 1985. *The Great Arch: English State Formation as Cultural Revolution.* Oxford: Blackwell.

Cumings, Bruce. 1995. "Colonial Formations and Deformations: Korea, Taiwan, and Vietnam." Paper presented at the Annual Meetings of the American Political Science Association, Chicago.

Czarniawska-Joerges, Barbara. 1997. *Narrating the Organization: Dramas of Institutional Identity.* Chicago: University of Chicago Press.

Davidson, James W. [1903] 1988. *The Island of Formosa, Past and Present.* Reprint, Taipei: Southern Materials Center.

Davies, Celia. 1996. "The Sociology of Professions and the Profession of Gender." *Sociology* 30 (4): 661–78.

Dirks, Nicholas, ed. 1992. *Colonialism and Culture.* Ann Arbor: University of Michigan Press.

Dunn, Fred L. 1976. "Traditional Asian Medicine and Cosmopolitan Medicine as Adaptive Systems." Pp. 133–58 in *Asian Medical Systems: A Comparative Study*, ed. Charles Leslie. Berkeley: University of California Press.

Duran-Arenas, Luis, and Michael Kennedy. 1991. "The Constitution of Physicians' Power: A Theoretical Framework for Comparative Analysis." *Social Science and Medicine* 32: 643–48.

Duus, Peter. 1989. "Japan's Informal Empire in China, 1895–1937: An Overview." Pp. xi–xxix in *The Japanese Informal Empire in China, 1895–1937*, ed. Peter Duus, Ramon H. Myers, and Mark R. Peattie. Princeton, NJ: Princeton University Press.

Duus, Peter, Ramon H. Myers, and Mark Peattie, eds. 1989. *The Japanese Informal Empire in China, 1985-1937.* Princeton, NJ: Princeton University Press.

———, eds. 1996. *The Japanese Wartime Empire, 1931–1945.* Princeton, NJ: Princeton University Press.

Eley, Geoff. 1992. "Nations, Publics, and Political Cultures: Placing Habermas in the Nineteenth Century." Pp. 289–339 in *Habermas and the Public Sphere*, ed. Craig Calhoun. Cambridge, MA: MIT Press.

Emirbayer, Mustafa. 1997. "Manifesto for a Relational Sociology." *American Journal of Sociology* 103 (2): 281–318.

Espiritu, Yen L. 1997. *Asian American Women and Men: Labor, Laws, and Love.* Thousand Oaks, CA: Sage Publications.

———. 1992. *Asian American Panethnicity: Bridging Institutions and Identities.* Philadelphia, PA: Temple University Press.

Fine, Gary A. 1998. "'Main Street' on Main Street: Community Identity and the Reputation of Sinclair Lewis." *Sociological Quarterly* 39 (1): 79–101.

Fix, Douglas L. 1993. "Advancing on Tokyo: The New Literature Movement: 1930–1937." Pp. 251–97 in *Riju shiqi Taiwanshi guoji xueshu yantaohui lunwenji*, ed. History Department at National Taiwan University. Taipei: National Taiwan University.

Foucault, Michel. 1979. *Discipline and Punish: The Birth of the Prison*. Trans. Alan Sheridan. New York: Vintage Books.

Frankenberg, Ruth. 1993. *White Women, Race Matters: The Social Construction of Whiteness*. Minneapolis: University of Minnesota Press.

Fraser, Nancy. 1987. "What's Critical about Critical Theory? The Case of Habermas and Gender." Pp. 53–71 in *Feminism as Critique: On the Politics of Gender*, ed. Seyla Benhabib and Drucilla Cornell. Minneapolis: University of Minnesota Press.

Freidson, Eliot. 2001. *Professionalism: The Third Logic of the Practice of Knowledge*. Chicago: University of Chicago Press.

———. 1994. *Professionalism Reborn: Theory, Prophecy, and Policy*. Chicago: University of Chicago Press.

———. 1986. *Professional Powers: A Study of the Institutionalization of Formal Knowledge*. Chicago: University of Chicago Press.

———. 1970. *Profession of Medicine: A Study of the Sociology of Applied Knowledge*. New York: Harper & Row.

Friedland, Roger, and Robert R. Alford. 1993. "Bringing Society Back in: Symbols, Practice, and Institutional Contradictions." Pp. 232–63 in *The New Institutionalism in Organizational Analysis*, ed. Walter W. Powell and Paul J. DiMaggio. Chicago: University of Chicago Press.

Gamson, William. 1992. *Talking Politics*. Cambridge: Cambridge University Press.

Gann, L. H. 1996. "Reflections on the Japanese and German Empires of World War II." Pp. 335–62 in *The Japanese Wartime Empire, 1931–1945*, ed. Peter Duus, Ramon H. Myers, Mark R. Peattie. Princeton, NJ: Princeton University Press.

Gaonkar, Dilip P. G. 1999. "On Alternative Modernities." *Public Culture* 11 (1): 1–18.

Gellner, Ernest. 1983. *Nations and Nationalism*. Ithaca, NY: Cornell University Press.

———. 1964. *Thought and Change*. London: Weidenfeld and Nicolson.

Giddens, Anthony. 1985. *The Nation-State and Violence*. Berkeley: University of California Press.

Gilroy, Paul. 1993. *The Black Atlantic: Modernity and Double Consciousness*. Cambridge, MA: Harvard University Press.

Gold, Thomas. 1988. "Colonial Origins of Taiwanese Capitalism." Pp. 101–17 in *Contending Approaches to the Political Economy of Taiwan*, ed. Edwin A. Winckler and Susan Greenhalgh. Armonk, NY: M. E. Sharpe.

Graham, Lawrence Otis. 1995. "'Head Nigger in Charge': Roles That Black Professionals Play in the Corporate World." *Business and Society Review* 94: 43–50.

Gutek, Barbara A. 1989. "Sexuality in the Workplace: Key Issues in Social Research and Organization." Pp. 56–70 in *The Sexuality of Organization*, ed. Jeff Hearn et al. London: Sage.

Haber, Samuel. 1991. *The Quest for Authority and Honor in the American Professions, 1750–1900*. Chicago: University of Chicago Press.

Habermas, Jürgen. [1962] 1989. *The Structural Transformation of the Public Sphere: An Inquiry into a Category of Bourgeois Society.* Trans. Thomas Burger, with Frederick Lawrence. Cambridge, MA: MIT Press.

———. 1984. *The Theory of Communicative Action.* Vol. 1. Trans. Thomas McCarthy. Boston: Beacon Press.

———. 1974. "The Public Sphere: An Encyclopedia Article (1964)." *New German Critique* 3: 49–55.

Halliday, Terence C. 1987. *Beyond Monopoly: Lawyers, State Crises, and Professional Empowerment.* Chicago: University of Chicago Press.

Hart, Janet. 1996. *New Voices in the Nation: Women and the Greek Resistance, 1941–1964.* Ithaca, NY: Cornell University Press.

———. 1992. "Cracking the Code: Narrative and Political Mobilization in the Greek Resistance." *Social Science History* 16: 631–68.

Haskell, Thomas L., ed. 1984. *The Authority of Experts: Studies in History and Theory.* Bloomington: Indiana University Press.

Hechter, Michael. 1975. *Internal Colonialism: The Celtic Fringe in British National Development, 1536–1966.* Berkeley: University of California Press.

Hechter, Michael, and Margaret Levi. 1979. "The Comparative Analysis of Ethnoregional Movements." *Ethnic and Racial Studies* 2 (3): 260–74.

Ho, Samuel Pao-San. 1984. "Colonialism and Development: Korea, Taiwan, and Kwantung." Pp. 347–98 in *The Japanese Colonial Empire, 1895–1945*, ed. Ramon H. Myers and Mark R. Peattie. Princeton, NJ: Princeton University Press.

Hobsbawm, E., and T. Ranger, eds. 1983. *The Invention of Tradition.* Cambridge: Cambridge University Press.

Hoffman, Lily M. 1997. "Professional Autonomy Reconsidered: the Case of Czech Medicine under State Socialism." *Comparative Studies in Society and History* 39 (2): 346–72.

———. 1989. *The Politics of Knowledge: Activist Movements in Medicine and Planning.* Albany: State University of New York Press.

Hohendahl, Peter U. 1979. "Critical Theory, Public Sphere, and Culture: Jürgen Habermas and His Critics." *New German Critique* 16: 92.

Horowitz, Donald L. 1985. *Ethnic Groups in Conflict.* Berkeley: University of California Press.

Hroch, Miroslav. 1993. "From National Movement to the Fully-Formed Nation: The Nation-Building Process." *New Left Review* 198: 3–20.

———. 1985. *Social Preconditions of National Revival in Europe: A Comparative Analysis of the Social Composition of Patriotic Groups among the Smaller European Nations.* Cambridge: Cambridge University Press.

Hunter, Janet. 1984. *Concise Dictionary of Modern Japanese History.* Berkeley: University of California Press.

Iriye, Akira, ed. 1980. *The Chinese and the Japanese: Essays in Political and Cultural Interactions.* Princeton, NJ: Princeton University Press.

Jansen, Marius. 1984. "Japanese Imperialism: Late Meiji Perspectives." Pp. 61–79 in *The Japanese Colonial Empire, 1895–1945*, ed. Ramon H. Myers and Mark R. Peattie. Princeton, NJ: Princeton University Press.

Jarausch, Konrad H. 1990. *The Unfree Professions: German Lawyers, Teachers, and Engineers, 1900–1950.* New York: Cambridge University Press.

Joffe, Carole E. 1995. *Doctors of Conscience: The Struggle to Provide Abortion Before and After Roe v. Wade.* Boston: Beacon Press.

Johnson, Terry. 1995. "Governmentality and the Institutionalization of Expertise." Pp. 7–24 in Health Professions and the State in Europe, ed. Terry Johnson, Gerry Larkin, and Mike Saks. New York: Routledge.

Kanter, Rosabeth Moss. 1977. Men and Women of the Corporation. New York: Basic Books.

Keene, Donald, ed. 1951. The Battles of Coxinga: Chikamatsu's Puppet Play, Its Background and Importance. London: Taylor's Foreign Press.

Kennedy, Michael D. 1991. Professionals, Power, and Solidarity in Poland: A Critical Sociology of Soviet-Type Society. Cambridge: Cambridge University Press.

———. 1990. "The Constitution of Critical Intellectuals: Polish Physicians, Peace Activists, and Democratic Civil Society." Studies in Comparative Communism 23: 281–303.

Kerr, George H. [1965] 1976. Formosa Betrayed. New York: Da Capo Press.

Kimball, Bruce A. 1992. The "True Professional Ideal" in America: A History. Cambridge, MA: Blackwell.

Kiser, Edgar, and Michael Hechter. 1998. "The Debate on Historical Sociology: Rational Choice Theory and Its Critics." American Journal of Sociology 104 (3): 785–816.

Kondo, Dorinne. 1990. Crafting Selves: Power, Gender, and Discourses of Identity in a Japanese Workplace. Chicago: University of Chicago Press.

Krause, Elliott. 1996. Death of the Guilds: Professions, States, and the Advance of Capitalism, 1930 to the Present. New Haven, CT: Yale University Press.

———. 1991. "Professions and the State in the Soviet Union and Eastern Europe: Theoretical Issues." Pp. 3–41 in Professions and the State: Expertise and Autonomy in the Soviet Union and Eastern Europe, ed. Anthony Jones. Philadelphia, PA: Temple University Press.

———. 1977. Power and Illness: The Political Sociology of Health and Medical Care. New York: Elsevier.

Kreckel, Reinhard. 1980. "Unequal Opportunity Structure and Labor Market Segmentation." Sociology 14: 525–50.

Lai, Tse-han, Ramon H. Myers, and Wei Wou. 1991. A Tragic Beginning: The Taiwan Uprising of February 28, 1947. Stanford, CA: Stanford University Press.

Larson, Magali S. 1990. "In the Matter of Experts and Professionals, or How Impossible It Is to Leave Nothing Unsaid." Pp. 24–50 in The Formation of Professions, ed. Rolf Torstendahl and Michael Burrage. London: Sage Publications.

———. 1984. "The Production of Expertise and the Constitution of Expert Power." Pp. 28–80 in The Authority of Experts: Studies in History and Theory, ed. Thomas L. Haskell. Bloomington: Indiana University Press.

———. 1977. The Rise of Professionalism: A Sociological Analysis. Berkeley: University of California Press.

Latour, Bruno. 1993. We Have Never Been Modern. Trans. Catherine Porter. Cambridge, MA: Harvard University Press.

Lee, Sophia. 1989. "The Foreign Ministry's Cultural Agenda for China: The Boxer Indemnity." Pp. 272–306 in The Japanese Informal Empire in China, 1895–1937, ed. Peter Duus, Ramon H. Myers, and Mark R. Peattie. Princeton, NJ: Princeton University Press.

Leslie, Charles. 1976. "Introduction." Pp. 1–17 in Asian Medical Systems: A Comparative Study. Berkeley: University of California Press.

Lo, Ming-cheng. 2000. "Confronting Contradictions and Negotiating Identities: Taiwanese Doctors' Anti-Colonialism in the 1920s." Pp. 210–39 in *Globalizations and Social Movements: Culture, Power, and the Transnational Public Sphere*, ed. John A. Guidry, Michael D. Kennedy, and Mayer N. Zald. Ann Arbor: University of Michigan Press.

———. 1994. "Crafting the Collective Identity: The Origin and Transformation of Taiwanese Nationalism." *Journal of Historical Sociology* 7: 198–223.

Lo, Ming-cheng M., and Christopher P. Bettinger. 2001. "The Historical Emergence of a 'Familial Society' in Japan." *Theory and Society* 30: 237–79.

Long, Susan. 1980. "Fame, Fortune, and Friends: Constraints and Strategies in the Careers of Japanese Physicians." Ph.D. diss. University of Illinois at Urbana-Champaign.

Macdonald, Keith M. 1995. *The Sociology of the Professions*. London: Sage Publications.

Manderson, Lenore. 1996. *Sickness and the State: Health and Illness in Colonial Malaya, 1870–1940*. Cambridge: Cambridge University Press.

Marcuse, Herbert. 1964. *One-Dimensional Man: Studies in the Ideology of Advanced Industrial Society*. Boston: Beacon Press.

Marshall, T. H. [1964] 1965. *Class, Citizenship, and Social Development*. Garden City, NY: Anchor Books.

Maynes, Mary Jo. 1992. "Autobiography and Class Formation in Nineteenth-Century Europe: Methodological Considerations." *Social Science History* 16: 517–37.

McClelland, Charles E. 1991. *The German Experience of Professionalization: Modern Learned Professions and Their Organizations from the Early Nineteenth Century to the Hitler Era*. Cambridge: Cambridge University Press.

Melosh, Barbara. 1982. *"The Physician's Hand": Work Culture and Conflict in American Nursing*. Philadelphia, PA: Temple University Press.

Melucci, Alberto. 1989. *Nomads of the Present: Social Movements and Individual Needs in Contemporary Society*. London: Hutchinson Radius.

Mendel, Douglas. 1970. *The Politics of Formosan Nationalism*. Berkeley: University of California Press.

Meskill, Johanna Margarete Menzel. 1979. *A Chinese Pioneer Family: The Lins of Wu-feng, Taiwan, 1729–1895*. Princeton, NJ: Princeton University Press.

Morris-Suzuki, Tessa. 1998. "Becoming Japanese: Imperial Expansion and Identity Crises in the Early Twentieth Century." Pp. 157–80 in *Japan's Competing Modernities: Issues in Culture and Democracy, 1900–1930*, ed. Sharon A. Minichiello. Honolulu: University of Hawaii Press.

Mosse, George. 1985. *Nationalism and Sexuality: Respectability and Abnormal Sexuality in Modern Europe*. New York: H. Fertig.

Mueller, Carol M. 1994. "Conflict Networks and the Origins of Women's Liberation." Pp. 234–63 in *New Social Movements: From Ideology to Identity*, ed. Enrique Laraña, Hank Johnston, and Joseph R. Gusfield. Philadelphia, PA: Temple University Press.

Myers, Ramon H., and Mark R. Peattie, eds. 1984. *The Japanese Colonial Empire, 1895–1945*. Princeton, NJ: Princeton University Press.

Nagel, Joane. 1994. "Constructing Ethnicity: Creating and Recreating Ethnic Identity and Culture." *Social Problems* 41 (1): 152–76.

Nairn, Tom. 1977. *The Break-up of Britain: Crisis and Neo-Nationalism*. London: NLB.

Office of the Chief of Naval Operations. 1944. *Taiwan (Formosa). Civil Affairs Handbook, Opnav 50E-12.* Washington, DC: Office of the Chief of the Naval Operations, Naval Department.

Ortner, Sherry B. 1989. *High Religion: A Cultural and Political History of Sherpa Buddhism.* Princeton, NJ: Princeton University Press.

Parker, Andrew, et. al., eds. 1992. *Nationalisms and Sexualities.* New York: Routledge.

Parsons, Talcott. 1968. "Professions." Pp. 536–47 in *International Encyclopedia of the Social Sciences.* Vol. 12, ed. David S. Sills. New York: Macmillan.

———. 1964. *The Social System.* New York: Free Press.

Passerini, Luisa. 1992. "A Memory for Women's History: Problems of Method and Interpretation." *Social Science History* 16 (4): 669–92.

Peattie, Mark R. 1984. "Japanese Attitudes toward Colonialism, 1895–1945." Pp. 80–127 in *The Japanese Colonial Empire, 1895–1945,* ed. Ramon H. Myers and Mark R. Peattie. Princeton, NJ: Princeton University Press.

Pieterse, Jan N. 1995. "Globalization as Hybridization." Pp. 45–68 in *Global Modernities,* ed. Mike Featherstone, Scott Lash, and Roland Robertson. London: Sage.

Quadagno, Jill, and Stan J. Knapp. 1992. "Have Historical Sociologists Forsaken Theory? Thoughts on the History/Theory Relationship." *Sociological Methods and Research* 20: 481–507.

Ragin, Charles C. 1992. "Introduction: Cases of 'What Is a Case?' " Pp. 1–17 in Ragin and Becker, eds. 1992.

Ragin, Charles C., and Howard S. Becker, eds. 1992. *What Is a Case? Exploring the Foundations of Social Inquiry.* New York: Cambridge University Press.

Reynolds, Douglas R. 1989. "Training Young Chinese Hands: Tōa Dōbun Shoin and Its Precursors, 1886–1945." Pp. 210–71 in *The Japanese Informal Empire in China, 1895–1937,* ed. Peter Duus, Ramon H. Myers, and Mark R. Peattie. Princeton, NJ: Princeton University Press.

Robertson, Jennifer. 1995. "Mon Japon: The Revue Theater as a Technology of Japanese Imperialism." *American Ethnologist* 4: 970–97.

Rockefeller, Steven C. 1994. "Comment." Pp. 87–98 in *Multiculturalism: Examining the Politics of Recognition,* by Charles Taylor et al., edited and introduced by Amy Gutmann. Princeton, NJ: Princeton University Press.

Rofel, Lisa. 1999. *Other Modernities: Gendered Yearnings in China after Socialism.* Berkeley: University of California Press.

Rothblatt, Sheldon. 1995. "How 'Professional' Are the Professions? A Review Article." *Comparative Studies of Society and History* 37 (January): 194–204.

Rueschemeyer, Dietrich. 1986. *Power and the Division of Labor.* Stanford, CA: Stanford University Press.

Sahlins, Peter. 1989. *Boundaries: The Making of France and Spain in the Pyrenees.* Berkeley: University of California Press.

Sciulli, David. 1986. "Voluntaristic Action as a Distinct Concept: Theoretical Foundations of Societal Constitutionalism." *American Sociological Review* 51 (December): 743–66.

Sewell, William H., Jr. 1992a. "A Theory of Structure: Duality, Agency, and Transformation." *American Journal of Sociology* 98 (1): 1–29.

———. 1992b. "Introduction: Narratives and Social Identities." *Social Science History* 16 (3): 479–88.

Shepherd, John Robert. 1993. *Statecraft and Political Economy on the Taiwan Frontier, 1600–1800*. Stanford, CA: Stanford University Press.

Sheppard, Deborah. 1989. "Organizations, Power, and Sexuality: The Image and Self-Image of Women Managers." Pp. 139–57 in the *Sexuality of Organization*, ed. Jeff Hearn et al. London: Sage.

Shimazu, N. 1989. "The Japanese Attempt to Secure Racial Equality in 1919." *Japan Forum* 1: 93–100.

Skocpol, Theda, ed. 1984. *Vision and Method in Historical Sociology*. New York: Cambridge University Press.

Smith, Anthony D. 1992. "Introduction: Ethnicity and Nationalism." *International Journal of Comparative Sociology* 33 (1–2): 1–4.

———. 1991. *National Identity*. London: Penguin.

———. 1986. *The Ethnic Origins of Nations*. Oxford: Blackwell.

Somers, Margaret. 1998. "'We're No Angels': Realism, Rational Choice, and Relationality in Social Science." *American Journal of Sociology* 104 (3): 722–84.

———. 1994. "The Narrative Constitution of Identity: A Relational and Network Approach." *Theory and Society* 23: 605–49.

———. 1992. "Narrativity, Narrative Identity, and Social Action: Rethinking English Working-Class Formation." *Social Science History* 16 (3): 591–630.

Steinmetz, George. 1993. *Regulating the Social: The Welfare State and Local Politics in Imperial Germany*. Princeton, NJ: Princeton University Press.

———. 1992. "Reflections on the Role of Social Narratives in Working-Class Formation: Narrative Theory in Social Sciences." *Social Science History* 16 (3): 499–516.

Stinchcombe, Arthur. 1978. *Theoretical Methods in Social History*. New York: Academic Press.

Stoler, Ann L. 1989. "Rethinking Colonial Categories: European Communities and the Boundaries of Rule." *Comparative Studies in Society and History* 31: 134–61.

Swidler, Ann. 1996. "From the Chair." *Newsletter of the Sociology of Culture* 10 (3–4): 1–3.

———. 1995. "Cultural Power and Social Movements." Pp. 25–40 in *Social Movements and Culture*, ed. Hank Johnston and Bert Klandermans. Minneapolis: University of Minnesota Press.

———. 1986. "Culture in Action: Symbols and Strategies." *American Sociological Review* 51 (2): 273–86.

Tanaka, Stefan. 1994. Review of *Cultural Nationalism in East Asia: Representation and Identity*, ed. Harumi Befu. *Journal of Asian Studies* 53 (May): 505–6.

———. 1993. *Japan's Orient: Rendering Pasts into History*. Berkeley: University of California Press.

Tanaka, Yuki. 1996. *Hidden Horrors: Japanese War Crimes in World War II*. With a foreword by John W. Dower. Boulder, CO: Westview Press.

Taylor, Charles. 1999. "Two Theories of Modernity." *Public Culture* 11 (1): 153–74.

———. 1990. "Modes of Civil Society." *Public Culture* 3 (1): 95–118.

Taylor, Charles, et al. 1994. *Multiculturalism: Examining the Politics of Recognition*, edited and introduced by Amy Gutmann. Princeton, NJ: Princeton University Press.

Tilly, Charles. 1992. *Coercion, Capital and European States, A.D. 990–1990*. Oxford: Blackwell.

Tiryakian, Edward A. 1997. "The Wild Cards of Modernity." *Daedalus* 126 (2): 147–82.

Tsurumi, Patricia. 1984. "Colonial Education in Korea and Taiwan." Pp. 275–311 in *The Japanese Colonial Empire, 1895–1945,* ed. Ramon H. Myers and Mark R. Peattie. Princeton, NJ: Princeton University Press.

———. 1977. *Japanese Colonial Education in Taiwan, 1895–1945.* Cambridge, MA: Harvard University Press.

Uno, Kathleen. 1993. "The Death of 'Good Wife, Wise Mother'?" Pp. 293–322 in *Postwar Japan as History,* ed. Andrew Gordon. Berkeley: University of California Press.

Weber, Max. 1968. *Economy and Society: An Outline of Interpretive Sociology.* Ed. Guenther Roth and Claus Wittich. Trans. Ephraim Fischoff and others. New York: Bedminster Press.

Weiner, Michael, ed. 1997. *Japan's Minorities: The Illusion of Homogeneity.* New York: Routledge.

Witz, Anne. 1992. *Professions and Patriarchy.* New York: Routledge.

Woods, James D., with Jay H. Lucas. 1993. *The Corporate Closet: The Professional Lives of Gay Men in America.* New York: Free Press.

Wray, Harry, and Hilary Conroy, eds. 1983. *Japan Examined: Perspectives on Modern Japanese History.* Honolulu: University of Hawaii Press.

Wuthnow, Robert. 1987. *Meaning and Moral Order: Explorations in Cultural Analysis.* Berkeley: University of California Press.

Young, Crawford. 1985. "Ethnicity and the Colonial and Post-Colonial State in Africa." Pp. 73–81 in *Ethnic Groups and the State,* ed. P. Brass. London: Croom Helm.

Young, Louise. 1998. *Japan's Total Empire: Manchuria and the Culture of Wartime Imperialism.* Berkeley: University of California Press.

Young, Robert. 1995. *Colonial Desire: Hybridity in Theory, Culture, and Race.* London: Routledge.

Zald, Mayer N., and John D. McCarthy. [1987] 1994. "Organizational Intellectuals and the Criticism of Society." Pp. 97–120 in *Social Movements in an Organizational Society,* ed. Mayer N. Zald and John D. McCarthy. New Brunswick, NJ: Transaction Publishers.

CHINESE MATERIALS

Cai, Peihuo, et al. 蔡培火等. 1983. *Taiwan minzu yundongshi* 臺灣民族運動史. 3rd ed. Taibei: Zili wanbaoshe.

Cao, Yongyang 曹永洋. 1996. *Dushi conglin yisheng—Guo Weizu de shengya xinlu* 都市叢林醫生——郭維租的生涯心路. Taibei: Qianwei chubanshe.

Chen, Junkai 陳君愷. 1992. *Rizhi shiqi Taiwan yisheng shehui diwei zhi yanjiu* 日治時期臺灣醫生社會地位之研究. Taipei: Institute of History, National Taiwan Normal University.

Chen, Yisong 陳逸松. 1994. *Chen Yisong huiyilu: Taiyangqi xia feng man tai* 陳逸松回憶錄:太陽旗下風滿台. Recorded by Wu Junying and compiled by Lin Zhongsheng. Taibei: Qianwei chubanshe.

Du, Congming 杜聰明. 1989. *Du Congming huiyilu* 杜聰明回憶錄. Taibei: Longwen chubanshe.

Fan, Yanqiu 范燕秋. 1993. "Rizhi shiqi Taiwan Zongdufu Yilan Yiyuan chutan 日治時期台灣總督府宜蘭醫院初探." *Yilan wenxian zazhi* 宜蘭文獻雜志 7: 3–38.

"Gaoling yishi zuotanhui—Fujin zhuixi 高齡醫師座談會——撫今追昔." 1978. *Yiwang* [Hope] 醫望 2 (1): 58–70.

Guo, Jinta 郭金塔. 1995. "Huiyi Taida diyi waike 回憶臺大第一外科." P. 113 in *Taida Yiyuan bainen huaijiu* 臺大醫院百年懷舊, Guoli Taiwan Daxue Yixueyuan Fushe Yiyuan. Taibei: Guoli Taiwan Daxue Yixueyuan Fushe Yiyuan.

Guoli Taiwan Daxue Yixueyuan Fushe Yiyuan 國立臺灣大學醫學院附設醫院. 1995. *Taida Yiyuan bainen huaijiu* 臺大醫院百年懷舊. Taibei: Guoli Taiwan Daxue Yixueyuan Fushe Yiyuan.

Han, Shiquan 韓石泉. 1966. *Liushi huiyi* 六十回憶. Tainan: Han Shiquan xiansheng shishi sanzhounian jinian zhuanji bianyin weiyuanhui.

He, Kaiqia 何開洽. 1995. "Huiyizhong de diandi 回憶中的點滴." Pp. 76–77 in *Taida Yiyuan bainen huaijiu* 臺大醫院百年懷舊, Guoli Taiwan Daxue Yixueyuan Fushe Yiyuan. Taibei: Guoli Taiwan Daxue Yixueyuan Fushe Yiyuan.

Huang, Fuqing 黃福慶. 1982. *Jindai riben zaihua wenhua ji shehui shiye zhi yanjiu* 近代日本在華文化及社會事業之研究. Taibei: Zhongyang Yanjiuyuan Jindaishi Yanjiusuo.

Huang, Xiuzheng 黃秀政. 1992. *Taiwan gerang yu yiwei kangri yundong* 臺灣割讓與乙未抗日運動. Taibei: Taiwan Shangwu yinshuguan.

Jian, Jiongren 簡炯仁. 1991. *Taiwan minzhongdang* 臺灣民眾黨. Taibei: Daoxiang chubanshe.

Lan, Bozhou 藍博洲. 1993. *Riju shiqi Taiwan xuesheng yundong* 日據時期臺灣學生運動. Taibei: Shibao wenhua chuban.

Li, Nanheng 李南衡, ed. 1979. *Lai He xiansheng quanji* 賴和先生全集. Taibei: Mintan chubanshe.

Li, Tengyue 李騰嶽. 1953. *Taiwansheng tongzhigao, zhengshizhi weishengpian* 臺灣省通志稿政事志衛生篇. Vol. 2. Taibei: Taiwansheng wenxian weiyuanhui.

———. 1952. *Taiwansheng tongzhigao, zhengshizhi weishengpian* 臺灣省通志稿政事志衛生篇. Vol. 1. Taibei: Taiwansheng wenxian weiyuanhui.

———. 1949. "Shijie dierci zhanzheng zhong Riben zhengfu duiyu Taiwan zhi yiyao guanli shishi gaiyao 世界第二次戰爭中日本政府對於臺灣之醫藥管理實施概要." *Taiwansheng wenxian weiyuanhui zhuankan* 台灣省文獻委員會專刊 1 (August): 32–39.

Li, Xiaofeng 李筱峰. 1986. *Taiwan zhanhou chuqi de minyi daibiao* 臺灣戰後初期的民意代表. Taibei: Zili wanbao.

Li, Xinfen 李欣芬. 1989. "Jidujiao yu Taiwan yiliao weisheng de xiandaihua—Yi Zhanghua Jidujiao Yiyuan wei zhongxin zhi tantao (1896–1936) 基督教與臺灣醫療衛生的現代化:以彰化基督教醫院為中心之探討." Master's thesis, Institute of History, National Taiwan Normal University.

Liang, Jinlan 梁金蘭 and Liang Yuming 梁育明. 1994. "Liang Jinlan, Liang Yuming jiedi fangwen jilu 梁金蘭, 梁育明姐弟訪問記錄." Interviewed by Xu Xueji, recorded by Cai Shuoli. *Koushu lishi* 口述歷史 5: 307–19.

Lin, Bowei 林柏維. 1993. *Taiwan Wenhua Xiehui cangsang* 臺灣文化協會滄桑. Taibei: Taiyuan yishu wenhua jijinhui.

Lin, Jiwen 林繼文. 1991. "Riben Jutai moqi (1930–1945) zhanzheng dongyuan tixi zhi yanjiu 日本據台末期 (1930–1945) 戰爭動員體系之研究." Master's thesis. Guoli Taiwan Daxue Zhengzhixue Yanjiusuo.

Lin, Kunyuan 林坤元. 1978. *Qishi zishu* 七十自述. Taizhong: Lin Kunyuan.

Lin, Ruiming 林瑞明. 1996. *Taiwan wenxue de lishi guancha* 台灣文學的歷史觀察. Taibei: Yunchen wenhua shiye gufen youxian gongsi.

Lin, Tianyou 林天佑. 1983. *Xiangya zhita chunqiuji* 象牙之塔春秋記. Taibei: Taiwan Shangwu yinshuguan.

Lin, Yanqing 林彥卿. "Gongxue 共學." Unpublished manuscript.

Lu, Xiuyi 盧修一. 1989. *Riju shidai Taiwan gongchandang shi, 1928–1932* 日據時代臺灣共產黨史. Taibei: Ziyou Shidai chubanshe.

Ng, Yuzin Chiautong 黃昭堂. 1989. *Taiwan Zongdufu* 臺灣總督府. Trans. Huang Yingzhe. Taibei: Ziyou Shidai chubanshe. Originally published as *Taiwan sōtokufu*. Tokyo: Kyoikusha, 1981.

Ohzuru, Masamitsu 大鶴正滿. 1995. "Mingzhi shidai de yiwei xianqu—Shankou Xiugao 明治時代的一位先驅——山口秀高." Pp. 8–10 in *Taida Yiyuan bainen huaijiu* 臺大醫院百年懷舊, Guoli Taiwan Daxue Yixueyuan Fushe Yiyuan. Taibei: Guoli Taiwan Daxue Yixueyuan Fushe Yiyuan.

"Shixin xiagu de Huang Wentao xiansheng 詩心俠骨的黃文陶先生." 1979. *Yiwang* 醫望 [Hope] 2 (February): 73–78.

Shozawa, Jun 所澤潤. 1995b. "Wode fangtan zhuti ji jingyan: Rizhi shidai Taiwan de 'ziwo suzaoshi' 我的訪談主題及經驗: 日治時代台灣人的自我塑造史.'" Tran.Huang Shaoheng. *Koushu lishi* 口述歷史 6: 229–44.

Sugatani, Shinji 菅谷新次. 1995. "Taibei zhiyi 台北之憶." P. 262 in *Taida yiyuan bainen huaijiu* 臺大醫院百年懷舊, Guoli Taiwan Daxue Yixueyuan Fushe Yiyuan. Taibei: Guoli Taiwan Daxue Yixueyuan Fushe Yiyuan.

Taiwan Zongdufu 臺灣總督府. 1988. *Taiwan shehui yundong shi* 臺灣社會運動史. Translated from Japanese to Chinese by Wang Naixin et al. Taibei: Chuangzao chubanshe. Originally published as *Taiwan Sōtokufu keisatsu enkaku shi (KE)*. 4 vols. (Taihoku [Taipei]: Taiwan Sōtokufu, 1933–1941).

Taiwan zuojia quanji (Riju shidai) 臺灣作家全集 (日據時代). 1991. Vols. 1–10. Taibei: Qianwei chubanshe.

Tu, Zhaoyan 涂照彥. [1991?]. *Riben diguo zhuyi xia de Taiwan* 日本帝國主義下的臺灣. Translated from Japanese to Chinese by Li Mingjun. Taibei: Renjian chubanshe. Originally published as *Nihon teikokushugika no Taiwan*. Tokyo: Tokyo Daigaku shuppankai, 1975.

Wei, Huoyao 魏火曜. 1990. *Wei Huoyao xiansheng fangwen jilu* 魏火曜先生訪問記錄. Interviewed by Xiong Bingzhen and Jiang Dongliang, recorded by Zheng Lirong. Taipei: Institute of Modern History, Academia Sinica.

Wu, Jifu 吳基福. 1978. "Ningwei jishou buwei niuhou 寧爲雞首不爲牛後." *Taiwan Medical Journal* 臺灣醫界 21: 53–55.

Wu, Micha 吳密察. 1990. *Taiwan jindaishi yanjiu* 臺灣近代史研究. Taibei: Daoxiang chubanshe.

Wu, Pingcheng 吳平城. 1989. *Taipingyang zhanzheng junyi riji* 太平洋戰爭軍醫日記. Taibei: Zili wanbao.

Wu, Wenxing 吳文星. 1992. *Riju shiqi Taiwan shehui lingdao jieceng zhi yanjiu* 日據時期臺灣社會領導階層之研究. Taibei: Zhengzhong shuju.

———. 1986. "Riju shiqi difang zizhi gaige yundong zhi tantao 日據時期地方自治改革運動之探討." Pp. 281–308 in *Taiwan shi yanjiu ji shiliao fajue yantaohui lunwenji* 台灣史研究及史料發掘研討會論文集. Taibei: Taiwan shiji yanjiu zhongxin.

———. 1983. *Riju shiqi Taiwan shifan jiaoyu zhi yanjiu* 日據時期臺灣師範教育之研究. Taipei: Institute of History, National Taiwan Normal University.

Wu, Xinrong 吳新榮. 1981. *Wu Xinrong riji* 吳新榮日記. Taibei: Yuanjing chuban shiye gongsi.

Xie, Zhenrong 謝振榮. 1989. "Riben zhimin zhuyi xia Taiwan weisheng zhengce zhi yanjiu 日本殖民主義下臺灣衛生政策之研究." Master's thesis, Zhongguo Wenhua Daxue Riben Yanjiuso.

Xu, Xueji 許雪姬. 1992. "Cai Dingzan xiansheng fangwen Jilu 蔡丁贊先生訪問紀錄." *Koushilishi* 口述歷史 3: 139–44.

Yang, Bichuan 楊碧川. 1988. *Taiwan lishi nianbiao* 臺灣歷史年表. Taibei: Zili wanbao chubanbu.

Ye, Shitao 葉石濤. 1987. *Taiwan wenxue shigang* 臺灣文學史綱. Gaoxiong: Wenxuejie zazhishe.

"Yiren zhuanlan 醫人專欄." 1980. *Taiwan Medical Journal* 臺灣醫界 23: 3–12.

Zeng, Yibiao 曾以標. 1995. "Huainian Taibei Yizhuan Juenei [Horiuchi] xiaozhang 懷念台北醫專奧內校長." P. 269 in *Taida Yiyuan bainen huaijiu* 臺大醫院百年懷舊, Guoli Taiwan Daxue Yixueyuan Fushe Yiyuan. Taibei: Guoli Taiwan Daxue Yixueyuan Fushe Yiyuan.

Zhang, Yanxian 張炎憲 et al., eds. 1987. *Taiwan jindai mingrenzhi* 臺灣近代名人誌. Taibei: Zili wanbao.

Zheng, Yizong 鄭翼宗. 1992. *Lijie guilai hua bansheng: Yige Taiwanren yixue jiaoshou de zizhuan* 歷劫歸來話半生: 一個臺灣人醫學教授的自傳. Taibei: Qianwei chubanshe.

Zhou, Jingyin 周景音. 1984. "Fang Wei Bingyan boshi 訪魏炳炎博士." *Taiwan Medical Journal* 臺灣醫界 27 (2): 57–60.

Zhou, Wanyao 周婉窈. 1989. *Riju shidai de Taiwan yihui shezhi qingyuan yundong* 日據時代的臺灣議會設置請願運動. Taibei: Zili baoxi wenhua chubanbu.

Zhuang, Yongming 莊永明. 1995. "Zhuanke yiyuan de xianqu: Han Shiquan yishi qirenqishi 專科醫院的先驅: 韓石泉醫師其人其事." Pp. 87–90 in *Taida Yiyuan bainen huaijiu* 臺大醫院百年懷舊, Guoli Taiwan Daxue Yixueyuan Fushe Yiyuan. Taibei: Guoli Taiwan Daxue Yixueyuan Fushe Yiyuan.

JAPANESE MATERIALS

Abe, Fumio 阿部文夫. 1932. "Taiwan ni okeru yūseiundō 台湾における優生運動." *Taiwan jihō* 台湾時報 (February): 6–9.

Anzu 杏.

Du, Congming [To, Sōmei] 杜聡明. 1940. "Taiwan ni okeru iji eisei no konjaku 台湾における医事衛生の今昔." *Taiwan Sōtokufu rinji jōhōbu buhō* 台湾総督府臨時情報部部報 (June): 26–30.

Haruyama, Meitetsu 春山明哲. 1980. *Nihon shokuminchishugi no seijiteki tenkai* 日本植民地主義の政治的展開. Tōkyō: Ajia Seikei Gakkai.

Hong, Yuru [Kō, Ikujo] 洪郁如. 1995. "Nihon no Taiwan shihai to fujin dantai 日本の台湾支配と婦人団体." Master's thesis. Tōkyō Daigaku Daigakuin Sōgō Bunka Kenkyūka.

Ide, Kiwata 井出季和太. [1937] 1988. *Taiwan chisekishi* 台湾治績志. Reprint, Tōkyō: Seishisha.

Jiayi [Kagi] igakkai zasshi 嘉義医学会雑誌. 1934–1935.

Kaminuma, Hachirō 上沼八郎. 1978. "Nihon tōchika ni okeru Taiwan ryūgakusei: Dōka seisaku to ryūgakusei mondai no tenbō 日本統治下における台湾留学生:同化政

策と留学生問題の展望." *Kokuritsu Kyōiku Kenkyūjo kiyō* 国立教育研究所紀要, no. 94 (March): 133–57.

Keibukyoku 警部局. 1941. "Jikyoku to kokumin hoken 時局と国民保健." *Taiwan Sōtokufu rinji jōhōbu buhō* 台湾総督府臨時情報部部報, no. 91: 2–7.

Kiribayashi, Shigeru 桐林茂. 1932. "Taiwan no eisei kanmon o mamotte 台湾の衛生関門を護って." *Taiwan jihō* 台湾時報 (July): 34–36.

"Kokka sōdōin ka no kenkō shūkan 国家総動員下の健康週間." 1939. *Taiwan jihō* 台湾時報 (June): 187–88.

Lin, Yushu 林玉書. 1935. "Hajimete hontōjin ishi to narite 始めて本島人医師となりて." In *Jiayi [Kagi] shisei goshūnen kinenshi* 嘉義市制5周年記念史, Jiayi shiyakusho. Jiayi: Jiayi shiyakusho.

Mori, Oto 森於菟. [1969] 1993. "Suna ni kakareta kiroku 砂に書かれた記録." Pp. 323–427 in *Chichi toshite no Mori Ogai* 父としての森鴎外. Reprint, Tōkyō: Chikuma shobō.

———. 1936. "Zuihitsu wa tōbun oyasumi: Jūjitsu ni doryokusuru yō 随筆は当分お休み; 充実に努力するよう." *Teikoku daigaku shinbun* 帝国大学新聞 (February 3): 6.

Morishita, Kaoru 森下薫. 1942a. "Nettai igaku to Taiwan 熱帯医学と台湾." *Taiwan jihō* 台湾時報 (August): 80–91.

———. 1942b. "Nanpōken kōsei seisaku no kōsō 南方圏厚生政策の構想." *Taiwan jihō* 台湾時報 (March): 42–54.

———. 1932. "Nettai no keiei to mararia 熱帯の経営とマラリア." *Taiwan jihō* 台湾時報 (October): 136–42.

Mukōyama, Hiroo 向山寛夫. 1987. *Nihon tōchika ni okeru Taiwan minzoku undōshi* 日本統治下における台湾民族運動史. Tōkyō: Chūō Keizai Kenkyūjo.

Naka, Shūzō 中脩三. 1936. "Taiwan no shizen to seishinbyō 台湾の自然と精神病." *Taiwan jihō* 台湾時報 (October): 15–16.

Nakamura, Takashi 中村孝志. 1991. "Kanton [Guangdong] hakuaikai iin o meguru shomondai—Taiwan Sōtokufu no taika bunka kōsaku (2) 広東博愛会医院をめぐる諸問題──台湾総督府の対華文化工作 (2)." *Tenri University Journal* 天理大学学報 166: 1–24.

———. 1990. "Kanton [Guangdong] hakuaikai iin o meguru shomondai—Taiwan Sōtokufu no taika bunka kōsaku (1) 広東博愛会医院をめぐる諸問題──台湾総督府の対華文化工作 (1)." *Tenri University Journal* 天理大学学報 165: 25–49.

———. 1989. "Suwatō [Shantou] hakuaikai iin no seiritsu スワトウ博愛会医院の成立." *Tenri University Journal* 天理大学学報 162: 15–28.

———. 1988. "Amoy [Xiamen] oyobi Fukushū [Fuzhou] hakuaikai iin no seiritsu—Taiwan Sōtokufu no bunka kōsaku アモイおよび福州博愛会医院の成立──台湾総督府の文化工作." *Nanpō bunka* 南方文化 15: 1–40.

Nakao, Katsumi 中生勝美. 1994. "Shokuminchi no minzokugaku: Manshū minzoku gakkai no katsudō 植民地の民族学: 満州民族学会の活動." *Herumesu* へるめす no. 52 (December): 135–43.

———. 1993. "Shokuminchi shugi to Nihon minzokugaku 植民地主義と日本民族学." *Chūgoku: Shakai to bunka* 中国: 社会と文化 no. 8 (June): 231–42.

Nanmei kaishi 南溟会志.

Nihon sekijūji-sha Taiwan shibu 日本赤十字社台湾支部. 1939. "Jihenka ni okeru sekijūji 事変下における赤十字." *Taiwan Sōtokufu rinji jōhōbu buhō* 台湾総督府臨時情報部部報 no. 55 (March): 2–5.

Oda, Toshio 小田俊郎. 1974. *Taiwan igaku 50 nen shi* 台湾医学 50 年史. Tōkyō: Igaku shoin.

——. 1964. *Igakusha nansenhokuba: Daigaku kyōju 40 nen no kaisō* 医学者南船北馬: 大学教授 40 年の回想. Ōsaka: Rokugatsu-sha.

Oguma, Eiji 小熊英二. 1998. *"Nihonjin" no kyōkai: Okinawa, Ainu, Taiwan, Chōsen, shokuminchi shihai kara fukki undō made*「日本人」の境界:沖縄、アイヌ、台湾、朝鮮、植民地支配から復帰運動まで. Tōkyō: Shinyōsha.

Ohkubo, Rokurō 大窪六郎. 1942. "Taihoku hokenkan hōmonki 台北保健館訪問記." *Taiwan Sōtokufu rinji jōhōbu buhō* 台湾総督府臨時情報部部報, no. 146 (May): 27–33.

Ozaki, Hotsuki 尾崎秀樹. 1971. *Kyūshokuminchi bungaku no kenkyū* 旧植民地文学の研究. Tōkyō: Keisō shobō.

Ryū, Meishū [Liu, Mingxiu] 劉明修. 1983. *Taiwan tōchi to ahen mondai* 台湾統治と阿片問題. Tōkyō: Yamakawa shuppansha.

Saitō, Tatsuru 斉藤樹. 1941. "Hijōji to kenkō 非常時と健康." *Taiwan Sōtokufu rinji jōhōbu buhō* 台湾総督府臨時情報部部報 (May): 4–7.

Senmon Gakkō Kōyūkai 専門学校校友会. 1924. "Taiwan isen sōritsu nijūgo shūnen, Horiuchi Tsuguo hakushi zaishoku nijūgo nen, shukuga kinengō 台湾医創立 25 周年、堀内次雄博士在職 25 年、祝賀記念号." *Taiwan Sōtokufu Igaku Senmon Gakkō Kōyūkai zasshi* 台湾総督府医学専門学校校友会雑誌 no. 53. Taihoku [Taipei]: Senmon Gakkō Kōyūkai.

Shen, Jie [Shin, Ketsu] 沈潔. 1996. *"Manshūkoku" shakai jigyōshi* 満州国社会事業史. Kyōto: Mineruva shobō.

Shimojō, Himakazu 下条久馬一. 1942. "Nanpōken to waga nettai igaku kenkyūjo 南方圏と我が熱帯医学研究所." 台湾時報 *Taiwan jihō* (January): 66–70.

——. 1931. "Nanshi no iji eisei no genjō to waga taigan no iryōshisetsu 南支の医事衛生の現状と我が対岸の医療施設." 台湾時報 *Taiwan jihō* (June): 40–50.

Shozawa, Jun 所澤潤. 1999. "Kikitori chōsa: Gaichi no shingaku taiken (VI): Tainan-shū no nōson kara chōrōkyōchūgaku, naichino Ebara Chūgakkō o hete Nihon Shika Igaku Sennmon Gakkō oyobi Tōkyō Igaku Shigaku Sennmongakkō Igakuka o sotsugyō 聞き取り調査: 外地の進学体験 (VI): 台南州の農村から長老教中学、内地の荏原中学校を経て日本歯科医学専門学校及び東京医学歯学専門学校医学科を卒業. *Gunma Daigaku Kyōiku Gakubu kiyō jinbun shakaigaku hen* 群馬大学教育学部紀要人文社会学編 48: 127–66.

——. 1998. "Kikitori chōsa: Gaichi no shingaku taiken (V): Sekkō Kōgakkō kara, Taihoku Kōkō jinjōka, dōkōtōka, Taihoku Kōkyū Chūgaku o hete, Taiwan Daigaku Igakuin sotsugyō 聞き取り調査: 外地の進学体験 (V): 石光公学校から、台北高校尋常科、同高等科、台北高級中学を経て、台湾大学医学院卒業." *Gunma Daigaku Kyōiku Gakubu kiyō jinbun shakaigaku hen* 群馬大学教育学部紀要人文社会学編 47: 183–266.

——. 1996. "Kikitori chōsa: Gaichi no shingaku taiken (III): Teikō no chi, Ryūtan kara, Kiirun Chūgakkō, Taihoku Kōkō o hete, Nagasaki Ika Daigaku sotsugyō 聞き取り調査: 外地の進学体験 (III): 抵抗の地、龍潭から、基隆中学校、台北高校を経て、長崎医科大学卒業." *Gunma Daigaku Kyōiku Gakubu kiyō jinbun shakaigaku hen* 群馬大学教育学部紀要人文社会学編 45: 97–163.

——. 1995a. "Kikitori chōsa: Gaichi no shingaku taiken (II): Taihoku Isshi Fushō, Taihoku Kōkō, Taihoku Teidai Igakubu o hete, Taiwan Daigaku Igakuin sotsugyō 聞き取り調査: 外地の進学体験 (II): 台北一師附小、台北高校、台北帝大医学部を経て、

台湾大学医学院卒業." *Gunma Daigaku Kyōiku Gakubu kiyō jinbun shakaigaku hen* 群馬大学教育学部紀要人文社会学編 44: 139–87.

Soda, Takemune 曽田長宗. 1937. "Taiwan zaijū naichijin no taikaku mondai 台湾在住内地人の体格問題." *Taiwan jihō* 台湾時報 (July).

"Sokoku no hanayome 祖国の花嫁." 1939. *Taiwan Sōtokufu rinji jōhōbu buhō* 台湾総督府臨時情報部部報, no. 55 (March): 1.

Taiheiyō Kyōkai 太平洋協会. 1942. *Nanpō igaku ronsō* 南方医学論叢. Tōkyō: Taiheiyō Kyōkai.

Taiwan igakkai zasshi 台湾医学会雑誌. 1902–1944.

Taiwan jihō 台湾時報.

Taiwan Kyōikukai 台湾教育会編. 1939. *Taiwan kyōiku enkaku shi* 台湾教育沿革誌. Taihoku [Taipei]: Taiwan Kyōikukai.

Taiwan minpō 台湾民報.

Taiwan shinminpō 台湾新民報.

Taiwan Shinminpō Sha 台湾新民報社編. 1934. *Taiwan jinshikan* 台湾人士鑑.

Taiwan Sōtokufu 台湾総督府. 1896–1918. *(MJST) Taiwan Sōtokufu minsei jimu seiseki teiyō* 台湾総督府民政事務成績提要 vols. 2–24.

Taiwan Sōtokufu 台湾総督府. 1919–1941. *(JST) Taiwan Sōtokufu jimu seiseki teiyō* 台湾総督府事務成績提要 vols. 25–47.

Taiwan Sōtokufu fuhō 台湾総督府府報.

Taiwan Sōtokufu kanpō 台湾総督府官報.

Teikoku daigaku shinbun 帝国大学新聞.

Tōneikai 東寧会. 1978. *Tōneikai 40 nen: Taihoku Teidai Igakubu to sonogo* 東寧会 40 年: 台北帝大医学部とその後. Tōkyō: Toneikai.

Tōnei kaishi 東寧会誌.

Wakabayashi, Masahiro 若林正丈. 1983. *Taiwan kōnichi undōshi kenkyū* 台湾抗日運動史研究. Tōkyō: Kenbun shuppan.

Xie, Chunmu 謝春木. 1930. *Taiwanjin wa kaku miru* 台湾人はかく視る. Taihoku [Taipei]: Taiwan Minpō Sha.

Yanaihara, Tadao 矢内原忠雄. 1929. *Teikoku shugi ka no Taiwan* 帝国主義下の台湾. Tōkyō: Iwanami shoten.

ARCHIVAL MATERIALS

From Gaimushō Gaikōshiryōkan archives 外務省外交史料館

"8420–1." Dōjinkai kankei zakken—Shinryō-han Shina haken kankei 同仁会関係雑件——診療班支那派遣関係 (1). File no. H-4-2-0, 3–4.

"Bōeki butai no shingun 防疫部隊の進軍," originally published in *Yomiuri shimbun* 読売新聞, April 23, 1938. Dōjinkai kankei zakken—Bōeki jimu kankei 同仁会関係雑件——防疫事務関係 (1). File no. H-4-2-0, 3–5.

"Bōeki kenkyū shoin wa denkenkei ga dokusen—Taniguchi kyōju Nankin de kataru 防疫研究所員は伝研系が独占——谷口教授南京で語る," originally published in *Iji eisei shinbun* 医事衛生新聞, May 18, 1938. Dōjinkai kankei zakken—Bōeki jimu kankei 同仁会関係雑件——防疫事務関係 (1). File no. H-4-2-0, 3–5.

"Bōgyaku jikokumin ni mukuyu 暴虐自国民に報ゆ," originally published in *Kokumin shinbun* 国民新聞, October 5, 1938. Dōjinkai kankei zakken—Bōeki jimu kankei 同仁会関係雑件——防疫事務関係 (1). File no.: H-4-2-0, 3–5.

"Buki naki ikusa 武器なき戦," originally published in *Dōjin* 同仁, vol. 2, no. 3, 1923. Byōin kankei zakken—Dōjinkai no bu 病院関係雑件——同仁会の部. File no. 3-11-3, 6–2.

"Dōjinkai kakuiin keiei chōsho 同仁会各医院経営調書." Byōin kankei zakken—Dōjinkai Jinan byōin kankei 病院関係雑件——同仁会済南病院関係 (3). File no. H-4-1-0, 1–4.

"Dōjinkai kisoku gaiyō 同仁会規則概要." Originally published in *Dōjin* 同仁, 2, no. 3 (1923). Byōin kankei zakken—Dōjinkai no bu 病院関係雑件——同仁会の部. File no. 3-11-3, 6–2.

"Dōjinkai Jinan iin junkai shinryō hōkoku 同仁会済南医院巡回診療報告," Byōin kankei zakken—Dōjinkai Jinan byōin kankei 病院関係雑件——同仁会済南病院関係 (4). File no. H-4-1-0, 1–2.

"Hankou chihō no jikyoku jōhō 漢口地方の時局情報." Byōin kankei Zakken—Hankou iin kankei 病院関係雑件——漢口医院関係. File no. H-4-1-0, 1–4.

"Hiretsu na teki no saikin senjutsu 卑劣な敵の細菌戦術," originally published in *Yomiuri shimbun* 読売新聞 (夕刊), October 4, 1938 (evening edition). Dōjinkai kankei zakken—Bōeki jimu kankei 同仁会関係雑件——防疫事務関係 (1). File no. H-4-2-0, 3–5.

"Hizoku no gyakushū to tatakau, ijutsu no senbuhan, mezamashii Dōjinkai no katsuyaku 匪賊の逆襲と戦う、医術の宣撫班、目覚ましい同仁会の活躍," originally published in *Tokyo nichinichi shinbun* 東京日日新聞, November 24, 1938. Dōjinkai kankei zakken—Bōeki jimu kankei 同仁会関係雑件——防疫事務関係 (1). File no. H-4-2-0, 3–5.

"Hokushi chūshi ni okeru Dōjinkai no shinryō bōeki jigyō ni tsuite 北支中支における同仁会の診療防疫事業について," in Hokuchūshi ni okeru shinryō bōeki jōkyō 北中支における診療防疫状況. Dōjinkai kankei zakken—Shinryō-han Shina haken kankei 同仁会関係雑件——診療班支那派遣関係 (2). File no. H-4-2-0, 3–4.

"Jihen chokuzen ni okeru hokushi chūshi no eisei shisetsu ni tsuite 事変直前における北支中支の衛生施設について." Dōjinkai kankei zakken—Shinryō-han Shina haken kankei 同仁会関係雑件——診療班支那派遣関係 (2). File no. H-4-2-0, 3–4.

"Kimitsu 机密 # 302." Byōin kankei zakken—Dōjinkai Jinan byōin kankei 病院関係雑件——同仁会済南病院関係 (3). File no. H-4-1-0, 1–4.

"Kimitsu 机密 # 88." Dōjinkai Jinan iin keiei hōshin ni kansuru ken 同仁会済南医院経営方針に関する件. Byōin kankei zakken— Dōjinkai Jinan byōin kankei 病院関係雑件——同仁会済南病院関係 (3). File no. H-4-1-0, 1–4.

"Kōfutsū 公普通 236 [August 3, 1934]." Kakkoku ni okeru igaku oyobi ijutsu kankei zakken—Manshū koku no bu 各国における医学及び医術関係雑件——満州国の部. File no. H-4-2-0, 3–5.

"Kōfutsū 公普通 544 [May 8, 1933]." Kakkoku ni okeru igaku oyobi ijutsu kankei zakken—Manshū koku no bu 各国における医学及び医術関係雑件——満州国の部. File no. H-4-2-0, 3–5.

"Korera no shinryō narabini Shanhai ni okeru Shinajin no shippei ni tsuite コレラの診療並びに上海における支那人の疾病について," Hokuchūshi ni okeru shinryō bōeki jōkyō 北中支における診療防疫状況. Dōjinkai kankei zakken—Shinryō-han Shina haken kankei 同仁会関係雑件——診療班支那派遣関係 (2). File no. H-4-2-0, 3–4.

"Minshū o i de senbu—Senkentai sudeni shuppatsusu 民衆を医で宣撫——先遣隊既に出発す," originally published in *Teikoku daigaku shinbun* 帝国大学新聞, April

25, 1938. Dōjinkai kankei zakken—Bōeki jimu kankei 同仁会関係雑件——防疫事務関係. File no. H-4-2-0, 3–5.

"Nanjing ni okeru shinryō taiken narabini shinajin no tokushu shippei ni tsuite 南京における診療体験並びに支那人の特殊疾病について," Hokuchūshi ni okeru shinryō bōeki jōkyō 北中支における診療防疫状況. Dōjinkai kankei zakken—Shinryō-han Shina haken kankei 同仁会関係雑件——診療班支那派遣関係 (2). File no. H-4-2-0, 3–4.

"Ryōkokumin no akushu 両国民の握手," originally published in Dōjin 同仁 2, no. 3, 1923. Byōin kankei zakken—Dōjinkai no bu 病院関係雑件——同仁会の部. File no. 3-11-3, 6–2.

"Shijiazhuang, Zhengding, oyobi Jinan ni okeru shinryō taiken 石家荘、正定、及済南における診療体験," in Hokuchūshi ni okeru shinryō bōeki jōkyō 北中支におけるる診療防疫状況. Dōjinkai kankei zakken—Shinryō-han Shina haken kankei 同仁会関係雑件——診療班支那派遣関係 (2). File no. H-4-2-0, 3–4.

"Shina haken Dōjinkai shinryō-han seryō kanja-hyō 支那派遣同仁会診療班施療患者表." Dōjinkai kankei zakken—Shinryō-han Shina haken kankei 同仁会関係雑件——診療班支那派遣関係 (2). File no. H-4-2-0, 3–4.

"Shina minshū ni jōnoshinryō 支那民衆に情の診療." Originally published in Tokyo asahi shimbun 東京朝日新聞, May 8, 1938. Dōjinkai kankei zakken—Shinryō-han Shina haken kankei 同仁会関係雑件——診療班支那派遣関係 (1). File no. H-4-1-0, 1–2.

"Shina no minshū nara, isshi dōjin ni, Dōjinkai kara kyūgohan 支那の民衆なら、一視同仁に、同仁会から救護班." Dōjinkai kankei zakken—Shinryō-han Shina haken kankei 同仁会関係雑件——診療班支那派遣関係 (1). File no. H-4-2-0, 3–4.

"Shōwa 7, Yoshizawa gaimu daijin 昭和 7、芳沢外務大臣." Byōin kankei zakken—Dōjinkai Jinan byōin kankei 病院関係雑件——同仁会済南病院関係 (2). File no. H-4-1-0, 1–2.

"Taishi bōeki kyūgo-han haken ni kansuru jigyō-an 対支防疫救護班派遣に関する事業案," Dōjinkai kankei zakken—Shinryō-han Shina haken kankei 同仁会関係雑件——診療班支那派遣関係 (1). File no. H-4-2-0, 3–4.

"Taishi iryōjigyō no tōitsu an: Dōjinkai wa yoroshiku korega chūshin tare 対支医療事業の統一案: 同仁会は宜しく之が中心たれ," originally published in Dōjin 同仁 2, no. 3 (1923). Byōin kankei zakken—Dōjinkai no bu 病院関係雑件——同仁会の部. File no. 3-11-3, 6–2.

"Teki no saikinsen bakuro—Wagagun tsuini kakushō o niguru 敵の細菌戦を暴露——我が軍遂に確証を握る," originally published in Tokyo asahi shimbun 東京朝日新聞, October 5, 1938. Dōjinkai kankei zakken—Bōeki jimu kankei 同仁会関係雑件——防疫事務関係 (1). File no. H-4-2-0, 3–5.

"Zakkan 雑感." Byōin kankei zakken—Dōjinkai Shanghai byōin kankei 病院関係雑件——同仁会上海病院関係 (1). File no. H-4-1-0, 1–5.

From Kokkai Toshokan 国会図書館

"Asami kyōju cho Nihon ishokumin mondai jo 浅見教授著日本移植民問題序." File no. 24-14-8. Gotō Shimpei bunsho 後藤新平文書.

"Gotō minsei chōkan enzetsu hikki 後藤民政長官演説筆記." File no. 7-28-3. Gotō Shimpei bunsho 後藤新平文書.

Index

Abbott, Andrew, 18–19n, 80, 107n, 185
Aboriginal Administrative Territory, 35
aboriginal tribes, 26, 29, 31, 34–35; anti-
  Japanese uprisings of, 44; campaign to
  contain, 36; conversion to Christianity
  of, 40
academic excellence, 126–28
administrative units, under Japanese rule,
  32–33
adoption, interethnic, 86
agency, relational view of, 13–14
air-defense groups, medical, 114
aiyong system, 34
Akashi, Dr., 59
Alford, Robert R., 186n
Algeria, 54
American Medical Association (AMA),
  189n
anticolonialism, 4–7, 8, 17, 19, 22, 51, 79,
  82, 108, 127, 181, 195; and development
  of civil society, 43–48, 64–69; of elites,
  48–50; group identity and, 70–76; in
  literary sphere, 88–89; market position
  and, 79
Anzu group, 120, 129n, 140n, 141–44, 147,
  204, 205
Arnold, David, 49n
assimilation, 6–8, 109–12, 119, 128, 130,
  183, 195–96
Austronesian people, 26
autonomy, professional, 51, 69, 80, 82, 115,
  177–78, 181–83, 189; compromise of, 95,
  107; group identity and, 72, 75; politicization and, 114; state regulation versus, 52–
  57
autopsies, 72–73

Bakumatsu period, 152n
Balzer, Harley D., 80–81

Barlow, Tani, 8, 10
Barth, Fredrik, 149
Becker, Howard S., 21
Beijing Dōjin Hospital, 155
Bettinger, Christopher P., 196–97
Bhabha, Homi, 198
Bible, 139
biological weapons, 163–64, 169, 170
birth control movement, 116
bōeki (immunization) teams, 158
"borderless medicine," 172–73
Bourdieu, Pierre, 11, 12
bourgeoisie, native, 103–5
Boxer funds, 154
Brint, Steven G., 81
Britain, 179–80; China and, 159, 160; colo-
  nialism of, 49n, 178–80, 191 (*see also*
  India)
bubonic plague, 53, 96

Cai, Dr., 140n
Calhoun, Craig, 19n, 190
Campaign for the Attainment of Local
  Autonomy, 44
capital, flow of, 103–4
career opportunities, opening of, 99–102,
  182; during wartime, 117–19
case-study approach, 21
categorical thinking, 11
causal emplotment, 12–14
Chatterjee, Partha, 198
chemical warfare, 114
Chen, Edward, 91n
Chen, Hanshen, Dr., 124–25, 128–29, 137n
Chen, Junkai, 64n
Chen, Qimai, Dr., 1–3
Chen, Yisong, 91n
Chiang Kai-shek, 85, 170n
Chikamatsu Monzaemon, 27n

identity formation *(continued)*
105–8; "deep structures" and, 185–88; hybridization in, 79–84, 108, 109, 136–45, 148; during Kōminka Era, 119–31, 136–38, 147–48
Iji eisei shinbun (journal), 163
immunization measures, 42, 53, 55, 95–96; in China, 157–58, 163, 167, 169, 174; wartime, 114
immunization *(bōeki)* teams, 158
Imperial Parliament, Japanese, 31
Independence Club of Korea, 17n
India, 49n, 54, 82; "sick zone" designation of, 95, 96
Indochina, 28, 134. *See also* Southeast Asia
Indonesia, 54; immigrants from, 22
inequality, ethnic, 51, 55, 59–61, 66; assimilation campaigns and, 111; overcoming, 125–29
infrastructure development, 36, 43, 191
Inoue, Kaoru, 25
institutional memory, revisiting of, 58–59
integration, ethnic, 59
Integration Rescript (1922), 59
Internal Affairs Bureau, 59n
International Service for Human Rights, 3n
Iriye, Akira, 151–52n
Ishibashi, Tanzan, 151–52n
Ishii, Shirō, 163–64
Islam, 17n
isshi dōjin ("universal benevolence"), 168
Izumi, Dr., 138

Japanese common schools *(kōgakkō)*, 62n
Japanese Medical Association, 121, 163
Jiang, Weishui, Dr., xi, 1, 66, 70, 108
Jiayi Medical Association, 73n, 74; magazines of, 105–6
Jinan Dōjin Hospital, 155, 158, 161, 161–62n, 167, 171, 172–74
Joffe, Carole E., 189n
Johnson, Terry, 177–78, 180
Journal of the Medical Association of Formosa, 20, 99–101, 116n
jukubanjin ("civilized savages"), 35
jurisprudence, medical, 53

Kanagawa, Treaty of (1854), 25n
Kanter, Rosabeth Moss, 187n
Kawaishi, Professor, 133
Kobayashi, Governor, 42
Kodama, Gentarō, 31, 32, 36
kōgakkō (Japanese common schools), 62n
Kokkai Toshokan (Diet Library), 20
Kokumin shinbun (Taiwan News), 72, 169
Kōminka Era, 6, 139–40n, 145–48, 150, 182, 198, 204, 205; assimilation policies

of, 10–12, 109–12, 128, 130, 194–95; identity during, 119–31, 136–38, 141, 147–48
Korea, 91n, 191, 192n, 193, 194n; assimilation campaign in, 110, 111; Dōjinkai projects in, 155
Koxinga (Zheng Chengkong), 27n
Krause, Elliott, 80, 179n
ku (wards), 32
Kuomintang (KMT), 92, 139–40n, 203
Kurosawa, Professor, 124–25
Kwantung Army, 85, 135n
Kyoto Imperial University, 163, 164; Faculty of Medicine at, 135n

Lai, He, Dr., 90n, 106–7
Lan, David, 40
landlords, 34, 37, 38, 44, 48, 61, 103–4; opium smoking among, 75; in Taiwan Cultural Association, 64, 65
language, national, 110, 111
Larson, Magali S., 80, 187n
Latour, Bruno, 10
Law for National Mobilization (*Kokka sōdōinhō*; 1938), 113
Law No. 63, 44, 45
League for the Attainment of Local Autonomy (Taiwan Chinhōjichi Renmei), 45, 47, 89, 90n
League of Nations, 74, 85
Lee, Sophia, 154n
legislative elections, Taiwanese, 1–4
Leslie, Charles, 6n
Li, Chen-yuan, Dr., 3
Li, Dr., 113–14
Li, Jingfang, 30n
Liang, Yuming, Dr., 134–35
Liang, Zai, Dr., 135
liberalism, 44, 45, 69, 141, 181, 183; anticolonialism and, 51, 65–67, 127; ethnic inequality and, 60–61; in professional culture, 57–58; traditional culture versus, 63–64
licensing, medical, 52, 54
Lifton, Robert Jay, 165
Lin, Jiwen, 93
Lin, Kunyuan, 66
Lin, Tianyou, 120–21, 123–24
Lin, Xiantang, 45
Lin, Yanqing, Dr., 121
Lin, Yushu, Dr., 57n
literary sphere, 88–90, 92–93, 106–7
Liu, Juchuan, Dr., 62, 63
local councils: elections of, 91–92; of Kōminka Era, 130; postwar, 130–31
"local literature" campaign, 89–90
Long, Susan, 6n

Text:	10/13 Aldus
Display:	Aldus
Compositor:	BookMatters
Printer and binder:	Sheridan
Indexer:	Ruth Elwell

CPSIA information can be obtained
at www.ICGtesting.com
Printed in the USA
JSHW061558030822
28854JS00001B/16